Manufactured Insecurity

Manufactured Insecurity

*Mobile Home Parks and Americans'
Tenuous Right to Place*

ESTHER SULLIVAN

University of California Press

University of California Press, one of the most distinguished university presses in the United States, enriches lives around the world by advancing scholarship in the humanities, social sciences, and natural sciences. Its activities are supported by the UC Press Foundation and by philanthropic contributions from individuals and institutions. For more information, visit www.ucpress.edu.

University of California Press
Oakland, California

Library of Congress Cataloging-in-Publication Data

Names: Sullivan, Esther, 1981– author.
Title: Manufactured insecurity : mobile home parks and Americans' tenuous right to place / Esther Sullivan.
Description: Oakland, California : University of California Press, [2018] | Includes bibliographical references and index. |
Identifiers: LCCN 2018003002 (print) | LCCN 2018006521 (ebook) | ISBN 9780520968356 (ebook) | ISBN 9780520295643 (cloth : alk. paper) | ISBN 9780520295667 (paper)
Subjects: LCSH: Mobile homes—Florida. | Mobile homes—Texas. | Mobile homes—Sociological aspects.
Classification: LCC HD7289.62.U6 (ebook) | LCC HD7289.62.U6 s85 2018 (print) | DC 333.33/8—dc23
LC record available at https://lccn.loc.gov/2018003002

27 26 25 24 23 22 21 20 19 18
10 9 8 7 6 5 4 3 2 1

In memory of
Daniel Sullivan, M.D. (1980–2016), who dedicated his
mind to alleviating human suffering

Contents

Illustrations

Acknowledgments

This book is indebted first and foremost to Javier Auyero, whose arrival on the scene at The University of Texas at Austin changed my scholarly life. His seemingly endless intellectual enthusiasm, incredible scholarly support, and the community of ethnographers he built at UT–Austin were instrumental in this project. Javier is an advisor *par excellence.* If you have been lucky enough to discuss your work with him, you know how generative even the simplest conversation with him can be and how you will come away from it filled with new questions and insight. I have been fortunate to have his questioning voice in the back of my head as I brought this book to completion and I gratefully know that it is a voice I will never be able to dislodge.

Special thanks to the community at The University of Texas at Austin, which is a wonderful place to become a sociologist. At various stages of this project, in formal and informal ways, those at UT–Austin have lent nuance and depth to the arguments in this book and support to me personally— thank you Maggie Tate, Travis Beaver, David Glisch-Sánchez, April Sutton, Danielle Dirks, Jessica Dunning-Lozano, Sergio Cabrera, Katie Sobering, Jorge Derpic, Caity Collins, Nino Bariola, and so many past and present members of the UT–Austin Ethnography Lab. I owe a debt to Liz Mueller, Peter Ward, Michael Young, and Sheldon Ekland-Olson for their input during early stages of this project.

Throughout this long process so many individuals have supported me, encouraged me, and helped me sharpen my understanding of the processes outlined in this book.

First, I have to thank the residents themselves. I am indebted to the many incredible people I have met over the last several years, not only for allowing me into their lives at one of their most trying moments, but also for their candor, insight, and wit that sustained me during this fieldwork and that I carry with me to this day. My time with the residents in this book changed me forever. I cannot name these people here, but I hope they know how grateful I am to them. I want to thank especially the residents I call Walter, Mattie, and Lupe for their friendship and lasting influence on my life.

Thank you to the many practitioners and nonprofits that are working to assist mobile home park residents and who have been incredibly helpful to this research. National organizations like Prosperity Now, the National Manufactured Home Owners Association (NMHOA), and ROC USA are doing incredible work to shine a spotlight on the issues facing mobile home residents. The many people working for these organizations have been incredibly helpful throughout this project. Thanks Ishbel Dickens and Dre Chiriboga-Flor for the endless energy you devote to stemming the tide of mobile home park evictions. Thanks especially to Doug Ryan of Prosperity Now, who applied his expansive knowledge of the manufactured housing industry to a close reading of this manuscript and supplied help no one else could have.

Thank you Edna Ledesma, who was along for the whole journey and who captured the evictions in the photos she took for this book. Thank you Ellen Berrey, who so felicitously fell into my orbit and who the stars aligned to make my companion. She lent support in so many ways; in all the regular academic ones—reading drafts, helping with manuscript advice, networking for me by proxy—but also by just being a damn dear friend. Thank you Brandon A. Robinson, who challenged me at various stages of this project and who came through for me at a most critical moment. At the stroke of midnight and just before the presses began to roll, Brandon swooped in to provide critical, challenging, and insightful feedback on every single page of this manuscript.

Thanks to my incredible sociology department at the University of Colorado Denver, especially to Jennifer Reich and Keith Guzik, who gave thoughtful advice during each stage of bringing this book to press, and to Terri Cooney, who as department chair has provided the most supportive environment a junior professor could hope for. I am grateful to have found an academic home at CU Denver among so many brilliant colleagues who never cease to offer help and, more importantly, to make me laugh.

Thanks also to Andrew Rumbach and Carrie Makarewicz at CU Denver, who helped me sharpen the arguments in this book as I engaged with their own research on mobile homes and disaster vulnerability. Members of the Women and Gender Studies group at CU Denver workshopped parts of this manuscript and scrutinized issues of narrative through a nonsociological lens. Gillian Silverman, Amy Hasinoff, Sarah Hagelin, Jo Luloff, Nicky

Beer, Al Martin, and Mia Fischer provided thoughtful feedback in this regard. Their attention to the written word helped me better showcase the stories entrusted to me by residents in this study.

Parts of this book were presented at meetings of the American Sociological Association, the Law & Society Association, the Social Science History Association, the American Anthropological Association, and the International Sociological Association. Arguments were also workshopped at the Chicago-Kent Law School symposium on dignity takings and at various meetings arranged through UT–Austin's Ethnography Lab. Thank you to all the individuals who workshopped parts of this book at these venues or at other points: Bernadette Atuahene, Randol Contreras, Andrew Deener, Matthew Desmond, Jaime Palomera, and Tom Slater. Thanks to Salvador Vidal-Ortiz for phrasing the concept "displaced in place," which so perfectly encapsulated the unique dislocation some residents felt.

This work was supported by funding from the Hogg Foundation for Mental Health, the American Association of University Women, and the William C. Powers Fellowship. Travel grants to present portions of the book were given by the National Science Foundation and CU Denver's Office of Research Support.

I also want to recognize the Austin, Texas wine bar that employed me on and off over the eight years it took to undertake this work and who made it possible for me to complete it. Vino Vino, that special spot, funded this research as much as any academic organization and its family of employees supported me personally in so many ways over these many years.

Finally, I thank my family. My mom, my rock, and my dad, my hero. I owe everything to their support, to their incredible work ethics, to the model they set, and to the family of siblings they gave me whom I get to love: Tina, Patrick, Daniel, Rosemary, Josie, and Elle. I am so lucky to have you.

For Stephen, my partner, who was with me every step of the way. Over all these years, in and out of parks, he has been a sounding board, a support system, and the better half of a two-man moving crew. He somehow finds a way to be there for me exactly when I most need it, and disagree with me exactly when I most need it. Stephen, you connect me to all the contradictions and all the kindnesses of this world. During this fieldwork, and every day of our life together, I have counted on you for a fresh and more beautiful way of seeing things. Thank you for all you do and for being the joy in my life.

This book is dedicated to my brother Daniel. We would talk on the phone on my long nightly walks around the towns of Jupiter and Alvin during my fieldwork; he would ask with genuine interest for updated descriptions of these places and then laugh and tell me I always described them the same exact way. He left us before I got to describe them in this book, but his influence is in every page because for as long as I can remember, his curiosity and sense of discovery were my model of what it meant to be a scientist. His wonder at the world and his drive to understand it inspired so many people, his little sister most of all. Because of this, but also because of so many uncountable things, having a brother like him was the greatest gift. I miss him every day and I think of him every time this world fills me with wonder.

Prologue

Kathleen's home sat at the end of the last lane of mobile homes inside her Florida mobile home park, near a row of trees that separated the property from the funeral home next door. A gregarious, Irish American woman in her 60s, Kathleen was a transplant to Florida. She lived most of her life in Binghamton, New York, where she worked for more than 25 years in a state public health office. When she retired from that job and her husband, Chip, retired from a career driving trucks as a teamster, the couple sold their house, bought a used mobile home, and joined 1.5 million residents in Florida and 18 million residents nationwide who live in manufactured housing. They downsized into an affordable singlewide, which was made all the more affordable because the home was installed in a mobile home park where they rented rather than owned the land.

Kathleen and Chip prepared to live a retirement dream on a budget. Paying off the $8,000 mobile home in cash installments, they were able to settle in three miles from the Atlantic Ocean in their own two-bedroom home for lot rent of $200 a month. With the purchase of the mobile home Kathleen and Chip became "halfway homeowners." They assumed the risks of living on land they did not own to gain the emotional and symbolic rewards of the American Dream of homeownership.

When the couple first moved to Florida, they made frequent use of the nearby beach, which was "just so nice." In those days, Kathleen would walk along the beach while Chip, who could no longer walk even short distances because of deterioration in his knees and back, would take a spot at a bench. However, three years after moving into the park, Kathleen was bitten by a brown recluse spider while gardening on the side of her mobile home. She remembered that day:

I was pruning my rosebushes three weeks before Christmas. Chip's kids were all coming down for Christmas. We had rosebushes out back. I felt a prick, but I thought it was from the rosebush. That night, oh my God, it started hurting so bad and burning. Then the kids all got here. Oh it was painful, terrible, but it got worse. When I went to the hospital they misdiagnosed it, not once but twice. It was downhill from there. It was four months and they did three surgeries to save it, but it ate my leg right away. You could see the bone. It was like a piece of meat left on the grill to burn. I went from 125 pounds down to 84 pounds. I couldn't eat, I couldn't do nothing, the pain was too excruciating. They put me on morphine. The burning and the pain was horrible but the worst part about it was the gangrene.

After multiple surgeries, her leg was amputated at the hip. Kathleen had been confined to a wheelchair ever since, but she tried not to let it limit her mobility, especially inside her mobile home park. She often sat outside, perched in her wheelchair at the top of the fiberglass steps on one side of her mobile home. On the other side of the home, a long wooden ramp led to a set of sliding glass doors. But those doors were broken. When she left the house she needed Chip, also disabled with injuries to his back and knees, to force open the sliding door so she could get out. On the other side of the home, she could wheel herself out onto the top of the fiberglass steps without help. She used the four-by-four-foot space at the top of the stairs like a balcony; it was her only independent exit to the outside. Sitting on her perch she called to neighbors nearby, sometimes inviting them in for a visit to pass the time or, more likely in the year I met Kathleen, to talk about the eviction.

From the first murmurs of a potential sale and closure of Kathleen's mobile home park in March of 2012, eviction was all anyone could talk about. The park was being purchased by a developer who planned to build apartments to replace the community, one of only two mobile home parks remaining in the city limits. If the sale of the park were finalized, every resident would be evicted within the legal limit of the law and forced to move both themselves and their homes. Kathleen and every one of her neighbors needed to figure out what to do next.

Like many of her neighbors (her park was a 55 and older community), Kathleen simply never expected to move again, even though she knew she only rented the land under her home: "A lot of people think, how can this be happening to me at my age? How can this really happen at my age? I thought I was settled. My health won't let me take any more stress. I don't want to leave." Before moving into the park ten years prior, Kathleen had never lived in a mobile home, although Chip had found cheap housing in mobile home parks essential in his younger years as a single working man. Kathleen had "no intention" of moving into a mobile home park initially. She hoped to find an apartment in South Florida; but on the couple's low fixed income they could not begin to afford going rents in the area.

Kathleen's son, a local carpenter, had found the home to help Kathleen and Chip relocate closer to him as they aged. A friend of her son happened to be selling the home inside the park; the couple could purchase it and take over the lot rent. "If he found an apartment or something for the same price that is probably where we would've landed." Of course, after her park was sold and she searched for other housing rather than pay thousands of dollars to move the home, Kathleen would learn that she simply could not find "an apartment or something for the same price." Not even close. Lot rent of $200 a month plus electric was the entirety of her and Chip's housing costs. Going rates in the area for a two-bedroom apartment were $1,200 that year. Chip summed it up, "Where else can you go in Florida? Here the rent is cheap and we don't pay for garbage."

Kathleen knew her mobile home was mocked by others—that is, those outside the park. She knew the stigma. But to her it was home. In the open living space at the center of the house she could move freely between the living room, dining room, and kitchen. She enjoyed hosting neighbors, never failing to offer a packet of cookies, ice tea, or a beer. She didn't drink, but tried to keep beer on hand for company. She would offer a spot at her glass-topped dining set, where she had reupholstered the chairs in a fabric patterned with martini glasses. "Don't spill my drinks," she liked to say each time a visitor pulled out a chair.

When I first entered Kathleen's home—five months after she learned her park was up for sale and three months before she would receive an eviction notice—she welcomed me in, immediately giving me a short tour. She took me into her bedroom, which had folding doors that opened wide into a large bathroom with a deep Jacuzzi bathtub. Kathleen's bathroom had been updated by the home's previous owner, who also had retiled the walls and floor. However, the weight of this upgrade was now a primary concern, Kathleen explained. To prepare for the potential sale of the park she had professional mobile home movers come to assess the home for relocation. They informed her the new tile might make the back part of the mobile home too heavy, which would mean the home could not be relocated to a new park.

For Kathleen and Chip, the news that recent upgrades to their home might cause them to lose everything was hard to digest, especially because the home was the second mobile home they had owned in the park and they had purchased it from a neighbor precisely because they believed the newer, upgraded home would be more suitable for relocation. Their former home, the one Kathleen's son found for them when they moved to Florida ten years prior, was a visibly aging, 1984 powder-blue singlewide with white aluminum shutters modeled to resemble real wood, each featuring a cutout of a sparrow. Her son had renovated the deck of the old powder-blue mobile home, turning it into a wheelchair ramp after Kathleen's hospitalization. She remembered, with clear affection for the landlord who would eventually evict her, "He told my son: do whatever you need to do to get her back home." But those renovations were part of what had made her old home "structurally unsound" for relocation.

That was the first time she had been through the process of having a home assessed for relocation. The mover told her unequivocally that the powder-blue home would never survive a relocation. Kathleen understood why—the home was aging. Still, hearing the news was tough. The home wasn't much, but it was hers. She took care of it, down to the rosebushes planted alongside the home on grounds that did not belong to her. From where Kathleen sat, the home was in fine shape for daily life and she could have comfortably lived out her retirement there. But as the movers explained, the home was in no shape to be hauled down a highway.

In this moment and in the many moments that made up her year-long eviction, the closure of the park and the loss of her home looked vastly different from Kathleen's perspective than from the perspectives of the many actors that structured the eviction process: the landlord who evicted her, the movers who moved her home, the city council who approved her park's closure, and the members of the board that set the policies for relocation in her state. From the perspective of Max, the mobile home mover who delivered the news that she would need to abandon the powder-blue mobile home, Kathleen's feelings of loss were simply an uncomfortable part of the job. Speaking with Max privately he explained that what he did for a living—hauling the homes of evicted homeowners—was sometimes so draining he often thought about leaving the business. He reflected, "People own these houses. This is where they live, and they have a right to live there." Agreeing with him, I answered that parks provided a primary source of poverty-level housing. "A lot of people are living in these homes, 10 percent of Florida, 1.5 million Floridians," I replied. He thought for a second and then changed his tone, "Maybe I should stay in the business then."

Indeed business was booming in Florida and around the nation, both for mobile home park operators and for the network of private actors like Max who profit when mobile home parks close. Kathleen's story and the stories of close to two hundred evicted Florida and Texas mobile home residents who contributed to this book exist at this intersection of poverty and profit.

When Kathleen learned that her powder-blue trailer could not be moved it was hard, but at least it made sense. She and Chip knew the home was aging. Shortly after first hearing news of the sale of the park, when their singlewide was deemed unmovable, they scraped together more of their retirement savings to purchase the home of their neighbor next door at a discounted price (he chose to sell the home and move in with a girlfriend rather than wait to be evicted). They purchased the home, the one with the Jacuzzi tub and the tile, and lived in the newer, upgraded model over the next six summer months as they anxiously waited for an official eviction notice and for the relocation company to return to give a final assessment on the movability of their home.

Because Kathleen and Chip had made what they thought was a sensible decision when they abandoned their former, aging home, the movers' initial, uncertain pronouncement about this new home seemed inconceivable. However, from the perspective of the mobile home movers contracted to clear out Kathleen's park, the likelihood that the home could not be moved was not surprising at all. The mobile home movers, brothers Max and Joe, only needed to enter and look around a mobile home, then quickly peer underneath, to deliver the devastating news that a home was not structurally sound for relocation. At a neighbor's home a street over from Kathleen, Max and Joe made one such quick assessment. Max told the distressed homeowner that so much had been redone on the inside of the house it had become too heavy to move. Joe then explained that the home appeared to have been previously moved and that "homes can be moved once, maybe twice, but not more than that."

For weeks after receiving her eviction notice Kathleen once again returned to waiting, this time to get the movers' official judgment on her second mobile home. This waiting was not new to Kathleen. By the time the official eviction notice was slipped under her door in October of that year, Kathleen had been living in a state of stalled uncertainty for eight months, a waiting that would continue long after her relocation was carried out. As she came to understand the implications of her halfway homeownership, the threat of eviction began to haunt her daily life.

Kathleen had been warned when she moved into the park that the property was for sale; the landlord handed all incoming residents a notice saying so. But that was 10 years ago and longtime park residents insisted the park had always been up for sale. All residents understood they only rented the land under their homes, but the park had been opened since 1954 and life had continued mostly unchanged for decades. Over the decade she lived there, Kathleen came to imagine that perhaps since the park had "always been" for sale, it might *always be* this way. Thinking back on her landlord's first warning that the park was for sale back when she purchased the powder-blue trailer, she remembered, "I just wasn't thinking at all about this as a possibility." She explained, "I wasn't comprehending whatever that could mean . . . I just didn't think about it closing. I don't know what other people thought but I just misinterpreted it. Just like you saw how somebody buys a home and turns it over and whatever. I didn't think it would be anything like this."

From the perspective of the mobile home movers Max and Joe, Kathleen's misinterpretation was simply naive. Leaning against the cab of his truck later that year as a crew worked to hook up a singlewide for relocation, Max asked me to look around at the amount of development occurring in the area outside the park. What were these people thinking, investing in mobile homes inside the park? He insisted, "They had to know it was going to go." Max estimated he had moved at least five thousand mobile homes over the years and about 80 percent of them were moved out of closing parks. Still, Max empathized with Kathleen. He surmised that her eviction was not just about urban growth, but about urban priorities: "These cities, they don't want this [gesturing to the park]. They want the la-de-da, the lights, the fancy bullshit." I pointed to the home Max's crew was hooking up to his truck, asking, "They don't want somebody's 1970s mobile home?" He thought and reflected, "Yeah. But you know what? That person still has to live too. That's the person that is working at 7–11, or the gas station down the street giving you gas, or the CVS where you get your medicine. Who is going to do that? Are you going to do that in your fancy la-de-da house? You're not going to do it. You've gotta have that person. You're only hurting yourself by not allowing them to be there. I don't get it."

Max believed that Kathleen and her neighbors had to look at their park and "know it was going to go." Still, he couldn't quite make sense of the community's eviction, concluding, "I don't get it." However, from the perspective of AJ Hirsh, a member of the board of directors for the state office set up to handle Florida's numerous park closures, it all made perfect sense. Sitting in his parked SUV as we watched a crew splitting a doublewide for transport out of a South Florida park, AJ explained that it was simple economics. AJ not only sat on the board of directors for the state mobile home relocation office, but also owned a mobile home moving company of his own. His drivers would eventually move Kathleen's home. Moving mobile homes out of closing parks was AJ's bread and butter, and from his viewpoint, park closures were simply inevitable. From the driver's seat of his

SUV he laid it out, using the closing park where we were parked as an example:

I'm going to give you a quick intelligence test. Gee, we are making $3 million a year profit on this mobile home park. We put a casino in here and we make $1 million a day. Duh, let me think, what do we want? I'd take 365 million over 3 million. That's what it is—it's when the land value and the cost of what you are doing in development make sense. And the bad thing is there's been the downturn so we are not seeing that many parks close. If that land value starts going up like this, you're going to see little parks closing, you know?

The park where we sat, like Kathleen's, was simply on the wrong side of the balance between development and cheap land.

But Kathleen and many of her neighbors did not have the same clarity, that their park inevitably "was going to go." The sale of the park needed to be finalized with a rezoning by their local city council. Over the summer months before the eviction notices were handed out neighbors frequented Kathleen's fiberglass steps, debating whether the city council might turn down the rezoning of the park and block the redevelopment. Kathleen imagined that their own landlord must, like them, be grieving the loss of their park, which was "special" and which had been owned by his family for six decades. She recalled a story of a tree in the park that was knocked down during a hurricane. The landlord had told her that he and his father planted the tree together. They used to eat lunch under it when he was a boy helping out in the park back in the 1960s. Kathleen believed her landlord must also love the park and be sad to see it close.

But from her landlord's perspective, the park closure looked different. The landlord resented that the rezoning of the park needed to be approved by the city at all. In his maintenance shed at the back of the park, the landlord sat on a John Deere riding mower and fumed, "Who would have ever thought that you would have such a hard time getting rid of a piece of property when it belongs to you? They [the residents] knew for 10 or 12 years that we were going to sell the property. You get people to sign a piece of paper that acknowledges that the park is for sale and then when they learn that the park is being sold they want to throw a fit! There goes your private property rights! You pay taxes on it, you maintain it, and then you can't sell it."

But the landlord's property rights were not in question. He could sell the park at any time and he easily did by fall of that year. Kathleen and her neighbors had hoped the rezoning of the park might be turned down by the city council. From where Kathleen sat, she believed the council must have known the incredible hardship—emotional, practical, financial—the community-wide eviction would cause her and many of her already-struggling neighbors. But from the perspective of the city council, a trailer park simply was not the optimal use of the property. In the city council meetings where Kathleen and her neighbors showed up to put a face on mobile home park eviction, city council members expressed concern for the hardships they faced. But in conversations with me, in official documents, and in the final rezoning decision, city officials discussed the park closure not as a mass eviction, but as a redevelopment option that was "consistent with the goals, objectives, and policies of the comprehensive plan" for the city. Indeed, a city council's job is to pursue these stated goals. City officials argued that rezoning Kathleen's park was not only compatible with the growing city's vision of itself but also "necessary because of changed or changing conditions" in the region. From their perspective, growth was inevitable and new apartments, not mobile home parks, could attract a skilled workforce and produce "substantial public benefits" for the remaining residents of the area. They voted unanimously to rezone the park. Eviction notices were sent out the very next day. Kathleen received hers and, defeated, reflected back on the six months she had been waiting: "The writing was on the wall."

Kathleen and her neighbors had held out hope for the city council process all throughout the spring and summer of that year. They were stunned at the ease with which the council approved the closure of their park once the rezoning was finally heard that fall. Still, Kathleen saw herself as a fighter and tried to stave off the indignation of eviction by standing up for her rights. She frequently repeated that she would be "one of the last ones out" of the park. She wanted to stay until the last date of the eviction period, May 1, 2013. She prided herself on being tough. She liked to remind me that she did not go to the doctor for eight days after the spider bite and did not stay in the hospital long despite developing gangrene. Instead, at night she would cover the gangrenous leg in a blanket and wheel out onto the deck of her mobile home, where she could grit her teeth and cringe in pain without anyone there to see her.

Throughout the eviction process Kathleen lived up to her conception of herself as a fighter. Chip had a stroke shortly after the first news of the eviction. After his stroke, and throughout his many hospitalizations, Kathleen prepared for the eviction on her own. Once her son constructed a ramp into the newer mobile home they purchased next door, she began the final stages of emptying the powder-blue trailer they were forced to abandon. Over the course of weeks, she moved boxes one by one, positioning them in her lap as she wheeled them down one ramp and up another.

She tried her best to remain informed about what eviction would entail (Who would move them? Where? What would it cost? How could she pay?) and by doing so she tried to exercise some degree of control over the process. Through repeated phone calls and hours spent online, she became a trusted source of information for neighbors who complained, "It's the *not knowing* that makes it hard." When I asked Kathleen's next-door neighbor Larry how he had found out a particular bit of information he answered, "My neighbor, she found it on the internet."

By 2013, another spring living under the shadow of eviction had arrived in Kathleen's park. More than a year had passed since the first news of the closure circulated. But now homes began to be moved and a sense of loss set in. After months of waiting for the assessment on the structural soundness of their home (and after receiving two contradicting assessments), Kathleen was relieved to eventually be told her new home could be moved. However, she was then devastated to find out that any built-on additions, including her wheelchair ramp, could not.

Kathleen still considered herself a fighter. She called area nonprofits for months to seek help. When she couldn't find a nonprofit to agree to rebuild her ramp, she hounded representatives from the development company to contribute to the cost: "This is what I said. I said, I expect that after 25 days that we're out or however many days [to set up the home in the new park], when someone comes to me and tells me that we can go back into the trailer, I expect to get up my ramp and into my trailer just like somebody that's got two legs and can walk up their front porch and get into their trailer."

But as time progressed Kathleen became increasingly unwilling—or in her estimation, unable—to fight for her rights. Part of this was due to the partial, contradictory, or just incorrect information she received from various actors involved in the sale of her park. Most often, she received no information at all and was left simply to wait and see what would happen to her and her home. "All you can do is sit tight," she sighed. She went as far as to seek help from the Legal Aid Society, convinced that because her park housed many poor, elderly, and disabled residents, they might have a case. Legal Aid did provide pro bono assistance at the rezoning hearings; but from the perspective of the Legal Aid lawyer who spoke at those meetings, delaying the closure was mobile home park residents' best hope. From behind his large wooden desk at the offices of Legal Aid of South Florida, the young lawyer recalled that he had represented residents of at least five other closing parks in the area: "A lot of times what you end up doing is just delaying. You come in here saying, you didn't take the right vote so I am going to sue, delay this, make you have to redo this . . . There is not usually a way to permanently stop [the closure]."

But the procedural delay, which the Legal Aid attorney had presented as the residents' last best option, only exacerbated the slow-motion trauma of the eviction. In the absence of information and without any sense of control, Kathleen experienced this delay as a profound sense of powerlessness, "There's nothing we can do." The constant waiting, confusion, and delay that stretched over a year of becoming evicted took a toll on Kathleen. Inside her home, surrounded by partially packed boxes, she said flatly, "Don't get me wrong, I will argue with the best of them, but if there isn't something to argue about, don't waste your breath. There was nothing to argue about over the sale of this park from day one." She had once claimed that she didn't understand what the sale of her park really meant; I asked how it felt now that she did. She answered, "Bitter, bitter, bitter."

This bitterness followed Kathleen after the eviction as she waited for her home to be installed in a park 20 miles away. She continued to return as long as she could to retrieve her mail from the bank of mailboxes inside the now deserted park. The names on the row of mailboxes were a reminder of the neighbors and friends she had lost (only three out of a hundred other households found available lots in the park where she relocated). Kathleen steadied herself in the months she spent in limbo after her home was removed from the old park and being set up in a new one. She tried to reimagine this time spent sleeping on her son's couch as "practice in staying away" from her former community. She explained, "I need time to wean myself away." When I saw Kathleen seven months after the eviction I questioned whether she had been successful in doing so.

Visiting Kathleen in her same home, at her same glass-topped table, in a wholly unfamiliar park, I was struck by an incredible change in a woman who had always prided herself in what she saw as an Irish mix of stubbornness and endurance. Kathleen broke down in tears several times that day when talking about the relocation, something this self-described "tough lady" had never done in the time I had known her. She appeared exhausted as she described the months after leaving the park. She first lived in a motel, but as time wore on she could no longer afford it. She moved into the TV room of her son's house, which she had tried to avoid. His home was not wheelchair accessible and she was forced to constantly ask for help to accomplish daily tasks. Kathleen loathed living in this state of dependence.

As soon as she was approved to reenter her mobile home, she and Chip moved back in. They were confronted with significant damage to the home, the result of the relocation. But their immediate needs were more pressing. Unlike the time when Kathleen returned from the hospital after the amputation and the landlord urged her son to "do everything you can to get her back home," Kathleen was now alone in a new park in an unfamiliar town. The managers of the park, which was owned by a national corporation, seemed to rotate and none provided information or assistance with rebuilding her ramp. The anticipated costs of rebuilding the ramp felt overwhelming, especially after the financial drain of the eviction. In the meantime she developed a "system" for getting in and out of the house using the only available exit, the fiberglass steps that used to be her perch. When she left the home she stood from her wheelchair on her one leg, carefully placed all her weight on Chip, who stood still for fear of reinjuring his own damaged knees, and she hopped down the steps one by one. When she reentered the home she slid from her wheelchair onto the bottom step and stabilized herself on her hands while she shifted into her home stair-by-stair on her backside.

The change that had come over Kathleen was not due only to the physical or financial hardships she endured. She told me matter-of-factly that the "second phase" of being evicted was worse than anything she had experienced in the months before her park closed. Her old next-door neighbor Larry had been right when he warned from a park 40 miles away in a distant county, "It's not going to be the same. No matter where you go, it's not going to be the same." Now she agreed, lamenting, "I'm not happy . . . I don't know anybody. Down there everybody knew everybody."

Just as she had done in the days before the amputation when she wheeled herself onto her deck to grit and bear the pain of her gangrenous leg in stubborn silence, Kathleen had tried to endure as she saw her community dismantled around her. Only after she was finally resettled in her old home in a new park did Kathleen acknowledge the full weight of this individual and collective loss.

Kathleen's experience was bitter, in her words, but it was not unique. It was shared by 180 evicted mobile home residents in Texas and Florida, the two states with the largest mobile home populations, who took part in this research. This book explores how the experiences of mobile home park residents like Kathleen are structured by historic social, legal, and market forces that intersect to manufacture housing insecurity for an entire class of low-income residents. It probes the production and consequences of the risk that is rooted in the very land where mobile home park residents live. Finally, it links the mass evictions occurring in U.S. mobile home parks to the broader processes of urban growth and redevelopment, the restructuring of state and federal housing policy, and the unique cultural place of mobile homes in the United States.

Introduction

Halfway Homeowners

Eviction day at Silver Sands Mobile Home Park. It was the final day the residents of Silver Sands could remain in the community where many had lived for decades. Every resident of Silver Sands owned his or her mobile home. Every resident rented—rather than owned—the lot under that home in a century-old land-lease model that has made the mobile home park a primary mode of affordable housing in the United States. That same land-lease model has also made the mobile home park one of the fastest-growing, most lucrative real estate investment tools for park property owners and one of the most precarious modes of housing for low-income residents.

Along the nine narrow streets of a hundred singlewides and doublewides that made up Silver Sands Mobile Home Park, the eviction process had begun.[1] The bare concrete foundations where homes had been hauled away stuck out like wounds in a green South Florida landscape. Remaining mobile homes stood in various states of readiness to be transported. Screened porches and wooden decks, additions made over many years to expand and enhance the homes, were torn off so that only the bodies of the trailers remained. Years of careful landscaping were uprooted to clear a path for a semi-truck to back in and hook up to the triangular hitch positioned at the front end of every mobile home. Skirting was torn away to reveal homes' metal transport axles and long-since-rotted tires, an undercarriage that embodies the central tension between mobility and rootedness that lies at the heart of the mobile home. Denuded homes waited to be strapped with a "Wide Load" banner and hauled to a new park if the homeowners were lucky, or to the dump if they were not.

Randall, a wiry, long-haired, 61-year-old resident of Silver Sands, was one such unlucky homeowner. His 1981 trailer, his pride and joy, was deemed too old to survive a relocation and would have to be abandoned in the park. The morning of the final day of tenancy at Silver Sands, I found Randall sitting with a pile of his belongings inside the screened-in porch that ran the length of my singlewide. He had showed up early at Labor Finders, the local day labor agency where he found work, but he was not sent out for a job: "I couldn't. I was crying . . . My manager saw me and said I'm not gonna send you out today. I said, I can't go out today. I think reality just fucking set in . . . God, look at me. I've never shook like this before . . . I still couldn't find a room this morning." The previous night, in preparation for the final day of the eviction period, Randall had slept in an abandoned building where he found a small pile of mats and used them as a bed. He insisted, "I'll adjust to it after a while. I figure I've got to find a room in the next month."

But Randall had been looking for a room for months, ever since he heard that Silver Sands Mobile Home Park had been bought by a development company and would close. On his long daily walks to and from Labor Finders he took circular routes in search of a For Rent sign. Without a car he asked for rides around town on scouting missions. He walked over to the only publicly subsidized housing project in the town, where the waiting list was two years long and not accepting new applicants. He scoured the local paper. He made calls to numbers from the only resource he had, a dog-eared and worn volume of organizations assisting low-income people that he had found in the park's laundry room. He sought out help from every contact in his small social circle, from fellow day laborers to regulars at a nearby bar. He fought embarrassment and asked for help checking listings online since he had never before used a computer. He dutifully followed up on every potential lead, but his efforts did not produce a single apartment or room that he could afford and that was close enough to the city to allow him to continue walking to his job at Labor Finders, a job he clung to desperately. On a good week, he could earn $240 if he were lucky enough to work 30 hours.

On the last day of the eviction Randall took the $1,500 mobile home abandonment fee supplied by the state of Florida and paid for a storage unit where he moved the contents of his unmovable mobile home. He listed out the things he made sure to store safely, a house-worth of accumulated furnishings, treasured objects inherited from his parents, and the ashes of his mother, which he had long planned to scatter over the ocean. He bought a new pair of sneakers and a new pair of jeans and then put $850 in cash into the storage unit and kept $100 on him. After a night of sleeping in an abandoned building he returned to Silver Sands for no other reason than he didn't know where else to go. Randall steadied his shaking hands to smooth his shirt and asked, "Do I look bad or rough or anything like that?" He was equally meticulous arranging and abandoning the home he had owned for three years. Knowing the home would likely be scrapped for metal, he still took care to make small repairs he had never gotten to while living in the home. He fixed the front door handle before he abandoned the home. He wanted the home to look "decent."

Eleven months before eviction day, when I first met Randall, he had proudly stated he lived in mobile homes "all my life, I love them." They were small, cheap, and he could work on them himself. He moved into Silver Sands after purchasing his used singlewide for $3,000 and became a homeowner for the first time in his life. He paid $250 each month to rent the lot under his home, an unmatched level of affordability in South Florida and most U.S. metro areas but still nearly half of his unpredictable monthly earnings. He offered a tour of his 1981 mobile home, pointing out his favorite features, like the parquet floors. He asked me to excuse the house which was "messy now" and I replied that, quite the contrary, it was spotless. He then admitted with a grin that he had actually just scrubbed the outside of all his cabinets.

During the four years after losing his home in the closure of Silver Sands, Randall would continue to experience homelessness. In the months after the park closed and neighbors were scattered in various directions, Randall's phone was disconnected and he failed to pay his storage unit fee. The storage company repeatedly called me (Randall had listed me as the emergency contact), explaining they were disposing of the unit's contents. I thought of the ashes of Randall's mother in there along with every other thing Randall owned. Despite his continued searching Randall was unable to find a place he could afford near enough to the city that he could continue to walk to Labor Finders and be sent out on jobs, his only source of income until he turned 62 and could file for Social Security. Four years prior Randall was a proud homeowner. Now everything he owned fit in a duffel bag, which he kept tucked between his legs to guard against thieves as he slept on a mattress behind a strip mall only half a mile from where Silver Sands once stood.

MANUFACTURED HOUSING AND MANUFACTURED INSECURITY

Manufactured Insecurity explores the contemporary face of poverty housing and the tenuous right to place that is a lived reality for millions of low-income residents in mobile home parks in the United States. It examines the historical processes and contemporary policies that structure mobile home residents' divided property rights and documents the consequences of the risky housing tenure that results. It probes the social-legal-political construction of housing crises through an up-close, long-term account of the housing insecurity nakedly on display during mobile home park evictions in Texas and Florida, the two U.S. states with the largest mobile home populations. Finally, it analyzes the fallout, both for mobile home park residents and for all of those attempting to access and hold on to housing they can afford in an era of rising housing costs, falling and stagnant incomes, deepening cuts to federal housing assistance, and increasingly entrepreneurial urban development.

At the beginning of the twenty-first century, manufactured housing, more often called mobile homes or trailers, was the fastest-growing form of new housing in the United States (Scommegna 2004).[2] Today mobile homes provide housing for about 18 million residents (U.S. Census Bureau 2016b). The prevalence of manufactured housing is largely due to its affordability. Mobile homes represent a significant, but often unacknowledged, portion of our nation's low-income housing supply (Beamish et al. 2001; Aman and Yarnal 2010; Dawkins and Koebel 2010). Indeed, manufactured housing provides the largest unsubsidized source of affordable housing in the United States (CFED 2015). Throughout the 1990s, manufactured housing was responsible for 66 percent of the new affordable housing produced in the country (Apgar et al. 2002). Nationally, 73 percent of households living in mobile homes earn less than $50,000 a year, with a median annual household income of about $30,000 in 2009 (CFED 2014). In short, mobile homes are a primary way that America's poor are housed.

The affordability of manufactured housing is the product of a unique form of land tenure: about one third of the nation's mobile homes are located in land-lease mobile home communities commonly called trailer parks, which are developed and owned by private landlords (Kochera 2001). Despite popular perceptions to the contrary, mobile home parks are an urban phenomenon, providing a crucial source of affordable housing in U.S. metro areas.[3] In addition to affordable rental opportunities, mobile home parks provide a crucial site for the placement of owner-occupied units for low-income homeowners like Randall and Kathleen. In 2011, mobile homes accounted for 30 percent of all new homes sold under $200,000, 50 percent of all new homes sold under $150,000, and 71 percent of all new homes sold under $125,000 (MHI 2012). A remarkable 80 percent of mobile home park residents own their homes, many of them outright (HAC 2011). These mobile homeowners are just that—homeowners. However, homeowning households living on privately owned land in mobile home parks are marked by "divided asset ownership," which means that residents own their mobile homes but rent the lots on which the homes sit (Hirsch and Rufolo 1999). Of the 80 percent of park residents who own their homes, only 14 percent also own the land beneath their homes (HAC 2011). This divided form of land tenure is fraught with risk.

Without rights to the land under their homes, mobile home park residents are *halfway homeowners*. Because of divided asset ownership, the housing security of mobile home residents depends on the decisions of private landlords to continue to maintain and operate mobile home parks. While living within mobile home parks, residents have few protections against excessive rent increases, inadequate park maintenance, and lack of written or long-term leases (Kochera 2001). Ultimately, mobile home park residents, even those who have long owned their homes, can legally be evicted at any time when parks are sold or closed.

Despite their misleading designation, "mobile" homes are quite *immobile;* once set in place their frames slacken and relocation can result in serious structural damage (Consumers Union 2001a). The Manufactured Housing Institute, the industry's national trade organization, boasts that more than 90 percent of today's manufactured homes never move from their original site. However, this estimate is misleading: when faced with park closure many homeowners are forced to abandon their homes, and for many of these homeowners their manufactured home is their primary asset. The cost of relocating a mobile home is prohibitive and can be more than the homeowner initially paid for the home. Estimates range from $5,000 to $10,000 with permitting and installation fees. According to one study, this represents five to seven years' worth of accrued equity for mobile homeowners (CFED 2010). Legally, these residents are entitled to only 30 days' eviction notice in most states. Meanwhile, the demand for affordable housing in mobile home parks means that new lot vacancies are hard to find. Vacancy rates are commonly in the single digits. A study of park closures in Oregon estimated it would take 14 years for local mobile home parks to accommodate the displaced homes from a single mobile home park closure (Sheehan and Colton 1994). Facing prohibitive relocation costs, short notice, and few vacancies, many homeowners sell their homes for a fraction of their appraised value or abandon them to park owners who collect additional profits by selling off deserted homes (Consumers Union 2001b).

All these factors limit choices for displaced homeowners like Randall who see their community, their equity, and their homes destroyed when parks are redeveloped for other uses. Despite their seeming attainment of the culturally cherished American Dream of homeownership, the social stability this dream implies remains beyond their reach. In mobile home parks, precarious land tenure exempts low-income residents from the benefits of homeownership and disposes them to dispossession.

Eviction has been called America's "hidden housing problem," and housing scholars estimate several million residents are likely evicted from their homes each year in the United States (Hartman and Robinson 2003). Despite the focus on negative outcomes associated with both forced and voluntary residential relocation (Sluzki 1992; Hagan, MacMillan, and Wheaton 1996; Hoffman and Johnson 1998; Tucker, Marx, and Long 1998; Pribesh and Downey 1999; Haynie and South 2005), within sociology eviction remains "the most understudied process affecting the lives of the urban poor" (Desmond 2012: 90). Gretchen Purser (2016: 395) summarizes: "We thus have no reliable figures on how many people are evicted each year, no clear understanding of the underlying causes of eviction, no detailed picture of how and under what conditions evictions are actually carried out, and no comprehensive sense of what happens to individuals, families and communities in the wake of eviction." Forced relocation has long been a problem for the urban poor and evictions are likely increasing in the United States due to a triad of housing pressures: rising rents and utility costs, especially as a percentage of income; stagnant and falling incomes, especially for the poor; and a shortfall of federal housing assistance, as the budget for the Department of Housing and Urban Development (HUD) has been slashed more than any other federal-level branch of government (Hackworth 2009). Meanwhile currently there is no state in the United States in which someone working full-time at minimum wage can afford a "fair market rent" two-bedroom apartment (National Low Income Housing Coalition 2017).

The nascent sociological study of eviction, which "represents a nearly unexplored area of research" (Pattillo 2013: 518), has argued that all those interested in fair housing access should focus "not only on the front end of the housing process—the freedom to *obtain* housing anywhere—but also on the back end: the freedom to *maintain* housing anywhere" (Desmond et al. 2013: 321). Sociologist Matthew Desmond's study of evicted renters in Milwaukee introduced the provocatively simple notion that eviction is a cause rather than condition of poverty, as residents themselves bear the costs of relocation, higher rents, and a mark on their tenant record (Desmond and Bell 2015; Desmond 2016). Yet eviction, and housing insecurity more generally, remain at the margins of the poverty debate. If sociologists are to understand not only *whether* but also *how* eviction acts to drive poverty, more research on various forms of housing insecurity is key.[4]

Housing is both a cultural object, a financial commodity, and a sociolegal artifact. The proliferation of mobile home parks in cities across the

United States is a material expression of broad shifts in U.S. housing policy that have occurred as part of welfare state retrenchment. Over the last four decades, housing has transformed threefold from a public institution (Mumford 1961), to a private commodity, to a complex financial instrument (Pattillo 2013). At the same time, under a cash-strapped and gutted system of direct federal aid, the provision of affordable housing has devolved from a responsibility of the social safety net to a resource for private investors. Only a tiny fraction, about two percent, of U.S. residents will ever access public housing and most will find a home in the properties of private providers. Exploring the political economy of the private poverty housing market is essential for understanding both the intersection of poverty and profit in the production of housing crises (Desmond 2016) and the lived experience of contemporary housing insecurity.

The ubiquity of the mobile home park in the American landscape and the insecure land tenure of its residents are both outgrowths of the expansion of this private poverty housing market. A budget crunch in federal housing assistance has been a financial boon for low-income housing in trailer parks where residents live "at the whim of property owners" (Consumers Union 2001a: 1). Attributing increased demand for space in parks to a lack of affordable housing elsewhere, a senior investment director at Marcus & Millichap boasted, "The demand right now for manufactured housing communities is at an all-time high."[5] Mobile home park owners have answered this demand in much the same way that inner-city landlords have capitalized on critical needs for rental housing in times of affordable housing scarcity. One of the nation's largest mobile home park owners explained that the mobile home park industry thrives precisely because it capitalizes on a captive and needy population. Summarizing his industry's capacity to wring profits from impoverished and effectively *immobile* mobile home park residents, he stated, "We're like a Waffle House where everyone is chained to the booths."[6]

LIFE INSIDE THE MOBILE HOME PARK

Walter, an 89-year-old World War II veteran and resident of Silver Sands, would bristle at the comparison between his mobile home park and a Waffle House. Instead, Walter nicknamed it Paradise. He pointed out, "We've got our own little slice of paradise right here." Walter had lived in Silver Sands for 20 years with his wife, Mattie. The couple's low monthly rent afforded them a slice of paradise on Walter's fixed Social Security income and military benefits.

Walter lived immediately across from my rented singlewide from 2012–13. The first time we met, I introduced myself as I would about 180 times in the next two years to residents facing eviction in 32 different mobile home parks in Texas and Florida. Like many other residents in these parks, eviction was forefront in Walter's mind on the day we met as neighbors.

By way of his own introduction, Walter gives me his name and immediately rattles off in a thick New England accent: "Well, I'm from Maine—a little island out off the coast of Maine. Well, I left there a little time ago. I was drafted into the army in 1942 and went to the war." Walter gives me his long housing history, then he asks me directly: "So you're gonna live over there for a while?"

Esther: "Yeah, I'm gonna live over there for a while, at least until we can't live here anymore."

Walter: "Well, ain't that something huh? [He shakes his head.] I lived right here, in this park, in a trailer for 20 years. I've got two sons here. One, his house is right there and his house is right there, the other." (He points to an RV right behind his own house and to a mobile home at the end of our street).

We wave to his great-granddaughter, who passes by and goes into his house to visit his wife, Mattie. His granddaughter is down visiting from Ohio and staying at his son's house, about three homes away.

Walter shows me around the extensive garden he has planted on a second lot that he rents next door to his home just so that he can have room to garden [bringing his total monthly rent for two lots to $350]. He uses the extra lot as a patio and spends much of his day out here, sitting or working in the shade. Mattie spends almost all of her time inside in her chair, since disabilities limit her mobility. Her chair is her "nest" where everything she needs for the day is tucked in a sleeve slung over the chair's arm; it holds the remote, crossword books, and snacks, plus a call button that alerts Walter if there is an emergency and he is outside. Out on the patio, Walter takes me to his favorite shady corner, "It's 20 degrees cooler over here." When you're in this spot, he insists, you're really in paradise.

Walter: "Oh we hate to move, but what can we do? That's the way it is."

Walter continues to work on an eight-pound pork roast he is smoking for Fourth of July dinner later this night. All of his family from the park are coming over.

I ask him how he's feeling about it, the move. Mainly, he says, it's just Mattie that he's worried about: "As long as she makes it through it," he believes they will be all right. He says, "We have been around quite a bit. But this place here, you hate to leave it."

The three generations of Walter and Mattie's family that came for the pork roast that night all lived within three streets of each other in Silver

Sands. Their son Sammy, a 63-year-old, disabled, soft-spoken Vietnam veteran, lived in an RV on the lot directly behind Walter and Mattie's mobile home. Sammy's younger brother Mike, a big-rig truck driver, and his wife, Gail, who ran a stall at the local flea market, lived down the street and their own 24-year-old son, RJ, lived one street over with his girlfriend.

Walter's daughter-in-law, Gail, had adopted his title for the park; in a potted plant outside her singlewide she stuck a wooden sign that read "Welcome to Paradise." But as the family members already knew, paradise was being dismantled by a developer who bought the park to build a 350-apartment mixed-use development. As Walter and Gail began to search for housing, they scoffed at the design plans for the apartments that would replace Silver Sands, the rent for the select number of units that would be deemed "affordable," and the idea that these apartments were superior to their mobile homes:

> Gail: "The way they have them built—I don't want to live in one of them. They are all stacked in there worse than sardines on top of one another. I don't want to live that way."
>
> Plus, Walter points out, based on the plans, the portion of the apartments reserved for affordable housing (capped at 30 percent of income) is completely unaffordable for anyone in their family.
>
> Walter: "They are going to take 30 percent of someone's income?! And if you make $2,000 a month, that's $600 a month!"
>
> Gail: "That's right. You might as well go to the trailer park. At least you have a yard. At least you have a yard and your grandkids can come and visit and have a little bit of room."

The yard was exactly the piece of their homes that Gail and Walter did not own. As their park closed, every household in Walter's family was evicted and scattered to parks where they could find vacant lots to rent. These parks were miles away from each other in neighboring counties to the north and south. To their relief, Walter and Mattie's home was deemed structurally sound for relocation. However, Sammy, Mike, Gail, and RJ all lost their homes and scrambled to find second- and thirdhand RVs and mobile homes to replace them. Yet, the financial losses they endured were eclipsed by a deeper emotional loss as they, like Kathleen, Randall, and hundreds of other residents who took part in this study, were dispossessed not only of their homes and communities but of their sense of dignity and their rights as citizens.

The experiences of Kathleen, Randall, and Walter, like the experiences of all those recounted in this book, reveal the complex intermingling of pride, stigma, investment, and uncertainty that are central to life on the private poverty housing market and in the mobile home park. There are no figures for how many residents are affected by the "epidemic of closures" (CFED 2011) occurring in mobile home parks. These closures likely impact a substantial number of low-income residents in a substantial range of community types. This ethnography was equally substantial, conducted among 180 evicted residents in 32 parks in two states: parks large and small, parks in city centers and on the urban fringe, parks filled with young families and parks filled with single men, parks where a majority of residents were elderly white retirees and parks where a majority of residents were undocumented Latino/a immigrants. Each of the residents who took part in this study faced eviction as their park was slated to close.[7] These participants included 113 residents of Silver Sands (where I lived), Sawgrass Estates, and six other closing parks in Florida and 67 residents of Ramos y Ramos (where I lived), Twin Oaks, Trail's End, and 21 other closing parks in Texas. A methodological appendix provides a description of how I found and took up residency in Silver Sands and Ramos y Ramos, details about the surrounding parks where I worked, descriptions of the participants, and reflections on my ethnographic approach.

In all cases I selected parks that were likely closing (which the residents knew) but where eviction notices had not yet been distributed. In that way I was able to enter parks and capture a picture of community life before it began to be dismantled. I then conducted ethnography over two consecutive years, including 17 months living within closing mobile home parks and being evicted alongside residents, and six months of follow-up visits with residents in new parks, family's homes, and a number of precarious housing situations. Like Kathleen, Randall, and Walter, these residents allowed me to accompany them in the heightened and sometimes desperate moments when they managed the practical aspects of their forced removal and in the intimate moments when they reflected on the meaning of their home, their community, and their eviction. Over time, residents became accustomed to my daily presence in the park and to our perpetual companion, a digital recorder on which I recorded every interaction we had. All field notes excerpts are pulled directly from transcriptions of those recordings and quoted passages are reproduced verbatim (see the methodological appendix for details of the collection and analysis of all data including the transcriptions of a thousand individual audio recordings from over three hundred hours of MP3 files).

During these years, I practiced a slow ethnography, waiting with residents to see how eviction would unfold. Residents knew me first as a researcher and only second as a neighbor. We all knew that when the final day of the eviction came, I would go home or to another park to repeat the process. Although I spent years as the neighbor of the people in this book I would never suffer the same losses, face the same stigma, or endure the same hardships. Over these years I was never in the same position as my neighbors and I never tried to become like them, to fill their shoes. Instead I chose to walk beside them as they navigated a difficult terrain. This was not an ethnography of becoming, it was an ethnography of "being there" (Geertz 1988).[8]

In my first weeks living inside the first park where I took up residence, a woman came knocking at the door of my singlewide. She had her eight-year-old daughter in tow, at home sick from school, helping her mom hand out flyers for the mobile home trucking company where the woman worked. The woman had been sent door to door to drum up business for the trucking company, which exclusively moved homes out of closing parks. I had moved into the park to get evicted but I had never heard of such an eviction service; the woman listed several competitor companies in the area. I had spent the last year in a university lab using Geographic Information Systems (GIS) to identify where park closures were occurring (see chapter 2); the woman rattled off half a dozen parks that were likely closing nearby. I peppered her with questions as if our encounter were a rare opportunity; she looked at me, off-put, busy, and slightly bemused as she explained she was only the first in a long line of movers and park owners that would be knocking on my door.

There is money to be made from poverty housing, and so in addition to following the paths of evicted mobile home residents, I followed the money and found, just as Kathleen had, that mobile home park evictions are trans-actional processes taking place within a field of interested actors. Kathleen had spent hours on the phone and the internet to map out these actors in a desperate search to find help rebuilding her ramp. I spent months and years tracing the web of actors, companies, and transactions involved in mobile home park evictions to understand their effects. As Kathleen's story illus-trated, the closure of the park looked different from her perspective than from the perspective of the landlord who evicted her, the movers who moved her home, the city council who approved her park's closure, and the member of the board that set the policies for relocation in her state. This ethnography reconstructs evictions from these multiple perspectives, focus-ing on the configurations of relations that make up a mass eviction. Thus in addition to the fieldwork conducted alongside 180 evicted residents, ethnographic fieldwork included interactions with almost two dozen pro-fessional players in the mobile home marketplace. This included participant observation and in-depth interviews with 15 expert key informants: park landlords, property developers, mobile home industry representatives, industry and public aid lawyers, and state officials. It included training at the for-profit Mobile Home University alongside 18 eager entrepreneurs seeking guidance in mobile home park investing. It also included days spent riding alongside and talking shop with 12 mobile home movers, installers, and company owners working with four different moving companies that split, hitched, and hauled mobile homes out of closing parks in both Florida and Texas.

It was this network of actors that shaped the byzantine process of dislocation that led Walter to ask powerlessly "what can we do?" as three generations of his family were evicted. In response to Walter's question, his soft-spoken son Sammy summarized the treatment of his family and neighbors by stating blankly, "We're trailer trash to them."

SPATIAL STIGMA AND "SITE EFFECTS"

Trash. The word encapsulates the disposability of mobile home park residents and the communities they call home. It also encapsulates the economic and political justification for their displacement—the perpetual pursuit of "highest and best use" in the legal language of real estate analysts and city planners. Finally, it encapsulates broader social processes by which the priorities of urban policy, the politics of metropolitan growth regimes, and the regulatory tactics of state governments redefine public responsibility for the poor. The very process of urban redevelopment and revitalization is a process of taking out the trash, what sociologist Loïc Wacquant (2008b: 198) calls "the cleansing of the built environment and the streets from the physical and human detritus wrought by economic deregulation and welfare retrenchment." Stigma is central in defining and then removing the "trash" from the urban environment. Processes of stigmatization are thus central to contemporary urban inequalities and, more generally, to the contemporary operation of power.

Tracing mobile home residents' paths into and out of eviction requires separating myth from reality in the mobile home park and tracing the historical roots of the marginality and stigma that attaches itself to the places they live. Stigma is rooted in the very spaces where trailer park residents make their homes. Thus, I conceptualize trailer park stigma in terms of the "spatial oppositions" that Pierre Bourdieu argues are central to our understanding of social space.[9] Social space organizes itself through hierarchical classifications and social distances that in turn are naturalized through the inscription of social distinctions into the physical world (Bourdieu 1999). Theorizing the production of inequality in the ghetto and the lower-class *banalieue*, Bourdieu uses the concept of "site effects" to describe how physical space both signifies and reproduces social power. He argues that marginalized spaces (spaces much like the derided trailer park) are most often perceived "not [as] 'realities'—largely unknown in any case to the people who rush to talk about them—but phantasms, which feed on emotional experiences stimulated by more or less uncontrolled words and images" (ibid., 123). The mobile home park demonstrates how these *subjective* images, narratives, and associations shape *objective* treatments of place, not only those that emerge in individual attitudes but those that are formalized in urban regulations and codified in law. The chapters that follow analyze "site effects" in the mobile home park by probing the relationship between spatial and social marginality, thereby "*emplacing*" marginalized space to understand how "the material and the interpretive, the physical and the semiotic … work autonomously *and* in a mutually dependent way" (Gieryn 2000: 467).

"Emplacing" place—borrowing phenomenological understandings of place from the fields of philosophy and human geography—helps us understand places as sources of identity (Relph 1976), as sources of security (Tuan 1977), and as sources of roots (Heidegger 1958). Emplacing place is one way to understand the real-life consequences that symbolic understandings of place can yield. The concept of place is *moralized* in value-laden understandings of home, hearth, and roots (see especially Cresswell 2001). These concepts are negatively reflected in the semantic distinction between a permanent community and a transitory mobile home "park." The moralization of place, roots, and permanence goes hand in hand with the *sociospatial stigma* that characterizes mobile home parks and their presumably mobile residents. Sociological theories of stigma refer to outward signs signifying a deficient or tainted moral status that discredits an individual and bars that person from full social participation (Goffman 1963). In Goffman's theory, stigma manifests as a discrepancy between an "actual" social identity and a perceived or "virtual" social identity that nonetheless shapes all social interaction with the stigmatized (ibid., 3). Yet, Goffman's theory only references individual disqualifying features of persons and never the disqualifying features of the places where they live.[10]

Wacquant (2016: 1078) updates Goffman and incorporates Bourdieu's understanding of site effects to argue that *territorial stigmatization* is a primary mechanism through which urban outcasts are "selected, thrust and maintained in marginal locations" (see also Wacquant, Slater, and Pereira

2014). These processes are central to how advanced urban marginality is produced and maintained in the "hyperghettos" of the United States (Wacquant 2008a). The halfway homeownership of mobile home park residents is a product of similar processes. The mobile home has been thrust to the nether regions of both the American city and the American housing hierarchy, while the mobile home park is maintained in its secondary status by financing laws that define homes in parks as non–real estate, by zoning codes that prohibit parks in single-family residential areas, and by municipal regulations that require parks be "visually screened" from outside view, "set back" minimum distances from public roads, and "buffered," fenced in, or walled off from the communities around them (Sanders 1986). Meanwhile, the same regulatory treatment of mobile home parks—their classification as a substandard land use, their spatial isolation in the urban fabric, and their lack of protection under current law—primes the pump for capital investment in park properties, contributing to their redevelopment.

In the reviled trailer park, territorial stigmatization and the moralization of place are flip sides of the same coin. In much the same way, the problem of manufactured insecurity is a double-sided dilemma. The visible trauma that unfolds when a park closes and an entire community is dismantled is only one side of a more constant, quotidian crisis—one in which an entire class of community members is effectively "zoned out" (Levine 2006) of collective metropolitan life. Much has been said about the social and semiotic processes that produce urban marginality and its spatial expression, territorial stigmatization (Wacquant 2009; Slater forthcoming). Less is written about the mutually constitutive relationship between the *perception* of place and the *regulation* of place, even while urban regulations provide a primary mechanism for establishing and maintaining spatial inequalities (Levine 2006; Rothwell and Massey 2010; Valverde 2012; Lens and Monkkonen 2016).

The process through which this occurs is intricately shaped by local and state laws. As the following chapters describe, the regulation of the private poverty housing market and regulatory responses to mobile home park evictions are characterized by a shift toward private-market solutions that characterize low-income housing policy specifically and poverty governance more generally. Mobile home parks, as the largest source of unsubsidized affordable housing and a lucrative, expanding U.S. industry, cannot be understood apart from this context. These private-market approaches are central to the program of contemporary neoliberalism.

In its most abridged form, neoliberalism is a term defined as a preference for free market exchange over government intervention (Centeno and

Cohen 2012). In its most expansive form, neoliberalism threatens to become "the next popular metaconcept in the social sciences" (Hackworth 2007: xi). In its most analytically useful form, neoliberalism describes techniques of national and urban governance that simultaneously dismantle redistributive public welfare policies (Greenhouse 2009) while constructing new policies, practices, and partnerships that sustain the functioning of private markets (Harvey 2005; Brown 2006; Hays 2003; Collins and Mayer 2010; Peck and Tickell 2012). It is in this final form that the concept of neoliberalism can be mobilized to understand the roles that the private poverty housing market and spatial stigmatization play in producing contemporary urban marginality.

These issues surrounding place, roots, power, and marginality come to the surface when parks are redeveloped and residents are removed, as the stories of Kathleen, Randall, and Walter begin to show. This book probes the relation between social and physical space, between social and physical marginalization. It explores how social and spatial stigma intersect to create a class of citizens for whom a precarious right to place is a daily reality.

"YOU WOULDN'T THINK IT WAS A TRAILER"

I met Tabitha for the first time when I was having lunch with her neighbor Betty and she insisted on bringing me along as she went to visit Tabitha in the singlewide next door. This was something Betty and Tabitha did often, as Tabitha's poor health kept her inside her home. Almost daily, Betty dropped by to check in on her neighbor:

> Betty insists I come with her next door and we walk about 15 feet to Tabitha's front porch. Tabitha is a tiny, frail woman, maybe only five feet tall and 90 pounds. The neck of her shirt keeps slipping around her slender shoulder. The shoulder is bandaged up where she recently had surgery after a fall in her home.
>
> Her house is immaculately clean. It feels very spacious inside, as Betty points out upon entering, telling me this is because the trailer is "so wide." The home is an "extrawide," which means it's about two feet wider than standard singlewides. Tabitha is very proud of her house. She keeps it clean and gives me a slow and detailed guided tour of everything in the house, even the bathrooms. She points out the built-in storage and the space for washer and dryer inside the home. Every corner of the house is spotless and lavishly decorated with items related to one of two themes: carousel horses or flamingos. Outside the front door, in Tabitha's screened-in porch, flamingos abound in the form of stuffed animals, yard ornaments, and hanging wind chimes.

Betty looks at me, nodding, during the tour to see if I appreciate the loveliness of Tabitha's home. She remarks, "It doesn't look like a trailer, it looks like a home."

Tabitha asks with earnestness, "You wouldn't think it was a trailer, would you?"

In her study of the effects of urban renewal on the cultural, economic, and emotional life of African American communities, Mindy Thompson Fullilove (2005: 20) emphasizes, "we cannot understand the losses unless we first appreciate what was there." Doing so in mobile home communities requires a picture of park life freed from the stigmatizing tropes that form the cultural effigy of the trailer park. Indeed the willingness, even eagerness, of residents like Tabitha to invite me inside, show me around, and discuss in detail the space of their home is both a product of deeply felt stigmatization and evidence of a conscious effort to counterpose the myths and realities of mobile home life. Tabitha's question, "You wouldn't think it was a trailer, would you?" exposes an attempt to dispel stigma or, to paraphrase Goffman (1963), to manage a spoiled identity. Tabitha's question also speaks to ambivalence over this stigma and knowledge of what is at stake in the symbolic representation of the home. The tainted and tainting image of the mobile home that produces this ambivalence originates in the complex history of manufactured housing as a uniquely American housing invention.

I explore the architectural and social history of the mobile home in chapter 1, which traces the historical roots of the mobile home as a techno-legal artifact and a national housing intervention. This architectural history introduces a central theme regarding the built-in tension between mobility and permanence that is fundamental to manufactured housing. The chapter highlights the adaptability and versatility that have made the mobile home an indispensable contribution to the American housing stock over the last century. The same versatility has contributed to the precipitous growth of manufactured housing in recent decades and to its current role as the largest form of unsubsidized low-income housing in the country. Yet, understanding the contemporary spread of manufactured housing also requires situating the housing form within an historic shift in the provision of affordable housing over the last four decades. This first chapter explores the past and recent history of the mobile home, illustrating that the spread of mobile home parks is a close contemporary of the retraction of the state from the provision of low-income housing under the neoliberal administration of the social security net.

Within mobile home parks, residents' housing insecurity is codified in housing regulations that make them halfway homeowners and in urban development priorities that make them and their homes disposable. Chapter 2 analyzes how the *social stigmatization* of park residents is tied to the *spatial stigmatization* of park properties, which is maintained through local ordinances and state regulations that geographically seal off, segregate, and screen parks from the cities outside their walls. Here I expand the conventional sociological concept of stigma that focuses on interpersonal dynamics (Goffman 1986) to explore the ways social and spatial stigma intersect to create and maintain a secondary legal status for mobile home park residents.

Chapter 3 turns to life within parks and to detailed interactions with evicted residents who invited me inside their homes even as they prepared to be forced out of them. Contextualized in the history of housing stigma, these invitations should be seen in terms of residents' attempts (like Tabitha's) to dispel myths of mobile home life, but they were also part of a broader effort to enlist me to bear witness to a deep sense of unease over eviction. Time and again residents offered to lead tours before they began to box up their homes, disassemble their patios, and say goodbye to their gardens. They expressed gratitude toward the technologies of ethnographic record—pulling the recorder toward their voice, requesting and posing for photos with their homes, confirming "did you get that on your device?" Without knowing it, they were creating a record of a life they would never recover. In these months of waiting to be evicted, they could not imagine the great changes these relocations would bring, not simply in new damage to repair, new neighbors to meet, and new communities to navigate but in people's very understanding of their place in the world and their rights as citizens. These changes began even before the catalytic moments of upheaval when homes were hauled out of closing parks. As chapter 3 explores, this subjective shift was produced through a daily process of living under the threat of eviction, under the *specter of dislocation*. The specter of dislocation meant that long before she was ever evicted from her home Christy, like so many others, came to experience an increasing sense of powerlessness in the face of her forced removal.

> Out on her deck, Christy lights up a cigarette. When asked if she has been smoking more since the relocation began, she answers, "Oh gosh yes, and drinking." She used to drink a beer or two occasionally but now she will have a beer and chase it with a shot of liquor. She expects this increase in drinking is because she is out of pain medication—she used up her regular prescription early with the physical and mental stress of moving. She is actually out of all of her medications currently, including her blood pressure medication because she ran through them and can't afford to refill them right now. She's saving for the relocation.

She feels out of sorts and can't put her finger on exactly what's going on emotionally. It's many things. She sighs, as if trying to get a handle on how she feels, "I've been a basket case." Over the afternoon she cries several times when attempting to describe the feeling of waiting to be relocated, but then she sniffles and tries to pull herself together. In a defeated voice she says softly, "I am so tired . . . It *weighs* on you."

This *weight*, as Christy terms it, the load of daily life lived under the specter of dislocation, is brought to the fore in the frustration and inefficacy residents experienced during the actual relocation process. Chapter 4 describes the upheaval of mobile home park evictions from inside multiple parks in both Florida and Texas. This chapter pays special attention to the community-wide effects of eviction, especially to the sustained sense of collective indignation that extended beyond the immediate and individual losses of property. Through detail of residents' attempts to reconstruct their lives in the face of dislocation, it builds a picture of eviction as both individual and collective trauma.

Chapter 5 details the broader impacts of eviction from both inside and outside of parks. It does so by following the day-to-day preparations, expressed anxieties, searches for new housing, and strategies for relocating in multiple different households. It also examines the process of relocation from the standpoint of moving crews and relocation service providers. Ultimately the shape of these residents' evictions was determined not by the residents themselves and not by the workers who pulled their homes from their foundations. Rather, the experience of eviction was foremost a product of differing state housing policies meant to manage the mass evictions of park residents and administer (or not) relocation assistance. While the preceding chapters explore the shared experience of life under the specter of dislocation, this chapter focuses on the differing experiences of eviction under different state regulatory regimes in Texas and Florida. It explores distinctive iterations of contemporary neoliberal housing policy in the two states and analyzes the effects for evicted residents.

Chapter 6 returns to the central paradoxes at the heart of manufactured housing to understand how park residents' housing insecurity is shaped by market forces that wring economic value out of an otherwise devalued housing form. Examining the mobile home park marketplace at multiple scales, this chapter maps the field of economic transactions that shape housing processes in mobile home parks. From the operations of individual companies working within the closing parks where I lived, to the California resort where I enrolled alongside eager entrepreneurs in the for-profit

"Mobile Home University," to the investment portfolios of some of the richest individuals in the United States, mobile home park housing insecurity is structured by forces far beyond individual closing parks. This chapter explores how the intersection between poverty and profit in the low-income housing market (Desmond 2016) operates well beyond the boundaries of individual neighborhoods or even cities and structures a national multibillion-dollar industry.

The conclusion outlines the broader picture painted by residents' experience of eviction, a picture that provides a snapshot of contemporary housing insecurity in the United States. While the conclusion provides policy recommendations specific to mobile home parks, ultimately the deeply felt dislocations described in these pages call for more than mere policy prescriptions. They call for a critique of the role of housing policy in the production of housing crises. Within research on contemporary urban marginality, sociologists have become concerned with a "growing heteronomy of urban research" (Wacquant 2008b: 198), which produces research driven by the priorities of policymakers and city officials. Imagining a solution benefits from thinking across disciplines, as human geographers remind us that *policy-relevant* research should not necessarily be limited to *policy-driven* research (Wyly 2004). An analytic solution hinges upon critical inquiry constructed to interrogate the role of policy in the production of inequality rather than merely appending policy prescriptions as an unavoidable ancillary to the research (Slater 2010). In other words, as geographer Robert Lake (2003: 463) argues, "a less constraining alternative to policy relevance is *policy critique.*"

The crisis of mass eviction in mobile home parks is *produced through* and then *managed by* the laws and policies put in place to regulate manufactured housing and its residents. As the following chapters describe, state housing regulations and land use ordinances are not impersonal forces or purely technological artifacts, they are social objects. This analysis of poverty housing and the social production of crises in mobile home parks borrows from architectural history, planning theory, legal scholarship, and critical geography, putting the insights of these disciplines into conversation with sociological theories of power. Our very understanding of home and community, and our experience when homes and communities are dismantled, hinge on the ways we regulate those spaces. These regulations in turn comprise complex cultural narratives with deep historical roots. I begin by exploring how these historical roots inform contemporary understandings of the mobile home park and the people who live there.

1. The Mobile Home in America and Americana

The owners of the singlewide on lot #83, Marta and George had abandoned their mobile home and their investment in a Florida retirement after they received the notice of an application for a rezoning of Silver Sands Mobile Home Park. At first, they debated whether to abandon the home or wait to see what the city council would decide with regard to the rezoning. The notice, delivered to every household in Silver Sands, was not an eviction letter but to many residents it signaled the probability of eviction. Marta and George decided they could not continue to invest $250 in lot rent each month while they waited to be evicted. They had banked on a Florida retirement on a budget. The weather would help with George's arthritis and the proximity to Marta and George's adult son would help them both as they aged.[1] They thought of attempting to sell the pre-owned, circa-1989 trailer, which they had purchased on site in Silver Sands, but any purchaser would need to commit to moving it at a cost of up to $10,000. The many For Sale postings in the Silver Sands laundry room indicated that the sale of their aging singlewide was unlikely. They signed over ownership of their home to Ron Silver, owner and landlord of Silver Sands, rather than pay continued rent or abandonment fines. In May 2012, Mr. Silver rented the fully furnished singlewide to me for $600 a month on a month-to-month basis so that he could continue to earn income on the lot in the months during which the sale of the park was finalized and the eviction was carried out. Over the next 11 months I would sleep in the couple's abandoned bed, eat off their abandoned mixed-matched plates, and work into the night transcribing that day's recordings on their old corduroy recliner.

On first arriving in the home I boxed up George and Marta's abandoned items, making note as I went: a prescription bottle of cholesterol medication, children's beach toys with price tags still on them, a hanging calendar marked with dates of doctor's appointments at the VA hospital (the month turned to April 2012), a guide to other Florida mobile home parks, a metal wall-hanging that read "Bless This Home." Outside in the screened-in porch that ran the length of the singlewide, I swept the linoleum floor, took a break in the aluminum patio furniture, dusted off and rearranged a sea-shell collection.

But what I learned about the owners of this Florida mobile home came less from the objects I found inside and more from the neighbors just out-side, many of whom could recount intimate details of George and Marta's life. The details were similar to others in the park. George and Marta were staging an incremental move into their mobile home, downsizing from their long-term home in New Hampshire. They were drawn to Jupiter, Florida, because they had a son who lived nearby; he had stopped by frequently to check on them. The extra help from their son was especially important now as Marta's Alzheimer's progressed. But Marta's illness and the expense they knew they would incur if they were forced to move their home also played into their decision to abandon the home in the face of eviction rather than continue to pay rent in a gamble that the rezoning of the park might not be approved. They gave up the singlewide and their investment rather than deal with eviction on top of their many health problems.

Neighbors were able to recount the details of George and Marta's life because of a unique closeness that existed in the parks where I lived, where homes might be only 10 feet away from each other. The social and spatial closeness I noted in every park where I spent time is constructed, in part, by the tools of urban governance. Zoning regulations, for instance, often restrict mobile homes exclusively to mobile home parks while also requir-ing a separation of uses between land zoned as a mobile home park and land zoned as single-family residential. Though overdetermined by local plan-ning, this closeness feels organic, creating an internal cohesiveness that leads many to define their neighborhood as the park rather than the sur-rounding community (Apgar et al. 2002). Historic zoning and restrictive covenants require separation between mobile home parks and "conven-tional" homes, but also lead to the development of self-contained commu-nities, walled off and separated from their neighbors, accessed by single entrance points that require residents to drive or walk past the homes of neighbors as they wind their way home. Municipal regulations that protect neighboring real estate values require parks to be visually screened or fenced off, but this often creates networks of safe internal streets where people can meet or children can play without the threat of through-traffic.

FIGURE 1.   Example of visual screening around a mobile home park. Photo by Helena Bowen, 2017.

FIGURE 2.   A man plays with his child on the street in front of his mobile home. Photo courtesy of *The Press Democrat,* 2009.

This chapter explores how the regulatory treatment of the mobile home park is intricately linked to the historical development of the mobile home as a uniquely American housing invention.[2] Planning and zoning regulations have shaped the development and proliferation of mobile home parks as well as the everyday life that occurs within them. By tracing the production and regulation of the housing form over the last century, this chapter helps to contextualize the social and spatial stigma that is central to constructing mobile home park residents' housing insecurity and disposing them to dislocation.

Paradoxically, the spatial containment and social segregation produced by a century of restrictive regulations also contribute to a sense of neighborliness found in parks. In both Texas and Florida, park residents used the open spaces inside parks as their personal playgrounds. In Twin Oaks and Trail's End in Alvin, Texas, even the most diligent parents let small children play freely in the park, out of eyesight, often in and out of neighbors' homes. In Silver Sands, elderly neighbors could be seen each evening riding alone or in pairs on the stable three-wheeled bicycles that were a popular item among residents. They biked their rounds along the park's nine internal streets, stopping to talk with neighbors while perched right in the center of the road.

Silver Sands resident Hanna did this each evening. She did not drive, seldom left the park, and dutifully rode her bike each night to stay active. At 80 years old she was tanned and toned and said, "I am feeling pretty good!" When I first met Hanna out on her bike she stopped to get the details on who I was and how I was able to move in to Silver Sands, which was one of Florida's many "55 and older" parks devoted to seniors. She guessed that the rules did not mean as much since the park was now up for sale. Hanna moved to Jupiter, Florida, from Switzerland in the 1950s at a boom time for mobile home parks in the United States. She lived nearby with an uncle while Silver Sands was being constructed, and in 1969 they decided to move into the park. In those years, the road outside Silver Sands was still unpaved and the park was on the outskirts of the town. By moving into Silver Sands, Hanna and her uncle were able to purchase a brand new, two-bedroom doublewide and live only three miles inland from the ocean. A mobile home cost $5,000 on average that year compared to $25,000, the median price of a new site-built home with land in 1969 (U.S. Census Bureau 2016a). Hanna's home joined the 3,799,730 mobile homes shipped from factories nationally in the years from 1967 to 1976 (Wallis 1991), a record that decade and a trend that would continue to grow.

In 1967, just two years before Hanna moved into Silver Sands, planner Margaret Drury concluded in her pioneer study of the mobile home industry: "Being forced out of the conventional market, the mobile home industry has been operating in an extraterritorial market where it has had free rein. The industry has thus produced an innovative low-cost housing unit, and indeed, mobile homes have effected an unrecognized revolution in American housing" (138). Drury's conclusion begins to encapsulate the inherent tensions that have characterized manufactured housing since its inception. Through a brief architectural and social history of the mobile home, this chapter explores these tensions: between innovation and defamation, necessity and marginality, demand and derision. These tensions are literally *built in* to the mobile home as a cultural object and a uniquely American housing invention. This chapter examines the historic roots of these tensions, and of the perceptions of trailer life they have produced. It traces the origins of the mobile home as a techno-legal artifact as well as a place that low-income Americans call home. Through emphasis on *modularity*—the standardized but flexible prefabrication systems that are critical to factory-produced housing—it documents the changing social and political needs the mobile home has been adapted to fill over the last century and demonstrates how, in filling these needs, the mobile home has come to hold a distinct and denigrated position in the iconography of Americana and the hierarchy of American housing.

HYBRIDITY AND MODULARITY

Throughout its history, design innovations and manufacturing technologies have shaped the production of manufactured housing and revolutionized its final product, the mobile home. Unlike conventional site-built housing, the rate of innovation in manufactured housing was accelerated by techniques of standardization and prefabrication that were introduced into home construction through factory production beginning in the 1920s. While standardized production methods facilitated affordability, the modular design of the mobile home facilitated innovation. Experimentation and flexibility were more practical and less risky within the strict parameters required to factory-produce a self-contained, transportable housing unit.

The concept of *modularity* describes the degree to which distinct functional units can be combined or interchanged to form a biological, electronic, or mechanical system. In manufacturing, modularity refers to the use of interchangeable parts in the fabrication of a product. But the importance of modularity in the system of mobile home production and the rise of the manufactured housing industry is best understood in light of definitions of modularity from other fields. In contemporary art and architecture, modularity refers to the use of standardized units of measurement to create larger compositions. In ecology, modularity is the organization of an ecosystem according to discrete, individual units that can increase the system's overall resiliency (Thébault and Fontaine 2010). In computer science, studies of modularity build off seminal work on complex adaptive systems, which "change and reorganize their component parts to adapt themselves to the problems posed by their surroundings" (Holland 1992: 18). Understandings of modularity and complex adaptive systems have been used to explain technological revolutions like the rise of the internet.

These concepts of modularity are useful for understanding the development and spread of other innovative technologies and industries, like the manufactured housing industry. Modularity in design parameters supports experimentation while still managing complexity and uncertainty (Baldwin and Clark 2000). In this way modularity is at the core of design evolutions that produce industry evolutions, which can be highly responsive to broader societal changes. Thus in the case of manufactured housing, itself a hybrid between the house and the automobile, the very concept of *modularity* has a hybrid meaning. It applies to the technical design and construction of mobile homes, those components which make them prefabricable, replicable, transportable, and incomparably affordable. But modularity also encapsulates the responsiveness of mobile homes to broader societal changes. As this chapter explores, mobile homes have filled multiple distinct roles throughout U.S. history as they have been adapted to respond to pressing social and economic needs of the times. This dual role, this hybrid *techno-social modularity*, has characterized manufactured housing since its inception and has served to anchor the mobile home in the American housing stock.

BUILDING A HOME ON THE FACTORY FLOOR

From its early beginnings, the history of manufactured housing was a ballet of innovative technological responses to new social needs. In the Americas, the first appearance of prefabricated housing was spurred on by the demands of "forty-niners" in the Gold Rush of 1848 (Peterson 1948). By 1850, five thousand prefabricated houses were contracted or produced in New York alone. The homes were produced at a cost of about $400 and shipped to California where they were sold for about $5,000 to prospectors who were in search of fortune and in need of housing (Kelly 1952).

These Gold Rush mobile dwellings demonstrate the globalism of early revolutions in prefabricated housing. Designed with sheets of corrugated iron—an 1830s English invention—mobile structures were being built and shipped all over the globe (Herbert 1978). The global prefabricated housing network had its roots in the demands of colonizing British forces, who expected to transport the comforts of a familiar home to new colonial settings. The response, corrugated iron "portable houses," was a technology of colonial expansion (ibid.). Indeed, factory production taking place in England shaped the built environments of colonies overseas. In the latter half of the nineteenth century corrugated iron became the most conspicuous building material in the colonial territory of South Africa, where whole towns were made of "iron houses" and the beams of the Johannesburg railroad station were factory-rolled in Birmingham, England (ibid.).

The period of importing prefabricated homes to the United States was brief. Enterprising U.S. manufacturers quickly intercepted the foreign export of housing demand and ramped up domestic production. Beginning in the 1860s, manufacturers throughout the United States introduced improved prefabricated designs that ranged from standardized wood-panelized cottages to a 1908 precast iron and cement multistory home proposed by Thomas Edison (Kelly 1952).[3]

In an example of the essential hybridity at the heart of manufactured housing, the technological innovations that eventually propelled the mobile home into a national place in American housing came not from the house-building trade, but rather from the automobile and aerospace industries. In 1919 Glenn Curtis, a founder of the U.S. aircraft industry, designed and built a "motor bungalow" that he named the Aerocar, a towable version of the factory-built home. The idea took off. Early 1920s trailer designs took the form of "covered wagons" and "autocampers" (Wallis 1991). The streamlined design and curved metallic edges of early mobile homes showcased the automotive lineage and factory precision of their construction. This aesthetic hybridity is referenced in the Airstream trailers popularized in the 1960s, which have experienced a rebirth as trendy recreational homes today.

The American popularity of the automobile catalyzed the popularity of the trailer. Meanwhile, the techno-social modularity of the mobile home meant that households quickly began to adapt the design to changing social needs. While the first factory-built trailers were a luxury item of the upper class, improvised knockoff models came to be increasingly used by lower-income households. In 1926, the *New Republic* termed an emerging mobile breed of residents "gasoline gypsies," noting that their passion for mobility led them to accept pop-up auto camps as "real" neighborhoods (Schneider 2005). Magazine and newspaper articles often mistook these households' pressing economic needs for a "passion for distance" that they believed characterized the early population of mobile home dwellers.

The manufactured housing industry of the time was equally misguided in its designs. Throughout the 1920s and 1930s high-tech, yacht-like designs were offered for sale, catering to the original class of luxury consumer. Yet the most common versions of the trailer were less expensive towable homes of wood and canvas developed by residents themselves. During these decades three out of four trailers were homemade (Wallis 1991). The techno-social modularity at the heart of the mobile home continued to allow a subset of the country's most impoverished residents to adapt the design to their own housing needs. This shift was illustrated by the changing face of the municipal campgrounds where these trailers were parked. By 1924 the municipal campgrounds originally designed to attract vacationing recreational vehicles were beginning to suffer: "A less desirable class of camper was moving in, encouraged by the free facilities . . . Unlike the vacationing camper, the 'hobo tourist' often had no permanent home and was likely to stay on in a campground for as long as possible" (ibid., 40).

This trend peaked in the Great Depression years. During the 1930s, the term "park" began to replace the former term "campground," illustrating the decreased mobility of the trailer and its increased use as permanent affordable housing. The techno-social modularity of the mobile home was fundamental to this shift. During the Great Depression, the technological product of an era of innovation and prosperity became a ready-made solution for a time of economic uncertainty and hardship. The mobile home was once again adapted to fill a crucial housing need, this time for a transitory population in desperate search of work.

This was especially true for the droves of families escaping the Dust Bowl in the Great Plains. They improvised trailer homes out of scrap metal, attached them to their automobiles, and moved west. In California, migrants escaping the Dust Bowl in search of work were problematic for an established system of migratory labor that had relied on a short-term, on-demand, harvest-time work force of single men, primarily Mexican laborers and itinerate tramps or hobos called "bindle-stiffs" (Cresswell 2001). Unlike the migratory agricultural laborers on which California's crops depended, the Dust Bowl migrants were in perpetual need of labor in the localities where they relocated. Unlike Mexican migrant workers who were segregated into "Jim towns" and transitory bindle-stiffs who rented a piece of floor in 10-cent lodging houses, these new migrants lived out of their "jalopies" in large "trailer camps." Eventually residents began to consolidate encampments into more stable communities; or, as historians of the Dust Bowl claim, they "convert[ed] squatters' camps that were located just outside towns into permanent suburban slums" (Stein 1973: 51).

The trailer park was born. These first trailer parks—permanent encampments of ostensibly mobile, deeply impoverished families—continued to proliferate. By the mid-1930s, an estimated 79 percent of U.S. households could not afford even a "low-cost" home priced with a lot at $4,000 (NRPB 1941). In 1933, at the peak of the Great Depression, house building had dropped to 10 percent of its 1925 peak. At this time, "the nation, struggling through a depression, turned anxious eyes towards the technical world in the hope that some mass-production miracle might occur" (Kelly 1952: 29). Radically low-cost manufactured housing provided just such a panacea: "Though born in the Depression, trailer manufacturing was an industry in which a relatively small investment could return an enormous profit" (Wallis 1991: 47). The effects of the Depression made mobility for employment central to residential choice at the same time that it led industries to scramble for new market opportunities in a deeply changed economy. The techno-social modularity of the mobile home meant that the housing artifact was once again adapted to fill an economic need, this time of the manufacturing industry. Across multiple industries, mobile homes were designed to use the maximum amount of whatever material their parent company produced (Kelly 1952: 44). In 1937, with other industries still reeling from the effects of the Depression, sales of mobile homes doubled from the previous year, reaching an estimated $55 million (Wallis 1991).

The use of mobile homes as permanent housing fueled by Depression-era production also fueled resistance to the homes and their residents. Communities became concerned that "trailerites, especially migrant worker families, would descend upon them *en masse*, draining local services" (Wallis 1991: 71). Trailer residents came to be seen as a destabilizing feature of local towns. Because they did not own the land under their homes, they did not pay individual property taxes like conventional homeowners and were seen as a drain on public services. Driven by their own subsistence needs and used in vast numbers to support the mercurial needs of the agro-industry, early trailer migrants were seen as expendable and unattached. The trailer parks where they lived "threatened to become a serious social and political dislocation in counties that could not possibly absorb a new population" (Stein 1973: 44). Park residents embodied the socioeconomic anxiety of middle-class residents at the time: "Wandering to the edges of the cities, idling in crude dwellings, unemployed, impoverished, these Americans and their tawdry trailers represented the threat that loomed in every citizen's life—the loss of job, social status, and a permanent home" (Hartman 2011).

These are the roots of the socio-spatial stigma that continues to shape housing insecurity in the mobile home park. Trailer park residents were viewed as outsiders in the civic life of local towns and a drain on overextended local resources. Meanwhile their numbers continued to grow. By 1938, the American Automobile Association estimated that there were 300,000 travel trailers in the United States and that 10 percent of them were being used for full-time housing: "It was this 10 percent of the so-called 'trailerite' population that became the focus of some municipalities around the country. Irate citizens, shocked by what they regarded as unsightly 'trailer slums' peopled by transients of questionable character, demanded their abatement. Before the end of the decade many towns and cities passed exclusionary zoning and ordinances that prohibited the use of trailers as housing, banished them from the city limits, or to commercial trailer courts, or required occupied trailers to be moved every few days" (Grissim 2003: 16). Public objections to trailer parks will be familiar to students of other forms of low-income housing and the Not In My Back Yard (NIMBY) activism that often accompanies its construction. City councils across the nation began to respond to public objections that trailer park occupants did not contribute their share of taxes for public services and that the parks threatened real estate values and housed a seedy, immoral, and socially threatening segment of the population; they did so by enacting restrictive ordinances and exclusionary zoning. Such actions followed the late nineteenth-century precedent of using zoning regulations to exclude socially undesirably ethnic minorities (Bernhardt 1981). Local regulatory bodies either prohibited mobile homes altogether or relegated them to the least desirable areas in their jurisdiction, primarily industrial or commercial zones that lacked city amenities (ibid.). This early restrictive regulation perpetuated the stigma associated with park residents, serving to socially and spatially marginalize trailer park residents up to the present day. During the Depression years, just as manufactured housing adapted to fill the most pressing social needs of the time, the concept of trailer trash was born.

FROM TRAVEL TRAILER TO MOBILE HOME

In the decade following the Great Depression, sociologist Robert K. Merton (1948: 165) described the essential conflicts engendered within housing: "Housing as a social institution is undergoing relatively rapid change. And, as in any institutional sphere subject to market change, the field of housing is rich in conflict and controversy. The type of housing to be built, for whom and by whom it is built—all these are matters involving great conflicts of interests and sentiments rooted in economy, society, and culture." Techno-social modularity is not only characteristic of mobile homes themselves, but also the systems designed to produce, transport, install, and regulate them. When the United States entered World War II the need for wartime housing exploded. Meanwhile, material and labor shortages slowed the conventional housing industry. The manufactured housing industry retooled to respond quickly to the sudden wartime demand for housing near the country's defense plants. At the same time, regulations shifted to facilitate the factory production of homes on a national scale.

The advantages of flexibility, mass production, and limited on-site labor lessened regulatory resistance to manufactured housing. In the preceding decade, the manufactured housing industry had responded to restrictive regulation by forming associations between larger manufacturers and more affluent users that sought to downplay the widespread use of trailers as permanent housing and highlight their use as recreational vehicles (Wallis 1991). Now industry representatives were forced to admit that the vast majority of mobile homes were being used as permanent housing. This realization and redefinition benefitted the industry's bottom line, as it allowed manufactured housing producers to receive rationed materials and continue to ramp up production (ibid.).

As regulatory resistance fell away alongside federal demand for prefabricated defense worker homes, the industry introduced the Spartan, an eight-foot-wide trailer complete with a kitchen and bathroom. The U.S. government embraced this ready-made solution to its wartime housing woes, constructing 8,500 trailer parks and purchasing 35,000 of these mobile homes at a price of $750 each (Grissim 2003). Over the course of the war, an estimated 200,000 trailers were used to house a portion of the 4 million workers who moved to defense employment areas. An estimated 80 percent of these trailers were privately owned (Wallis 1991). Wartime needs temporarily relaxed the constellation of zoning restrictions that had established the trailer home as a housing pariah.

As in previous decades, the manufactured housing industry adapted to meet the nation's changing housing demands. The modularity of the housing invention allowed for adjustments to both physical homes and manufacturing systems that rapidly responded to the need for affordable, flexible housing for a mobile wartime workforce. The forced recognition of the mobile home as permanent housing forever changed the manufactured housing industry, which began to produce "mobile homes" rather than road-ready trailers. However, in the WWII years, the sudden overhaul of regulatory resistance and the expectation that the industry produce thousands of units to meet sudden demand ultimately contributed to shoddy construction. The wartime housing demand was met, but the quality of the final product suffered. The lasting image of the mobile home (and mobile home residents) bore the consequences of this low-quality wartime housing. Negative public opinion of the mobile home became further entrenched in the postwar years. Writing during the time, Kelly (1952) determined that beyond the stigma already attached to the mobile home during the Depression era, negative public opinion stemmed mainly from public distaste for the minimum standard manufactured units built under government contract during the war emergency.

From the early history of manufactured housing, the techno-social modularity of the mobile home proved uniquely suited to respond to various boom and bust cycles in U.S. housing, from the Gold Rush of the forty-niners to the migrants of the Dust Bowl. In the WWII years, the mobile home was once again adapted to respond to a pressing social need, but the hurried design and production of the trailer homes used to fill wartime demand further contributed to the stereotype of the mobile home as substandard and disposable housing.

REGULATING THE MODERN MOBILE HOME

Despite these negative stereotypes, interest in the mobile home has continued to grow from the postwar years to the present day. A foreword to a 1952 study by the Bemis Foundation for manufactured housing research at the Massachusetts Institute of Technology begins by noting the "intense" interest in prefabricated housing that had amplified in the postwar period so that "[t]he Foundation was frequently sought out by visitors, especially from abroad, who were seeking the truth about a business concerning which many half-truths or untruths were being said" (Kelly 1952: viii). The report summarizes the sentiments of the time:

> Prefabrication, or the factory manufacture of houses, means many
> different things to different people . . . the seeker for a house who finds
> that what he does not want costs more than what he wants to pay
> imagines that houses produced like automobiles or radios ought to be
> nearer his heart's desire; the entrepreneur imagines that he may be
> another Ford . . . a national president faced with depression may look to
> it as a new industry to lead from the morass; the opponent of subsidized
> housing may see a chance of arresting the tide if the cost of the housing
> unit can be materially reduced through factory methods. And all these
> hopes have some justification if only the successful commercial
> manufacture of housing on a large scale could be achieved. (Kelly
> 1952: ix)

By 1955 consumer demand, industry innovation, and regulatory shifts once again intersected to revolutionize the manufactured housing industry. As postwar housing shortages began to level off, mobile home manufacturers searched for new ways to compete for consumer demand and found an opportunity by lobbying for changes to regulation that allowed for the transport of wider mobile homes. The resulting shift in regulation produced another boom in manufactured housing when the officially named "mobile home" was manufactured at a width of 10 feet in 1955 (Schneider 2005).

This year marks a turning point in the history of the mobile home since this wider unit could not be pulled behind a personal vehicle. From this year on, mobile homes became increasingly *immobile*, creating the many challenges residents in this study faced when they were required to move themselves and their homes following the closure of their parks. The continued production of larger-model mobile homes would increasingly require specialized trucking, increase the expense of transport, and result in a shrinking portion of mobile homes ever being moved from their original site from that year forward (Drury 1972).

At the same time market opportunities, themselves created by changes to current law, contributed to the increased development of mobile home parks where residents could locate these homes. In 1956 Congress bestowed federal recognition on the mobile home park by authorizing the Federal Housing Authority to insure loans (up to 60 percent value) to finance new mobile home park construction. Prior to this legislation (and contributing to their socio-spatial stigmatization), mobile home parks had the legal status of unimproved land (Willat 1955). This legislative shift in federal insurance had the practical effect of legitimizing mobile home parks as a community form and opened up opportunities for property owners to capitalize on the housing needs of growing postwar American families.

By 1959 a 12-foot-wide mobile home ("12-wide") was put into production despite state highway laws that opposed this wider model. By 1964, 42 state highway departments allowed the 12-wide to be transported on their roads and by 1966 the 12-wide accounted for 65 percent of mobile home sales (Drury 1972). Finally in 1967 manufacturers introduced the doublewide, transported in two units and joined on site at the peak of a pitched room, which resembled the roofline of site-built homes. By 1966, 4 million Americans lived in these homes (Schneider 2005).

The federal recognition of the mobile home as a form of single-family housing and federal financing in the form of FHA loans to park owners contributed to another boom for manufactured housing, a boom time when most of the parks profiled in this book were first developed. During the 1950s mobile homes were housing so many Americans and trailer parks were comprising so many American communities that a series of sociological and popular studies became warranted. The deep influence of cultural ideals of American single-family privatism can be seen in the orientation of these studies, which found that the spatial arrangement of the "trailer slum" effectively "robs a family of any sense or actual practice of privacy, or any opportunity for real withdrawal into itself, so essential to healthy family life" (Wellington 1951: 421). Yet these pioneer studies also contain a trace of surprise, noting that research findings differed from initial expectations. In his study of "trailer living" among construction workers and their families, sociologist Alvin Schorr (1954: 60) notes that despite the unrooted nature of the housing form, these communities and their residents "possess characteristics that are generally prized by all American communities . . . They view themselves as community assets and, therefore, are extremely sensitive to charges that they are irresponsible."

In 1965 a headline in *Forbes* magazine declared: "Trailers No More: Mobile Homes Have Grown into a Billion-Dollar Industry." By this time, parks showed significant consolidation and community amenities. A 1959 survey of 1,629 mobile homeowners sampled from the readership of *Mobile Home Journal* found that a majority of parks had paved streets, underground power lines, laundry facilities within the park, and newer model mobile homes (seven out of 10 of the households surveyed had purchased their home new). Park residency during these decades seems to have been driven more by preference than by financial need. The same survey reported that 45 percent of residents chose a mobile home as a dwelling unit because it best suited their household's needs, while only 20 percent did so because they believed they would spend less in household expenses (Edwards 1963). A 1960 U.S. Census survey of 800,000 households, including mobile homeowners, found similar incomes between the conventional and mobile home household heads (cited in Drury 1972).

Despite its increased prevalence in the U.S. landscape, the mobile home continued to be built on land zoned "nonresidential," where local regulations permitted park development and where inexpensive land benefitted park landlords' bottom lines. Because parks remained relegated to the margins of cities, park residents remained at the margins of city life. The conclusion to Margaret Drury's 1967 dissertation on mobile homes could just as well describe the mobile home park residents profiled in this book. Drury concludes that despite ever-increasing production, "The public image of the mobile home resident was one of social undesirability, rootlessness, and lack of community responsibility . . . some of the public still attached the stigma of second-class citizenship to current mobile home residents" (16).

During the manufactured housing boom of the 1950s and 1960s, many of the closing parks described in the following chapters were first developed. In 1952 in Alvin, Texas, Trail's End opened on an unused plot of land behind park owner Christine Perch's family home. Twin Oaks open in 1970 when a property owner converted one city block in Alvin to a mobile home park by allowing trailers to line the perimeter. Silver Sands opened in Jupiter, Florida, on formerly agricultural land in 1954. Ocean Breeze, initially formed as a makeshift seaside park in 1938, was incorporated as its own South Florida town in 1960. Sawgrass Estates was built in 1969 by the Seminole Tribe of Florida to provide revenue for the tribe by renting lots to Florida retirees before it shifted focus to casinos.

Park development at the time was an ad hoc affair. Mr. Silver, the owner and operator of Silver Sands, had inherited the park from his father. He recalled the work that he and his brother had done pouring the original concrete slabs for the mobile home lots, which reappeared as flat white rectangles dotting the property once eviction began in Silver Sands: "People used to ask my father why he didn't rent a backhoe to spread the concrete. He would laugh, point to us boys, and say, 'Why should I? I got them boys.'" Silver Sands, like other mobile home parks featured in this book and like mobile home parks throughout the country, continued to operate at full capacity over the next six decades right up to the date of its closure. Over those decades the property produced a steady income for Mr. Silver, who rented to tenants like 80-year-old Hanna, above, who had lived in the park since the 1960s. Mr. Silver had no trouble filling a rare Silver Sands vacancy with a new homebuyer who would purchase the mobile home on site (paying about $10,000 for the used mobile home) and be happy to pay the impossibly low South Florida rent of $250 a month.

Lot rents in Twin Oaks, Trail's End, Silver Sands, and Sawgrass Estates are similar to rents paid in parks across the nation, which average $200 to $300 per month (Rolfe 2011). Low monthly rents and factory production costs that are on average half that of conventional housing (Genz 2001) have contributed to the explosive growth of the mobile home as a form of low-income housing and have fueled the continued spread of the mobile home park. Yet the ubiquity of the mobile home park must also be understood as an historical and political outcome of the last four decades of housing policy.

As early as 1970, President Richard Nixon acknowledged in his message to Congress on national housing goals that "for many moderate income American families, the mobile home is the only kind of housing they can reasonably afford" (cited in Wallis 1991: 207). That year Nixon included mobile homes as housing units in his address to Congress on the state of the nation's housing stock. This inclusion was instrumental; it allowed Nixon to state that his administration had exceeded the housing goal of 2.6 million new units set by the HUD Act of 1968. Excluding mobile homes would have forced Nixon to report that his administration was 17 percent short of this goal: "At the time of Nixon's message, mobile homes accounted for approximately one third of new housing starts in the nation and over 90 percent of all new housing selling for under $15,000. Despite mobile homes' prominent contribution, the Department of Commerce had not included them in its housing production figures; until the 1960 Census, they had been lumped in with 'other' types of housing, a category containing house-boats, tents, and converted railroad cars. The mobile home, to many federal agencies, was still 'temporary' housing at best, and totally invisible at worst" (Wallis 1991: 207).

This federal recognition speaks to the political expediency that manufac-tured housing has continued to provide in more recent decades. As further evidence of its techno-social modularity, manufactured housing has stemmed the tide of affordable housing need that began when the Nixon administration inaugurated unprecedented cuts to federal subsidies for affordable housing. Since Nixon's term, the proliferation of manufactured housing has grown precisely in tandem with the decline in direct federal support for affordable housing. Indeed, the spread of mobile home parks is a close contemporary of the retraction of the state from the provision of low-income housing. These processes are not coincidental and must be understood as mutually constitutive.

Production of mobile homes increased in the post-WWII decades, but it was not until Nixon's New Federalism that manufactured housing saw a dramatic *quadrupling* in its total numbers. By the end of Nixon's first term and at the time of his moratorium on all federal affordable housing in 1973, manufactured housing had grown from 315,000 units nationwide in 1950 to 3.3 million housing units nationwide and 4.4 percent of the nation's housing stock (Wallis 1991). The two primary ideological components of Nixon's New Federalism—the consolidation of numerous federal grant programs initiated by prior Democratic administrations and the devolution of administrative control over federal programs to state and local governing bodies—began large-scale retrenchment from national efforts to address housing inequalities that continues in the neoliberal housing policies of today (see chapters 5 and 6). This approach was renewed by the Reagan administration and never reversed by any subsequent president (Hays 2003). The post-Reagan decades have seen a continued transfer of the pro-vision of affordable housing from the state to private developers (primarily through Section 8 New Construction, the Low-Income Housing Tax Credit [LIHTC]), and demand-side private solutions, i.e., housing vouchers).

Within this context, contemporary mobile home parks must be seen, not as accidental enclaves of low-income individuals making similar housing choices, but as the practical outcome of a dismantled public housing safety net. As a result of new modes of affordable housing production under a system of increasing reliance on private housing developers, residents of various forms of low-income housing are compelled to become "smart shoppers" (Klinenberg 2002) of affordable housing products, balancing meager, fixed, and uncertain incomes with their need to secure decent housing. This squeeze has spurred the continued spread of mobile homes across the nation, so that they now provide 66 percent of the new affordable housing produced in the United States, making manufactured housing the fastest-growing mode of new housing in the country (National Conference of State Legislatures 2007).

The shift from the federal allocation of affordable housing as a public good to a neoliberal model of private affordable housing provision is rendered visible in the homes of mobile homeowners who live on the properties of private landlords, who in turn can close mobile home parks and force residents to move themselves and their homes at any time. As a privately produced and operated mode of affordable housing, mobile home parks provide a particularly precarious form of low-income housing that is opened, operated, and oftentimes closed with no federal and little state or local oversight.

The ubiquity of the mobile home park in the American landscape and the insecurity of land tenure for residents living there are both an outgrowth of the expansion of the private market into the field of affordable housing production. In recent years, as the budget of HUD has been slashed more than any other federal agency (Glynn 2009), mobile homes constitute one in every three new homes sold (Burkhart 2010). Today mobile homes house about 6 percent of the nation's population, about 18 million people.

CONSTRUCTING MARGINALITY

The ubiquity of manufactured housing has not resolved a central tension characterizing the mobile home since its origin—the tension between necessity and marginality. This tension is evident in the current regulatory treatment of the mobile home, especially in the ways it is zoned and financed. Just as the history of manufactured housing production is central to the contemporary status of the mobile home, current mobile home zoning and finance are integral to constructing marginality in the mobile home park.

Zoning

Since the 1920s, regulatory changes allowed for innovations in manufactured housing and new legislation contributed to the growth of parks. At the same time, regulation was used to prohibit, divide, and isolate parks from surrounding communities and the effects of this are still felt today.

Alongside the marked growth in manufactured housing that began after 1955, there came a marked increase in ordinances, resolutions, covenants, statutes, and municipal regulations that restricted the placement of mobile homes and the development of mobile home parks (Drury 1972). From 1966 to 1969, production of mobile homes nearly doubled and one out of every two new single-family homes constructed in the United States was a mobile home, leading the author of a 1973 law review of mobile home park regulation to state: "For a while it has become apparent that a large number of persons are willing to live in house trailers; it has become equally obvious that many people are unwilling to live near mobile homes, especially when they are concentrated in trailer parks" (Moore 1973: 2). Decades of zoning laws have been utilized to address this discrepancy.

By the 1970s a majority of states authorized local municipalities and townships to regulate mobile homes within their jurisdictions, setting the stage for the regulatory treatment of mobile home parks for decades to follow (Moore 1973). Court cases challenging these regulations and ordinances had the effect of further institutionalizing the socio-spatial stigma of mobile home park residents. An Alaska case considering a private covenant to exclude mobile homes from a subdivision of conventional homes was upheld on the basis that using the land for a mobile home park would violate a covenant against "noxious or offensive trade or business."[4] A Colorado case called the domesticity of mobile homes into question, ruling that a private covenant could be used to legally bar them because the covenant held that land "will be used for dwelling houses only."[5] In Iowa, the court in *Jones v. Berber* stated that no "garage, trailer, shack or hut shall be used for living purposes."[6] In *McBride v. Behrman*, the court upheld a covenant that banned mobile homes based on language which prohibited "temporary dwellings" and "unsightly structures" and counterpoised them with the attractiveness and relative affluence of the existing community.[7] "In general, the court rulings of this period had the effect of defining the trailer as a temporary and mobile residence. Someone moving from place to place in a trailer was treated as a transient, not unlike a person staying in a hotel. Like a hotel, the trailer park could be classified as a permanent land use, but not the trailers in it. The ambiguity of these rulings reflects legal traditions that assume that proper dwellings are *attached* to land" (Wallis 1991: 74). In the absence of a national ruling on exclusionary zoning of mobile homes, an array of approaches enacted by state and local governments has created a patchwork of restrictions and regulations that severely limit the location of mobile home parks in practice. A 1980 national survey of zoning practices found the following municipal techniques most commonly used to restrict the placement of mobile homes: complete exclusion of manufactured housing, restriction of mobile homes to mobile home parks, and exclusion of mobile homes from residential areas (into commercial or industrial zones). At the time of that survey, each of these practices had become more frequent over the preceding 13 years (Bernhardt 1981).

Today, jurisdictions continue to restrict and direct the development of mobile home parks through a variety of planning and regulatory tools (Pendall, Puentes, and Martin 2007; Dawkins and Koebel 2010). The American Planning Association found that historic zoning processes relegating mobile home parks to undesirable nonresidential areas have resulted in contemporary spatial arrangements in which parks remain "mislocated" in commercial and industrial districts (Sanders 1986). In a national study of metropolitan plans and regulations, Dawkins and Koebel (2010: 74) found that many jurisdictions had adopted restrictive or exclusionary regulations to discourage or prohibit the use of mobile homes. Current American Planning Association policy guides specifically address the "unfair regulatory treatment of manufactured homes" that "unnecessarily limit" mobile homes among other forms of housing. However, the historically restrictive regulatory treatment of mobile homes is still felt in mobile home parks, which are disproportionately located in areas where lax building and zoning codes may further contribute to the vulnerability of their residents (Sanders 1986).

The historic regulation of mobile home parks structures the housing insecurity and eviction risk of mobile home park residents today. The use of exclusionary zoning and restrictive covenants effectively blocked mobile home parks from developing within city centers but encouraged their development on lands along the fringes of municipal boundaries. A 1960 Housing Census indicated that the majority of parks were on the fringe of urban areas (cited in Drury 1972). The parks described in the following chapters were developed during this period and in precisely these areas. The subsequent growth of cities has meant that parks are incorporated into urban areas, but urban growth further entrenches the housing insecurity of park residents. As cities expand, park lands become absorbed into more central urban areas, and this puts parks at heightened risk of redevelopment and closure. Today's mobile home parks (as opposed to individual mobile homes on private land) tend to be located in metropolitan areas, where about half of all parks are found (Apgar et al. 2002) and where the risk of redevelopment has spread to residents' front doors.

Urban growth can directly lead to mobile home park evictions, as in the case of Silver Sands and Sawgrass Estates, both of which closed to be redeveloped into higher-density, higher-value housing apartments and single-family housing. Growth can also indirectly contribute to closures, as was the case of Twin Oaks and Trail's End. There, population growth led the city to "improve" the conditions in mobile home parks by instituting a new ordinance, which proved so onerous that park owners were forced to close and the city was able to effectively regulate its aging mobile home stock out of city jurisdiction. In all cases in this book, historic zoning and contemporary urban regulation played a part in manufacturing the insecurity of mobile home park residents.

Financing

Historic exclusionary zoning has continued to locate mobile home parks on inferior, nonresidential, and hazard-prone land outside of city jurisdictions. Meanwhile, an equally damaging form of regulation has come from the treatment of manufactured homeownership as an inchoate or halfway mode of homeownership by financing institutions that finance mobile homes as personal property or "chattel."

The discriminatory financing of mobile homes stems from their origins as travel trailers and temporary wartime housing. Despite the crucial role that mobile homes have played from the Dust Bowl through the post-WWII housing boom, the mark of impermanence plagues the mobile home to the present day and has barred it from mainstream housing finance and the protections that come with it: "[A]fter the war the Federal Government turned away from the use of this kind of [manufactured] housing and focused its attention, except in cases of emergency, on the more permanent conventionally built housing that it advanced with FHA and VA loans. The foundation of government support and subsidy for housing has been based on 'permanence.' Because of this commitment to permanence, and since the mobile home is considered a temporary unit, the government, for all practical purposes, disengaged itself from support of the mobile home unit when it no longer considered the unit a necessity" (Drury 1972: 131).

The perception of impermanence is durable. It continues to impact the regulatory treatment of the mobile home even though a dwindling percent of mobile homes are ever moved after being sited on a lot (U.S. Department of Housing and Urban Development 1998). Even in cases of park closure and eviction, homes are often abandoned because they are too difficult or too costly to move. In fact, mobile home residents are less likely to move than residents of site-built housing. The average period of ownership is more than 10 years for mobile homeowners and only six years for site-built homeowners (Burkhart 2010). When parks remain open, rental households in mobile homes are also less likely to move than their counterparts. Annual resident turnover in rental mobile home parks is only 5 percent compared to 60 percent for apartments (Burkhart 2010).

Contemporary financing fails to reflect these fundamental facts, continues to treat mobile homes as transient, and serves to anchor the prejudicial treatment of mobile home residents. Due to restricted access to traditional mortgages, the vast majority of mobile homes are financed as private property through chattel loans that resemble automobile financing (NCMH 1996). These loans have shorter terms, higher interest rates, higher default rates, and fewer consumer protections than traditional mortgages. Their classification as private property, or "chattel," means mobile homes are more vulnerable to predatory lending practices and that they depreciate each year like a car rather than appreciate like a site-built home. The negative impact to the housing stability and wealth creation of low-income households is immense. Housing scholars have argued, "We need to promote and codify an understanding that manufactured housing is not mobile, not chattel, not disposable, and not a special case . . . Every housing advocate knows the gospel about homeownership . . . If we believe it, we should ask ourselves why it is acceptable to overlook millions of owner-occupied, depreciating homes that are cut off from the rest of the housing stock in a parallel legal universe" (Genz 2001: 408–9).

Just as in the case of federal recognition and municipal zoning, these lending classifications have implications far beyond the financial for all mobile home residents, whether they own or rent, whether they live in parks or on private land. The legal classification of their homes as chattel, from the Latin word for "head" meaning head of cattle, is based on its legal distinction from "real" property. This classification detaches a primary source of low-income housing from the powerful associations related to home, hearth, and community. It dichotomizes real homes and mobile homes, stable communities and trailer parks, the locals and the trailer trash.

The financing of mobile homes like heads of cattle is only a final broad brushstroke on a cultural effigy stained by a century of social stigma, political neglect, and regulatory bias. The *techno-social modularity* of the mobile home has allowed the housing artifact to adapt to some of the nation's most pressing housing challenges, from the mercurial housing needs of the Great Depression to the contemporary withdrawal of federal support for the public housing safety net. In responding to some of these very challenges the mobile home industry has experienced several episodes of explosive growth. But the proliferation of mobile homes during these times has also led to waves of restrictive regulations that have cemented the socio-spatial stigma of the mobile home park. As the history of the mobile home shows and as the following chapters argue: the way we regulate translates into the way we perceive. The cultural effigy of the trailer park and the trailer trash resident is constructed through regulations that ensure a separate and secondary social status. As the following chapters explore, these perceptions have consequences for the rights of residents to remain in their own communities.

2. Socio-Spatial Stigma and Trailer Trash

On the wooden front porch of her singlewide in Alvin, Texas, Señora Reyes rested in the shade on a plastic chair while her 16-year-old grandson sat in the corner of the porch on his cell phone with his homework opened on his lap. Señora Reyes's son, a carpenter in nearby Houston, built the porch for her when she installed the home in Twin Oaks Mobile Home Park about 10 years earlier. Twin Oaks was a small park of a dozen singlewides aligned along the perimeter of one city block in Alvin, Texas. The park was developed on a vacant block owned by Ed Romo, who "managed" the community. As in many other mobile home parks, management was interpreted loosely. Most residents had never met Ed Romo. They dropped their rent off at a neighbor's mobile home and once a month she brought the rent checks down to the local storage facility that Ed Romo also owned. Several residents of Twin Oaks were unable to recall their landlord's name.

Residents of Twin Oaks were equally in the dark regarding a new municipal ordinance instituted by the City of Alvin, which had cited Twin Oaks "in violation." The new Mobile Home Park Ordinance was intended to clean up the city's many mobile home parks by requiring infrastructural and aesthetic upgrades to all park properties located within city limits. To comply with this new ordinance, each landlord needed to complete costly upgrades or else close the park and evict residents. The deadline for these changes was July 1, 2013.

Nonetheless on May 25, 2013, Señora Reyes, like her neighbors, had no idea if she would be evicted: "They haven't told me anything yet." She was unsure of the extent of the violations in Twin Oaks and did not know if the ordinance would affect every home in the park or only some: "Some other trailers may have to leave. They haven't told me anything about my neighbor's house or mine. They haven't removed any trailers yet . . . The owner hasn't told me anything. But I give the neighbor my rent." She seemed anxious over these developments; she had experienced eviction in another Alvin mobile home park a decade earlier. There she had been displaced because the owner wanted to upgrade the park; he "wanted to put new trailers in the *parkedero*." She did not know if her home would survive another move; she knew it was at least 15 years old. That was the length of time she had lived in the home, which she purchased used from one of the many mobile home dealers that lined local Highway 6 just outside of town. Señora Reyes pointed to her grandson on the other side of the small wooden porch, remarking that he grew up in this trailer since he was "just this high," a small toddler. Her grandson looked up from his phone to confirm this, saying that the trailer "has been here forever."

Señora Reyes was originally from Nuevo Leon, Mexico, and had moved to Alvin, Texas, after her husband's death to be near six of her 11 children who lived in Houston: "Since I moved from there, I've been here." She spent much of her time on the open front porch just outside the mobile home's front door. From her plastic chair on the wooden porch she could watch the road and look out on her deceased husband's 1985 navy and white Ford F150. The handsome truck was perpetually parked on her lot just in front of the home and kept in pristine condition, always washed and waxed although she refused to let it be driven or put it up for sale: "It reminds me of him." She owned her singlewide outright and the low lot rent she paid in Alvin allowed her to live in her own home, for a total housing cost of $200 a month. She liked the independence her home and her lot afforded her, plus the ability to remain near her children, about a 25-minute drive, while living away from what she saw as the congestion and traffic of neighboring Houston.

But Alvin was changing. It was experiencing growing pains as a ripple effect of Houston's rapid population growth. During the years Señora Reyes lived in Twin Oaks, Houston—already the fifth-largest city in the country—was quickly becoming one of the fastest-growing cities in the United States. As the suburbs of Houston spread to Alvin's front door, the city became interested in assessing its previously neglected mobile home parks. In keeping with a century of municipal practices used to zone mobile homes out of desirable land near the city center, Alvin used its 2012 Mobile Home Park Ordinance to force decades-old parks out of its jurisdiction. Alvin's ordinance proved so difficult and costly for park owners to get up to code that many were eventually forced to shut down. One week after Señora Reyes stated on her front porch, "They haven't told me anything," she received an eviction notice.

This chapter explores the development histories and redevelopment pressures that put mobile home parks at risk of closure. I first give a brief history of the parks chronicled in the following chapters. Then, utilizing macro-level geospatial analysis and drawing on ethnographic fieldwork during city council rezoning debates, I explore how the restructuring of urban space that facilitates park closures is tied to the cultural structuring of "trailer trash" as a secondary class of urban citizen. First the geospatial analysis highlights how parks are being redeveloped into other forms of affordable housing that—despite housing low-income populations—are still prioritized over mobile home parks. This process offers an alternative to traditional definitions of gentrification and shows that while residents are evicted from closing parks, parks themselves are also evicted from areas near the urban core. The second half of the chapter ties these macro-level processes to the micro-level stigmatization of trailer residents that occurs as city councils debate decisions to close trailer parks. The spatial stigma of park properties discussed in the preceding chapter and the social stigma of park residents discussed here work in tandem to deprive residents of their claim to their communities. Meanwhile, residents' inefficacy in the face of city council decisions shows how deeply they internalize economic valuations of their property and social valuations of themselves as trailer trash.

URBAN DEVELOPMENT AND PARK REDEVELOPMENT

The histories of the mobile home parks that are the focus of this book tell an emblematic story of mobile home park development and redevelopment. These parks—Silver Sands in Florida, Twin Oaks and Trail's End in Texas— were prototypical of the modern-day urban mobile home park. Located in the center of towns and cities they were nonetheless set apart from the social, spatial, and civic life of the surrounding urban fabric. For decades they had existed in the "parallel legal universe" (Genz 2001) that has established a subjacent zone of development, finance, and operation for mobile home parks. In this parallel legal universe, local ordinances and planning regulations are used to reinforce the invisibility and marginality of park properties. Eventually, for Silver Sands, Twin Oaks, and Trail's End, the forces of local politics that had maintained their secondary status were also mobilized to remove them from their respective cities.

While mobile home parks are often represented as a rural phenomenon (see Salamon and MacTavish 2017 for a discussion of rural mobile home parks), parks are an important form of urban housing. Although the mobile home park is often ignored in urban scholarship and left out of prevailing narratives of the American city, parks have long been and remain a primary source of affordable housing for the urban poor. However, if you live in a U.S. metro area, you might not know that. In South Florida parks like Silver Sands and Sawgrass Estates, homes were shielded by high walls. These parks were accessible only by a single entry point. No person who did not have business in the park had reason to enter. In Alvin, parks like Trail's End were shrouded by a perimeter of shrubbery enclosing the park. As the landlord of Trail's' End herself admitted, "When I tell people that I own a trailer park they don't even know that the trailer park was there behind all the trees and stuff." This is a direct result of the zoning regulations and planning ordinances discussed in the previous chapter, which place parks in less desirable nonresidential areas and require that they be "visually screened" from view (in the language of Alvin's new ordinance).

The history of these parks illustrates the urban growth pressures and shifting urban priorities that lie at the heart of park redevelopment. Silver Sands, for instance, was opened in 1954 during the single-family housing boom described in the previous chapter. The park was built on formerly agricultural land that had served as a yam farm on the periphery of the city of Jupiter. As Jupiter grew and the demand for housing grew alongside it, the property owner converted the farm to a mobile home park. Over 60 years it operated near full capacity. Each one of the hundred lots arranged along nine short streets was filled with an occupied singlewide or doublewide; a few lots housed RVs. While many Silver Sands homeowners remained in their mobile homes for decades, those who chose to move were able to sell their homes in the park with few problems. Hank, for instance, had waited 18 months to get into his first home in Silver Sands and had owned three homes in the park during the 18 years he lived there. Each time Hank, who used a wheelchair, had purchased a larger or more handicapped-accessible model and each time he had found it easy to sell his former home: "We had no trouble selling the homes. This park is a very demanded park. A lot of people want to get in."

Over the years, longtime Silver Sands residents watched the town around their park grow into a large South Florida city. They saw the city's population grow to about 55,000 and watched the paving of the dirt road out front, the building of a hospital across the street, and the erection next door of a massive master-planned community made up of 14 subdivisions of luxury homes. The master-planned community boasted "stunning architecture and lush landscaping . . . for Florida home buyers who are looking for a quaint community with a classic small town feel." The symbolic interpretation of this "classic small town feel" was precisely what was

FIGURE 3.   Singlewides inside Silver Sands in Jupiter, Florida. Photo by Esther Sullivan, 2012.

at stake in 2012 as the Jupiter city council considered the rezoning of Silver Sands.

Alvin, Texas, was a similar metro-centered community with a "small town feel." Like Jupiter, the town's mobile home parks had provided a key source of low-cost housing over many decades. Like Silver Sands and many other Alvin parks, Trail's End Mobile Home Park was opened in the decade following WWII. The park's landlord, Christine, was the third-generation owner of the park, which was opened by her grandmother in 1952. Since that time, the operation of the park had passed from her grandmother, to her mother, to her. Like other Alvin parks, Trail's End was located on a shady block next to a variety of other land uses—single-family homes, a hair salon, and a small laundromat.

Like its neighboring urban center, Houston, Alvin had developed without zoning and this meant that urban form followed function. Without zoning, various land uses cropped up organically, developing to meet housing need (single family, multifamily, mobile homes, motel residences). My own rented trailer in Ramos y Ramos Mobile Home Park in Alvin, Texas, was sandwiched between railroad tracks and a residential motel renting rooms long term for rates by the week. From my trailer, I could walk to both Trail's End and Twin Oaks, passing several single-family homes, a church, a mechanic, and a small cemetery all within the first few blocks. In a meeting with the attorney for the city, she explained, "When you get a community like Alvin, which has never had master planning and people have been here forever, things just pop up everywhere." She meant that

FIGURE 4.   Homes inside Ramos y Ramos in Alvin, Texas. Photo by Esther Sullivan, 2013.

mobile home parks proliferate without the zoning constraints that have long been used to "unnecessarily limit" manufactured housing among conventional housing (APA 2001). In Alvin, a city of about 24,000 residents and 9,645 occupied housing units, there were 32 mobile home parks. Without the artificial restraints of zoning, the city was a veritable laboratory in the use of manufactured housing to meet the demand for affordable housing. The city attorney herself had grown up in the town in a mobile home. From Ramos y Ramos, I could walk to a dozen small parks (including Twin Oaks and Trail's End) all within a mile.

The historic location of parks on undesirable properties has allowed park owners to develop a profitable land use on lower value land or land along the urban fringe. The development of parks on these marginal lands *reproduces* the socio-spatial stigmatization of park residents. It also *produces* housing insecurity. As cities grow, urban development priorities and rising property values on once-peripheral properties increasingly put mobile home park residents at risk. This process is well known among mobile home park insiders. Indeed, a niche industry of mobile home park brokers—real estate agents who deal exclusively with park properties—has arisen to facilitate the commercial sale of mobile home parks, often for redevelopment. One Florida mobile home broker explained that he rarely needs to look for clients when selling off parks, which offer attractively large tracks of land near the urban core. Instead, clients come to him. One of his clients worked in property acquisition for Walmart and frequently called him in search of park properties ripe for redevelopment into big box stores. This broker regularly worked with this client because, as he pointed out, "I'm the mobile home park guy and he's the Walmart guy." For him the symbiosis was clear and the sale of parks was lucrative business. Indeed, Sunny Acres, the closing Miami park discussed in chapter 3, was closed after the property was bought by Walmart.

Although mobile home park brokers might take this process for granted, the extent and parameters of mobile home park redevelopment and eviction have never been documented. As with the dearth of data on eviction more generally (Hartman and Robinson 2003; Desmond 2016), there is currently no systematic data recording the frequency, location, or socio-spatial patterns of mobile home park closures. The nascent sociological study of eviction has demonstrated that it is a relational process between landlords, residents, and the legal frameworks that structure their interactions (Desmond 2016). Eviction is also a relational process between larger redevelopment decisions, land use priorities, and housing needs. While the ethnographic account presented in the following chapters investigates the former, it cannot grasp the latter because these processes operate at the level of larger metropolitan areas. Painting a broader picture of eviction, understanding the pressures that lead to the dislocations that the following chapters explore, requires tools that can map these processes at the metropolitan scale.

MAPPING MASS EVICTION

To map a macro-level picture of the urban pressures that contribute to mobile home park closure before moving into closing parks and investigating how these evictions played out, I utilized Geographic Information Systems (GIS) mapping technologies to conduct a geospatial case study of park closures in one U. S. county.[1] I mapped and analyzed the location and turnover of all mobile homes parks over one decade in the case study region of Harris County, Texas. Harris County contains the broader Houston area and is the center of the Houston-Woodlands–Sugar Land metropolitan area where Alvin, Texas, is located. Harris County contains a larger portion of the state's mobile home residents than any other metro area; about 7 percent of Texas mobile home residents live within Harris County. Texas in

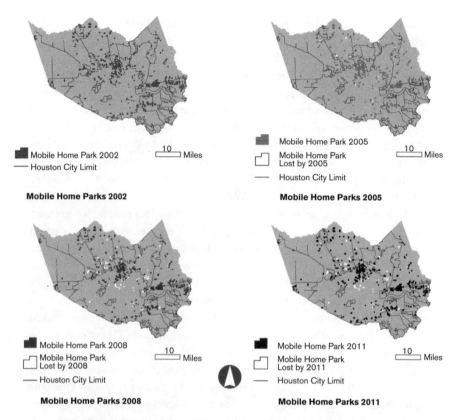

MAP 1. All Mobile Home Park Parcels by Year Range. Houston, Harris County, Texas, 2002–2011. Map author: Esther Sullivan. Map projection: NAD 1983 State Plane Texas – South Central FIPS 4204 feet. Sources: Harris County Appraisal District, U.S. Department of the Census, Houston-Galveston Area Council, and Environmental Systems Research Institute.

turn is home to the largest mobile home population in the United States.[2] In 2013, the year that Twin Oaks and Trail's End were slated to close, Harris County grew by more residents than any other county in the United States (U.S. Census Bureau 2014). This rapidly expanding metro area therefore provided an optimal case study to investigate the relationship between mobile home park closures and urban growth.[3]

Using GIS, I mapped the land use records of every parcel (about 1.2 million parcels in Harris County) at three-year intervals over a decade.[4] I isolated all parcels where the land use was entered as "mobile home park" (see Map 1) and subsequently changed to an alternative land use over time, using this recorded land use change as a proxy for a mobile home park closure on that parcel.[5]

I found clear indication that mobile home park parcels were being lost (i.e., mobile home parks were being closed) in Harris County, Texas. From 2002 to 2011, 119 park parcels (each containing numerous mobile homes) were lost. The spatial distribution of lost parks was not randomly distributed throughout the county. Rather, lost park parcels dotted the perimeter of Houston's distinctively shaped official city limits (see Map 2), and statistically significant clusters of lost park parcels were located along the city limit in the northeastern portion of the county (see Map 3).[6]

This spatial record demonstrates that while residents and individual households are evicted from closing parks, parks themselves are also, in a sense, evicted from areas near the urban core. Parks that closed during the years studied dotted the perimeter of Houston's city limits. Within the hierarchy of urban spaces, existing parks are relegated to ever-outer reaches of the city, primarily in county jurisdiction. Documenting these closures raises a central question: When parks are closed, what new land uses appear in their place?

To answer this question, I then mapped the land uses that appeared in the vicinity of parks that had closed from 2002–11. Surprisingly, this analysis revealed no tendency for new mixed-use developments or condominiums to appear near lost mobile home park parcels (see Map 4). While these land uses are often associated with displacement due to gentrification, they do not comprise the form of urban redevelopment that led to park closures in Harris County, as they almost exclusively appeared within the city center and well outside areas where mobile home parks closed. Instead, the residential redevelopment taking place on and near closed mobile home park properties included lower-income properties such as (1) lower-than-county-average residential development and (2) Low-Income Housing Tax Credit (LIHTC) properties (Map 4).

The most common land use code *on* parcels where parks closed was a code denoting that development was still taking place ("residential with improvement") (see Map 4).[7] In cases where new residential development *was* completed and coded, this development was not substantially different in value from the mobile home residences it replaced. For parcels where a park was replaced by new residential construction, the average 2011 value (including land and improvements) for the residence was only $59,941. This home value is low when compared to (a) the median home value ($130,100) for all of Harris County for that year, (*Houston Business Journal* 2011) and (b) the average sales price of a new singlewide manufactured home without land

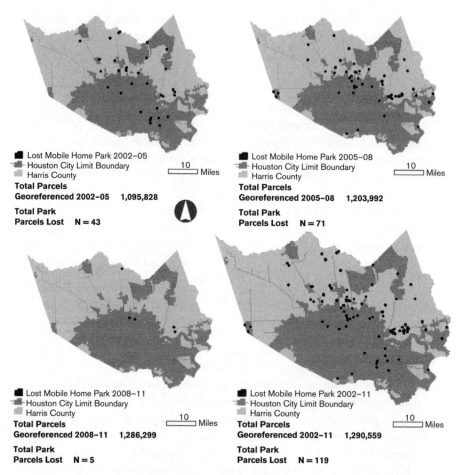

MAP 2.   Lost Mobile Home Park Parcels by Year Range. Houston, Harris County, Texas, 2002–2011. Lost mobile home parks are calculated by (1) georeferencing HCAD (Harris County Appraisal District) land use codes for each parcel in the county and (2) identifying parcels for which the land use code changed from "mobile home park" to an alternate land use code during each given year range. Map author: Esther Sullivan. Map projection: NAD 1983 State Plane Texas – South Central FIPS 4204 feet. Sources: Harris County Appraisal District, U.S. Department of the Census, Houston-Galveston Area Council, and Environmental Systems Research Institute.

($40,600) (U.S. Department of Commerce 2015). Indeed this new residential development, while out of reach for many mobile home residents, would be considered affordable for other low- and moderate-income residents.

A common land use *surrounding* parcels where a mobile home park closed between 2002 and 2011 denotes Low-Income Housing Tax Credit

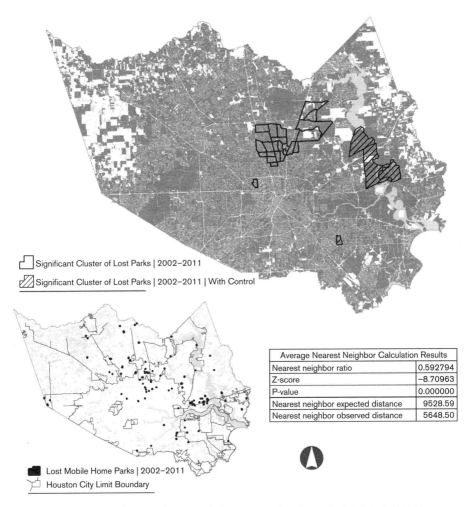

Significant Cluster of Lost Parks | 2002–2011

Significant Cluster of Lost Parks | 2002–2011 | With Control

Average Nearest Neighbor Calculation Results	
Nearest neighbor ratio	0.592794
Z-score	–8.70963
P-value	0.000000
Nearest neighbor expected distance	9528.59
Nearest neighbor observed distance	5648.50

Lost Mobile Home Parks | 2002–2011

Houston City Limit Boundary

MAP 3. Significant Clusters of Lost Mobile Home Parks (Getis-Ord Gi* and ANND Analyses). Harris County, Texas, 2002–2011. Map author: Esther Sullivan. Map projection: NAD 1983 State Plane Texas – South Central FIPS 4204 feet. Sources: Harris County Appraisal District, U.S. Department of the Census, Houston-Galveston Area Council, and Environmental Systems Research Institute.

(LIHTC) development (see Map 4 insets). The presence of LIHTC properties is significant; LIHTC provides the primary mode of federally backed affordable housing development in the United States. While LIHTC properties were not developed directly on parcels where mobile home parks had closed, the presence of LIHTC properties surrounding significant clusters of lost mobile home parks gives context to the finding that low-value

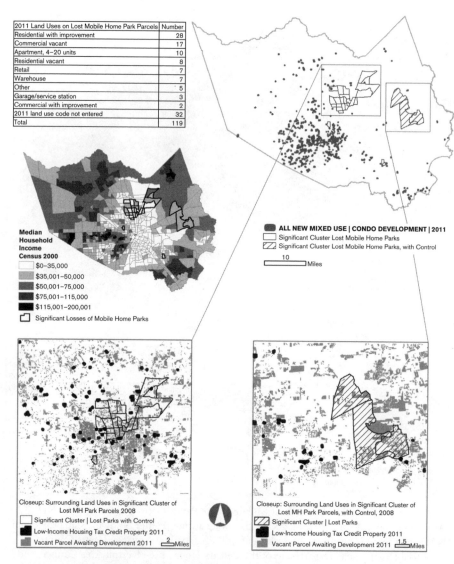

2011 Land Uses on Lost Mobile Home Park Parcels	Number
Residential with improvement	28
Commercial vacant	17
Apartment, 4–20 units	10
Residential vacant	8
Retail	7
Warehouse	7
Other	5
Garage/service station	3
Commercial with improvement	2
2011 land use code not entered	32
Total	119

Median
Household
Income
Census 2000
$0–35,000
$35,001–50,000
$50,001–75,000
$75,001–115,000
$115,001–200,001
Significant Losses of Mobile Home Parks

ALL NEW MIXED USE | CONDO DEVELOPMENT | 2011
Significant Cluster Lost Mobile Home Parks
Significant Cluster Lost Mobile Home Parks, with Control
10 Miles

Closeup: Surrounding Land Uses in Significant Cluster of
Lost MH Park Parcels 2008
Significant Cluster | Lost Parks with Control
Low-Income Housing Tax Credit Property 2011
Vacant Parcel Awaiting Development 2011   2 Miles

Closeup: Surrounding Land Uses in Significant Cluster of
Lost MH Park Parcels, with Control, 2008
Significant Cluster | Lost Parks
Low-Income Housing Tax Credit Property 2011
Vacant Parcel Awaiting Development 2011   1.5 Miles

MAP 4.   Harris County Land Use by Parcel, New Development, 2011 (Inset: Median Family Income 2000). Harris County, Texas, 2002–2011. Map author: Esther Sullivan. Map projection: NAD 1983 State Plane Texas – South Central FIPS 4204 feet. Sources: Harris County Appraisal District, U.S. Department of the Census, Houston-Galveston Area Council, and Environmental Systems Research Institute.

residential development did appear on parcels where parks closed. Together these findings suggest that low-income residential development is the land use encroaching on closed mobile home park properties. In other words, this particular loss of affordable housing appears to take place as low-income housing displaces and replaces other low-income housing.

This complicates traditional understandings of the processes of gentrification and urban residential displacement. While urban theorists see the replacement of lower-income groups by higher-income groups as foundational to the definition of gentrification (Galster and Peacock 1986; Zukin, 1987; Hackworth 2002; Lees, Slater, and Wyly 2013), these maps highlight how low-income uses also contribute to gentrification and displacement. While this analysis does not establish direct displacement of mobile home parks by federally subsidized housing, the notable presence of LIHTC around lost mobile home parks points to a need to better understand how publicly funded affordable housing might compete with and displace affordable housing that is developed without federal subsidy. Indeed during my fieldwork a local LIHTC developer contacted me, seeking help communicating with mobile home park residents he was evicting on a parcel where he was developing an LIHTC property. This geospatial analysis indicates that urban pressures resulting in mobile home park closures are simultaneously tied to local land markets, municipal priorities, and for-profit development of federally subsidized low-income housing. In the hierarchy of urban space, even government-subsidized low-income rental properties, themselves the object of stigma and NIMBYism, are privileged over and have the power to displace the mobile home park from the urban core.

THE MOBILE HOME PARK AND THE HIERARCHY OF URBAN SPACE

The geospatial analysis of Harris County demonstrates that almost any other land use is more *spatially* desirable than a mobile home park. The municipal debates over the closures of Silver Sands, Twin Oaks, and Trail's End show that other land uses are more *socially* desirable as well. In Alvin, Texas, the tension between the city's vision for its future and its citizens' investments in their mobile homes played out on Señora Reyes's front porch. In Jupiter, Florida, the tension between municipal land use priorities and mobile home residents' right to place played out in the city council's public hearing over a developer's application to rezone Silver Sands.

The development company "Flagler Inc." had targeted Silver Sands for redevelopment. Capitalizing on recent growth in Jupiter, the company wanted to build a large apartment complex with street-level retail space. Flagler Inc. approached the owner of Silver Sands at the right time. After almost 60 years of his family operating Silver Sands, Mr. Silver was tired of his dealings with residents and ready to retire to his cattle ranch about an hour inland from Jupiter. He insisted, "I'm just done dealing with people. When I go home at night to the ranch guess what I like about my cows? They don't talk back." He also took issue with the personal comportment and the state of the homes of some of the residents in the park: "Some of the people you just wouldn't believe. They say 'trailer trash' and some of them fit exactly into that."

The stereotype of *trailer trash* is inseparable from the concept of *white trash*, which scholars point out "is not just a classist slur—it's also a racial epithet that marks out certain whites as a breed apart, a dysgenic race to themselves" (Wray and Newitz 1997: 2). The term white trash rests on the racist assumption "that color and poverty and degenerate lifestyle 'automatically' go together, so much so that when white folks are acting this way, their whiteness needs to be named" (Bettie 1995: 140). The phrase *trailer trash* lacks the explicit racial referent of white trash, but both terms set apart those who are not adequately performing normative middle-class whiteness.[8]

Racialized views of class are at the root of the trailer trash stigma: "this term is most often used by Whites in order to distance themselves from other Whites whom are feared and despised because of their economic and physical proximity to minorities" (Kusenbach 2009: 402). The raced and classed roots of the term continue to be important today despite the modern use of mobile homes among a range of racial and ethnic groups (especially those of Latino / a descent). The very existence of the terms white trash and trailer trash demonstrate how class divisions between whites are articulated in racialized ways. Like white trash, the existence of trailer trash illuminates persistent inequalities and threatens the illusion of a classless U.S. society: "The presumed inherent superiority of whiteness, as well as the ideology of upward mobility, is challenged by the existence of white trash, and thus the difference of class *as class* is made visible" (Bettie 1995: 140).

Conceptions of trailer trash as "transient and deficient" (Kusenbach 2009: 400) undergirded the landlord's decision to sell Silver Sands. Mr. Silver's lament that the residents of his park acted like trailer trash was tied to class. When I asked Mr. Silver if he had always thought of the residents as trailer trash, even since his father opened the park, he mused that this shift had mainly been within the last 15 years: "The quality of people is just really going down ... maybe it is the economy, people just looking for places that are cheap like it is in here."

This assessment played into Mr. Silver's plan to sell Silver Sands to Flagler Inc., contingent upon the Jupiter city council approving Flagler's application for a rezoning of the property. In April 2012, residents of Silver Sands received notice that Flagler had applied for the rezoning. In most municipalities zoning changes must be approved by an appropriate governing body, but Florida statutes specifically mandate that before approving a land use change that will cause a mobile home park to close, a local governing body must also find that other adequate parks exist for the relocation of park residents.[9] In the public meetings where Jupiter city council considered the rezoning of Silver Sands, representatives from Flagler Inc. showed the city council a PowerPoint slide that juxtaposed the current Silver Sands property and their proposed redevelopment. On one side, under a heading for Proposed Development, the slide listed: "35,000 square feet of medical space, 25,000 square feet of office space, and 351 apartments" complete with "neighborhood commercial uses engaged to the street" and a "necklace of green space" that included a lake path, clubhouse, pool, playground area, and dog park. On the other side, under the heading Current Development, the slide simply listed: "100 mobile home sites." The developer presented the redevelopment of Silver Sands as an opportunity to intensify the use of the property by increasing commercial and residential density. The developer pointed out to a receptive city council that the proposed project embodied the city's municipal priorities; the city's own comprehensive plan had "set the stage for this kind of development." Articulating the city's final decision on the rezoning, the mayor reiterated the developer's logic and agreed that the park was primed for redevelopment: "It is a great location for the reasons that we heard. So I think that's going to be quite good!" The council voted unanimously to approve the rezoning of Silver Sands and evict its 130 residents.

In Alvin, Texas, similar urban priorities resulted in the closure of Twin Oaks and Trail's End. Even though these properties were not being purchased for redevelopment, the city's recently instituted Mobile Home Park Ordinance required that all the city's mobile home parks, many developed decades prior, be in compliance with costly new code enforcement standards or else close. While the city's lack of zoning had proved fertile ground for the development of parks, the new Mobile Home Park Ordinance proved prohibitive for park operators. Landlords protested to the city council; they estimated the cost of the improvements required to be up to code would force them to close. Park owners believed this was the intent of the ordinance. The city attorney confessed the same: "I think what happened was that some people got on city council and they said: the place is all trashed, the city is trashed, there's trailers everywhere. [She shrugs] Say, I own a nice house next to a trailer park, this is an example: if it is shut down, my property will have better property value than if it is not."

Landlords in Alvin assessed the new mobile home park ordinance in much the same way. Christine, the owner of Trail's End, lamented: "These new council people are coming in and they just want a change: so they're just trying to oust all the parks . . . And for them, I understand, they'll make the town look better." Like many of the other owners of the 32 Alvin parks originally cited in violation of the new ordinance (almost every park in the town), Christine could not afford to make the required upgrades to Trail's End. Like many residents of her park, she felt defenseless in the face of the city council:

> Christine talks about her frustration with the city and her worries for the families she is evicting. Shaking her head she tells me, "I don't think it's right. I don't know where they get off saying that someone can live in a trailer park or somebody can't live in a trailer park. Why do they have trailers if people can't live in them? I don't understand that . . . It's been horrible, just in the sense that you know that you are displacing families. . . . And I'm not saying that the park doesn't need to be upgraded but kicking families out is not the way."

The understanding that mobile home parks are an inevitable casualty of urban growth was not only expressed by public officials and private land-lords. It was acknowledged by residents themselves. In both Florida and Texas, residents demonstrated a nuanced understanding of how historic municipal marginalization and contemporary municipal priorities worked in tandem to deprive them of their right to their community. Their inter-pretations of their respective city's actions demonstrate a lay understanding of taken-for-granted assumptions about the maximum economic and social value of land, or in the language of real estate, the "highest and best use."

The city council actions in both Jupiter and Alvin were conducted, explic-itly and implicitly, in the interest of highest and best use. Assessments of highest and best use were seen in the considerations of city councils as they instituted (in the case of Alvin, Texas) or implemented (in the case of Jupiter, Florida) ordinances and zoning decisions that shaped future urban growth. Developers like Flagler Inc. played an important role in constructing notions of highest and best use, as evidenced in Flagler's slide juxtaposing Silver Sands's mere "100 mobile home sites" with the future development's "35,000 square feet of medical space, 25,000 square feet of office space, and 351 apartments." Yet, city councils are also complicit. This was evidenced in the Alvin city attorney's admission that at the heart of the new mobile home park ordinance was the city's simple valuation: "If it is shut down, my property will have better property value than if it is not." It was evidenced in the mayor of Jupiter's enthusiastic closing words when approving the redevelopment of Silver Sands: "It is a great location for the reasons that we heard. So I think that's going to be quite good!"

The concept of highest and best use originates from the real estate appraisal field, where it is the valuation of land in which an appraiser identifies the optimal combination of physical, legal, locational, and capital attributes that can maximize the wealth of the owner (Detzour et al. 1990). The Appraisal Institute defines the highest and best land use as the use that is (1) physically possible, (2) legally permissible, (3) financially feasible, and (4) maximally productive (McKenzie 2013). However, much of the determination of these factors rests on local municipal decisions regarding how properties are zoned. These decisions are made as part of the land use planning process (especially within a city's comprehensive plan) and are then regulated in zoning ordinances. In planning and zoning decisions, local governments often share the work of determining the highest and best land use with property owners, realtors, and developers—in other words, with the constellation of actors that stand to profit from development, an assemblage that urban political economy theorists have termed "the growth machine" (Logan and Molotch [1987] 2007). Logan and Molotch argue: "'Highest and best use' is the conveniently vague phrase so often invoked by planning professionals as a rationale for their recommendations. Because 'highest and best use' means whatever the market circumstance dictates—if it means anything at all—the phrase serves to align the work of planning officials with the needs of local growth machines" (ibid., 156).

Urban theorists have pointed to the role such assessments play in a range of urban property dispossessions (Roy 2003; Blomley 2004; Slater 2015). Nicholas Blomley (2004: xviii) argues that gentrification is spurred on by "'common-sense' assumptions about property, such as the 'naturalness' of displacement." This common sense is infected with economic valuations that become normalized as property valuations, so that they appear to be objective characteristics of place. But highest and best use is more than simply real estate or planning jargon; it is a rationale used to justify the cleansing of the built environment (Wacquant 2008) from those who are not seen as contributing to the economic and social vitality of urban regions. Mobile home park residents in both Texas and Florida recognized this. They understood that the city had a stake in the highest and best use of the land under their home. Not only did they witness how this rationalized and justified their expulsion, they internalized the economic valuation of their community.

In the final city council meeting where the rezoning of his community was heard, Silver Sands resident Hank spoke during public commentary. Hank moved slowly to the podium at the front of the small auditorium using his cane. He reflected on his happiness during his 18 years at Silver Sands. He described the orderly, well-tended grounds and neighborly atmosphere in the park, and, finally, he noted the futility of imagining that Silver Sands might survive in the face of new, more intensive development:

> Hank finishes his public statement by noting: "This project is a good project for the town—it'll bring big revenue in, it'll bring higher taxes in, it'll give the opportunity of a clean slate for a great piece of property that is not being used in its optimal use right now . . . I as one don't look forward to moving but I will accept the fact."

Hank did not want to move from his home. In fact he said, "I thought I would die here, in this unit." But he internalized the language of highest and best use in his own assessment that the community he loved was not the "optimal use" of the property. Other residents did not outwardly rationalize the city's conduct as Hank did, but their understanding of the city's pursuit of highest and best use nonetheless dampened their sense of efficacy and their willingness to fight in much the same way.

Silver Sands resident Kathleen had also spoken during public comment at the city council meeting. She hoped by expressing her love for her home of 10 years and detailing the difficulty of moving her disabled husband and herself she might influence the council's decision. After attending the city council meeting, Kathleen discussed the process with her husband Chip:

> Kathleen: "It's too late. It's a done deal."
> Chip: "What I was hoping for was that the Town of Jupiter would make it tough for them. But the Town of Jupiter—and Palm Beach County—doesn't want trailer parks. You can tell that. Since we lived here, how many trailer parks have closed up? Three?"
> Chip names the three trailer parks that have closed in this area.
> Kathleen says softly that the reason that people don't like mobile home parks is because they've never been inside a mobile home: "They just see them on the outside and they think the people that live in them are trailer trash."
> Kathleen points out, "It's sad but the community wants us out of here. They just don't want a trailer park."

Josefina, a neighbor of Kathleen's and a Guatemalan woman in her 60s, reflected the same sentiment, challenging the economic logic at the heart of the city council's decision:

Reflecting on the processes she witnessed at city council, where she attended all three of the lengthy council meetings, Josefina says, "What else can I do—if I say something, they won't pay attention to me. Because the sad thing in Florida—I really don't like Florida—the sad thing here is that I think people consider more the money than the people. They care more about money than anything else."

Silver Sands resident Sammy, a soft-spoken Vietnam veteran, put the same sentiment more bluntly when he stated that the city would not help them: "we're trailer trash to them."

Sammy's mother, 90-year-old Mattie, felt much the same about the inevitability of redevelopment after living in Silver Sands for 20 years:

> Mattie points out that she was not really surprised when she received the notice that a developer had applied for a rezoning of Silver Sands. This was not only because she had heard rumors in the park that the property was for sale, but especially because of the amount of development that had occurred along the road where Silver Sands sits.
>
> "It's property that people naturally want to build on. And, as we know, they don't want trailers, campgrounds, whatever you want to call them, mobile homes. They don't want them in the town. Now this is an upscale town.
>
> "I think that they think that the people that live in mobile homes—of course I still go back to saying trailers because that's what they usually were called—are not wealthy enough or do not have enough money or enough income or a good enough job to be average citizens. I think that's why this company [Flagler Inc.] can mess over so many people. They think that they don't have any rights or that they can't protest for what they want. That kind of stuff.
>
> "It's scary when you stop and think about it. When you have been settled and you own your own home and you think everything is going nice and smooth and everything, then all the sudden somebody says: Get out. Well, how am I going? Where am I going to? What's it gonna cost me? Will I like the place I'm going to? One question after another. And you can't find out! That's the way it is. [Sighs.] Yeah."

Mattie articulates the confusion and helplessness she faced as her park began to close. She also articulates a deep sense of disposability and stigma she associates with being a mobile home park resident.

In Alvin, Texas, this disposability and stigma were further complicated by the ethnicity of the majority of the city's mobile home park residents. There, the affordable owner-occupied housing provided by mobile home parks was preferred by many of the town's low-income Latino/a residents. Many of the city's parks, including Twin Oaks and Trail's End, were over 90 percent Latino/a. In Ramos y Ramos where I lived, I was the only non-Latino/a resident. Indeed, some residents seemed to believe that that the trailer trash stigma was drawn from the fact that, as one resident insisted, "only Mexicans live in parks." Additionally, since vacant lots in parks were filled via word-of-mouth referrals, many recent and long-term undocumented immigrants (most from Central American countries) had found housing in parks based on networks of friends and relatives they contacted when first moving to Alvin. These residents felt that being Latino/a generally and being an immigrant specifically limited their options to resist relocation or fight the city's new ordinance. In Alvin only landlords, who had a vested interest in the city's decision, and one or two residents (both non-Latino/a) showed up at the city council meetings where changes to the city's mobile home park ordinance were heard.

Alvin residents were direct in describing their fear of protesting the park closures. Lupe was a 22-year-old resident of Trail's End who often acted as a translator for neighbors when they needed it. Lupe's entire family was affected by the eviction at Trail's End; three separate households lived in the park. In Lupe's own family, her mother was a naturalized citizen, her father was a legal resident, her husband was a legal resident, her middle sister had received Deferred Action for Childhood Arrivals (DACA), her older sister was planning to apply for DACA but was currently undocumented, and Lupe was born in the United States.

> Lupe explains that her neighbors discussed talking to the city, but most dismissed the idea. She says, "If they are illegal, they're scared. That the city is just going to call the cops and have them arrested. And we are basically the only ones that have papers here (in Trail's End). My parents and I . . . I know for a fact that we're the only ones that have papers here, and my sister, because everyone is kind of connected here. A lot of the other people are all from where my mom was born [Morelos, Mexico] so they all know each other from Morelos."
>
> She continues, "Some people actually did go to the city to ask what year the trailers have to be and everything [in order to move them]. But they don't want to make a scene and everything. Because they just want to do everything they have to do. Because they are scared. This weekend even [Fourth of July weekend] when they had the cops out asking for licenses. Everyone was scared to go out of the park."

This trepidation was not only felt among the city's undocumented mobile home park residents, but among Latino/a park residents more generally, as Emilio, a Mexican American man in his 50s, described:

> It's been about a week since Emilio's family received their notice. We are discussing moving plans in their living room. Emilio (a Twin Oaks resident and father of four) is frustrated by the city.

I ask Emilio if he has thought about organizing with his neighbors to ask the city for help. He responds, frustrated, "The majority of us that live here are Latinos. How can you go against the city and what it says? How can we go to the city and have the city listen to us? . . . The city has all the power and Latinos don't have a voice right now."

Esther: "Is that the problem? Is it because the majority of the park is Latino?"

Emilio: "Yes! We're all Latinos, everybody. No white people. No Black. Only Latinos."

Next to Emilio, his daughter Camila repeats and summarizes her father: "We don't have a voice right now."

These residents' own assessments of their lack of political clout and their very real fears of deportation limited their interaction with the city. While the Florida residents were willing to show up at city council and voice their concerns, these concerns did not ultimately win them any concessions. Nonetheless, the Latino/a residents of Alvin's mobile home parks felt that even an appearance in front of their city council was an unimaginable risk. The stigmatized status acknowledged by the residents in Florida parks was deeply compounded by the marginality faced by the Latino/a residents in Texas parks.

SOCIO-SPATIAL STIGMATIZATION

Urban theorists have described how commonsense assumptions about the economic valuation of land and the naturalness of displacement spurs urban redevelopment (Blomley 2004; Slater 2015). The city council decisions in both Alvin and Jupiter demonstrate how notions of highest and best use are also influenced by the socio-spatial stigmatization of mobile home parks and their residents. Goffman (1963) originally conceptualized stigma as an outward sign that marked a tainted social status. Goffman distinguished three primary forms of stigma: bodily abominations, blemishes of individual character, and tribal stigma (those associated with race, religion, and nationality). Wacquant (2007) argues that a key oversight in Goffman's work is his failure to consider how a "blemish of place" infects the inhabitants of certain physical spaces, a process he terms "territorial stigmatization."

Wacquant's important expansion of Goffman's stigma updates the concept to include the myriad ways the ghetto, the project, the barrio, and the favela impart an independent social stain on their inhabitants. The concept of territorial stigma joins Goffman's understanding of a "spoiled identity" to Bourdieu's theory of symbolic power to better articulate how the blemish of place shapes inequality and marginality in the modern city (Wacquant,

Slater, and Pereira 2014). A logical next step is to examine the relationship between the spatial stigmatization of certain residents and the "revitalization" of their communities. Making these connections reveals the political utility at the heart of socio-spatial stigmatization. As Kallin and Slater (2014: 1351) argue: "territorial stigmatisation and 'regeneration' through gentrification form two sides of the same conceptual and policy coin: the 'blemish of place' becomes a target and rationale for 'fixing' the area . . . The state's role in creating the very stigma it then insists on scrubbing highlights a major contradiction in contemporary urban policy." Residents' recognition that they are trailer trash to city officials at precisely the moment they seek help from the city encapsulates this contradiction. Residents' inefficacy in the face of city council decisions shows how deeply they internalize economic valuations of their property and social valuations of themselves as trailer trash.

Understanding this connection between socio-spatial stigmatization and economic valuations of property helps to conceptualize park closures not only as incidences of contemporary housing insecurity, but also as examples of an essential tension between residents' rights to their own communities and the competing claims of those who have an interest in the highest and best use of the land under their homes. Ultimately, even mobile home residents' socio-spatial stigma has economic utility. It facilitates their expulsion and works in the interest of those who wish to develop and divide the city in the interest of capital. As Mattie aptly summarized, "They think that the people that live in mobile homes are not wealthy enough or do not have enough money or enough income or a good enough job to be average citizens. I think that's why this company can mess over so many people."

The geospatial mapping of park closures illustrates that mobile home parks exist at the very lowest rungs of the hierarchy of urban land use and are spatially relegated to ever outer reaches of urban areas. The municipal debates over the closure of mobile home parks reveal the effects for residents, demonstrating how socio-spatial stigma becomes embedded in the cognitive structures of residents like Hank, who came to city council to defend his home and ended up defending the city's right to rezone his community in the interest of the property's "highest and best use." The next chapter explores the subjective restructuring of residents' understanding of themselves and their communities, probing the depths of socio-spatial stigma and its effects in the days leading up to eviction.

3. Daily Life under the Specter of Dislocation

By early April, Mattie and Walter had begun packing their home in Silver Sands. Walter (89) was purposefully taking it slow; Mattie (90) was confined mostly to her chair and could only pack boxes from there. Walter laid out a plan for the rooms he would pack in their larger model "extrawide." He began in the guest bedroom and moved from there. He would work slowly over the six-month eviction period he and Mattie were given under Florida law. When the moving date approached, he got help from his adult children for the more demanding tasks: moving furniture over the axles of the home for stability and disassembling the built-on screened-in porch that had been the most used room in the house. In the weeks before the move, he and Mattie concentrated on boxing up any items that could shift or break when the home was hauled. This was a big task. They had lived in the home for 20 years and thought Silver Sands would be the last place they ever lived. The home was filled with a lifetime of their accumulated belongings: pictures of the children, grandchildren, and great-grandchildren; mementos from the years Walter was stationed in Okinawa where they raised their young family after WWII; plants and bonsai trees that Mattie learned to craft in flower arranging school during their years in Japan; collectables from the 19 years the couple spent traveling the United States and Canada in a Volkswagen van after Walter retired from the military.

One afternoon, Walter took a break to bring me something he had found while packing—a 2004 newspaper clipping from the local paper, the *Jupiter Courier*. The clipping featured a large photograph of a ravaged street in Silver Sands following a series of devastating hurricanes: homes were blown from their foundations; aluminum siding was ripped from homes and scattered in puddles around the park property. The article discussed the fallout of Hurricane Jeanne, which made landfall just north of Silver Sands.

That hurricane season, which included Hurricanes Charlie, Frances, Yvonne, and Jeanne, cost $18 billion and became the costliest Atlantic hurricane season on record (until it was surpassed the following year). Although the devastation from these multiple hurricanes was widespread and affected multiple forms of commercial and residential properties, the newspaper article solely featured the damage in Silver Sands. As with coverage of many other hurricanes, images of the destruction in the trailer park served as shorthand for the hurricane's widespread damage elsewhere.

Reading over the article, I noted the last name of the main resident interviewed for the piece, Silverton. The name was familiar; it hung on the first mobile home near the entrance to Silver Sands. There, next to the front door of a white singlewide, a little sign in a blue frame announced: "The Silvertons." The article read: "Burt Silverton says he isn't budging. The 1963 graduate of Jupiter High School says it will take much more than the one-two thrashing of hurricanes like Jeanne to pry him from South Florida . . . 'Hey, I grew up here, this is my home,' he said standing next to his blue and white mobile home at Silver Sands Park in Jupiter, 'I'm staying.'" The quote from Burt Silverton and the image of him standing proudly by his damaged mobile home was striking. In the face of a natural disaster, Burt Silverton articulated his commitment to his roots and his right to stay put. In the article, he and other Silver Sands residents asserted their intention to rebuild. In doing so they affirmed their emotional and economic investment in their homes. But by the time Walter found the newspaper clipping and brought it over, Silver Sands had been the subject of a six-month rezoning process and residents were about three months into the eviction period. Indeed by the time I read the article, Burt Silverton had already packed up and abandoned his home. The blue and white trailer referred to in the article sat empty, unable to be relocated. The little sign reading "The Silvertons" still hung on the abandoned singlewide.

What explains this change? How do residents shift from affirming their intent to rebuild in the face of adversity to abandoning their home in the face of eviction? This chapter explores this change, its roots and its realization. Focusing on the period before parks close, I show how the physical uprooting that takes place during eviction is only a final symptom in a more generalized disequilibrium that comes to haunt life in these communities. In the mobile home park, residents' unique land tenure (their divided right to the land under their home) shapes a more pervasive subjectivity of insecurity. This chapter explores how housing insecurity acts as a haunting: a *specter of dislocation* that reshapes residents' understandings of their homes, their communities, and even their rights as citizens.

Burt Silverton abandoned his older model singlewide with the sign reading "The Silvertons" still hanging by the front door. Unlike many of his neighbors he had the financial means to purchase a newer model pre-owned mobile home in a different park. Like the owners of the home I rented, he had cut his losses instead of paying lot rent in the months leading up to the eviction. He was among only a handful of Silver Sands households that could afford to do so. Most could not, and the shift from affirming their right to stay put to abandoning their claim to their community was a more gradual and creeping transition.

Down the street from the Silvertons' trailer, Christy lived as the primary caregiver for her aging mother. Christy was 50 years old with dark hair, an easy laugh, and a pack-a-day habit that kept her outside on the wooden deck that ran the length of her mother's singlewide. She loved it out there, her own space. She cared deeply for her mother and devotedly fed her, bathed her, administered her medicines, and looked after her daily routine. But she enjoyed her alone time and time with friends who frequently dropped by the porch. The first time I visited Christy on her porch, in August shortly after I moved into Silver Sands, she made sure I knew the park might close.

> "You know they're going to sell this park eventually?" she says, looking me in the eye as if to make sure I know this important piece of news.
>
> She follows up, telling me that we haven't even gotten the notice yet and we are still fighting it: "We have a lawyer and everything."
>
> In rapid succession she tells me that a bunch of residents got together and signed a petition, that they have a Legal Aid lawyer, that the city council meeting for next month was supposed to take place this month but it was canceled and moved to September, that this does not mean that the sale went through, and that their Legal Aid lawyer said that the developer is "running scared." She summarizes—leaning back in her chair, apparently satisfied—that all this means that it could be one year or it could be two years before we need to leave.

Christy maintained this attitude over the course of the six months it took for the Jupiter city council to review the rezoning of Silver Sands. But, like Burt Silverton, by the following April her attitude had completely changed:

> Today when I see Christy she is unusually quiet. She is looking out at her street from her porch. She tells me she's felt depressed lately.
>
> "When I drive through here I'm like, oh my God, this can't be happening. But, I'm going to have to deal with it, it's just the way it goes." . . . She follows in a defeated voice, "I said I was going to try to get Channel 5 News here [Christy had said this a number of times] but I am so tired . . . It weighs on you."

Christy's shift from "fighting" to feeling "defeated" was catalyzed by both the *wait* and the *weight* of daily life lived under a threat of becoming uprooted, under the specter of dislocation.

Desmond argues that eviction reveals the essential nature of poverty and inequality in the contemporary U.S. city. Thus far, he states, "We have failed to fully appreciate how deeply housing is implicated in the creation of poverty" (2016: 5). Yet, an understanding of the experience of both poverty and inequality needs to transcend bounded moments of crises, like eviction. In mobile home parks threatened by redevelopment, the constraints of residents' land tenure shape a more creeping subjectivity of insecurity. In the mobile home park as well as in poor urban neighborhoods like those in Desmond's study, a divided, contested, and insecure relation to place underlies a sense of powerlessness and expendability that effectively haunts residents, shaping their thoughts and actions in ways that ultimately reinforce their disposability. The production of powerlessness in mobile home parks is a slow and sometimes contradictory process. In other words, it's complicated.

Avery Gordon (2008: 3) argues that the study of any social world should be equally complicated: "That life is complicated may seem a banal expression of the obvious, but it is nonetheless a profound theoretical statement . . . the power relations that characterize any historically embedded society are never as transparently clear as the names we give to them imply. Power can be invisible, it can be fantastic, it can be dull and routine." She contends that the sociological study of people's complicated lives must account for what is lost and hidden, what haunts them and appears ghostly. These "ghostly matters" are central to how power operates, especially to how power is shaped by class, race, and gender. Gordon asserts that only by "thinking in terms of shadows . . . can [we] broach the effectivity of marginality and invisibility, its pall and its spell . . . Only such a context can approach the intermingling of fact, fiction, and desire as it shapes us" (195). In short, to understand how the facts of place, the fictions of stigma, and the desire for roots shape the lives of low-income residents (those within parks and those without, those actively evicted and those living under the shadow of eviction) we must look to ghosts and to their hauntings. Gretchen Purser (2016: 394–95) does so in her ethnography of eviction crews in Baltimore, arguing that evictions in poor communities are both dramatic and routine, representing both a reality and a threat. Examining how daily life unfolds under a specter of dislocation requires understanding both the reality and the threat of eviction. The specter of dislocation and the realities of residents' divided property claim structure a subjectivity of insecurity that not only predisposes residents to dispossession but also structures their ability to fight for their rights.

BLOWN AWAY

Understanding the threat of becoming uprooted requires first acknowledging the cultural importance attributed to roots. Since the beginnings of urban sociology, roots have been seen as vital to social integration and community life, while rootlessness is argued to be central in the production of social problems (Fischer 2002). The few contemporary scholars who have studied mobile home parks have identified an essential rootlessness as part of a pathology affecting residents living there. "As shelters and places, mobile homes and trailer parks are inherently settings of transience, whether in reality or psychologically" (MacTavish, Eley, and Salamon 2006: 107). In their recent book *Singlewide,* Salamon and MacTavish (2017: 5) find "a central belief among young families is that a trailer park is only a temporary address." They interpret their ethnographic findings to conclude that residents see their mobile homes as "'second best' housing" that is "occupied on the way to something better" (ibid.). In doing so, these scholars mistake the effects of socio-spatial stigmatization and housing insecurity for an inherent culture of transience. Like classic culture of poverty arguments (Lewis 1959), which attempted to explain conditions in midcentury slums by highlighting the pathological effects of poverty on individuals, these contemporary studies attribute the effects of structural inequalities in mobile home parks to an essential rootlessness in residents themselves.

The few mobile home park studies that currently exist make this mistake. Medical anthropologists Huss-Ashmore and Behrman (1999) argue that a sense of home, place, and permanence is essential for emotional well-being and anathema to the sense of impermanence and rootlessness they find in mobile home parks. They conclude that park residents live within a "permanently transitional community." In their study of rural mobile home parks MacTavish, Eley, and Salamon (2006: 107) likewise state:

> Rural people typically possess a strong sense of place and attachment derived from generations of the same families sharing a history and culture. Mobile-home owners and renters in the parks we studied uniformly self-identified as rural and small-town people, but lacked attachment to the place where they lived in the manner we would expect of small-town residents. It seems that parks are not sources of place identity because residents prefer moving on to something better,

epitomizing the American cultural ideal of social mobility. Their dedication to mobility—a sense of transience—exerts a distancing mechanism on daily life. Park residents neither feel rooted in place nor have a sense that their homes are permanent.

In one exception to this body of research, Margarethe Kusenbach (2017: 30) found that Latino/a mobile homeowners experience upward mobility, desire to remain in their homes, and view mobile home ownership as "a positive marker of their personal and collective identities." Likewise, mobile home residents in this study expressed a deep commitment to the cultural ideals of roots and permanence, as Burt Silverton did after the hurricane when he said, "Hey, I grew up here, this is my home. I'm staying." The above assessments fail to comprehend that a sense of impermanence is not created by residents' desire for "something better," their "dedication to mobility," or their "sense of transience" (MacTavish, Eley, and Salamon 2006: 107). The "essential restlessness of trailer-park life" (Salamon and MacTavish 2017: 2) is inscribed into the very land where residents make their homes. The impermanence these scholars describe is not inherent in this housing form—it is constructed via legal land tenure and urban priorities that ensure eviction continually haunts the mobile home park.

These scholarly treatments, like popular characterizations of the mobile home, imagine an essential rootlessness found in mobile home parks. Associated images, like the one in the newspaper clipping Walter brought to my front door, are smeared across TV screens following natural disasters. You may have seen these images in the wake of a natural disaster; they may be the primary images you have encountered of the mobile home park. Aerial images in the aftermath of hurricanes show flooded trailer park properties dotted with the telltale outline of singlewides. Trailers seem to float; their unmooring is testament to the weakness of their anchor. Coverage in the aftermath of tornadoes and severe storms shows trailers ripped from their foundations. The impact of heavy wind exposes the frailty of their roots. These images shock the viewer not only because of the deep poverty they reveal, but also because of the deep affront to the American value of rootedness they represent.

These images are commonplace in the popular iconography of the mobile home park, and they are well known to park residents. Residents of parks in Jupiter (in hurricane-prone South Florida) and Alvin (25 miles inland from the Gulf Coast) were accustomed to seeing such coverage in the aftermath of hurricanes and floods. But residents' reactions to these images do not confirm the culture of transience Salamon and MacTavish (2017) find; instead they demonstrate a deep anxiety over the strength of the roots they had planted. In Florida, where hurricanes are more common, this anxiety manifested in the way residents used the phrase "blown away" to refer to the idea that mobile homes could be blown apart by high winds. As the following passages show, this phrase came up frequently in conversations, where it was alternately incorporated by residents, resisted by them, and most frequently employed to characterize outsiders' views of their homes.

Tabitha and Betty had lived next door to each other for six years in Silver Sands. Betty, a transplant from Georgia, described herself as very Christian and very Southern, but she liked Tabitha's dry wit and forgave her tendency to curse. Tabitha, a retired medical transcriptionist who had moved down from Massachusetts, was never married and lived alone with a failing kidney. Betty checked in on her almost daily. After a recent tropical storm, Tabitha and Betty talked in Tabitha's living room about upsetting messages they had seen in the news and in Tabitha's Facebook feed regarding the destruction in a local mobile home park. The two women disputed what they saw as the common public perception that trailers are simply blown away during storms:

> Tabitha: "I saw some e-mails on Facebook where people said: 'What do you expect, you live in a trailer!' You know 'it's going to get blown away.' And they said [about] the ones that got blown away in the hurricane, 'They are not worth anything anyway.' It was very degrading."
>
> Betty: "Absolutely. And there are good people that's living here!"
>
> Tabitha is agitated.
>
> Tabitha: "Some comments were very, 'Oh these poor people that lost their homes.' But there were others that were very degrading just because it was a mobile home park that got destroyed. We take as much pride in our houses as anybody else!"
>
> Betty: "Now there are some like old red face (she means a neighbor who is known in the park for his heavy drinking) that are kind of low class but (she takes a pause to think), so what? Every neighborhood has them."
>
> Tabitha: "It doesn't mean, if you bought a $60,000 home, that you are any better than us just because your income is better than us."
>
> Betty: "That's right. You're still human."

In the days leading up to a different tropical storm, Silver Sands resident Gail also complained about local news coverage she had recently seen. Gail was sick of the heavy news coverage of mobile homes in the area as residents were being told to evacuate. She was incensed by a particular local news anchor who voiced the opinion that people living in mobile homes along the Florida coast needed to "wake up." Gail pointed out that during the then-recent Superstorm Sandy "homes all over the East Coast were blown away" and that in the end it seems that "they are not any stronger than a mobile home."

Residents' rejection of these words and images exposed a concern that extended far beyond the structural integrity of their homes. The popular assumption that their homes could simply be "blown away" affirmed public perceptions of their own inconsequence, of the ease with which they might become uprooted. Residents' resistance to the words and images of being blown away speaks to their understanding that roots are foundational to full citizenship, to being "equal" in Betty's words, or "human" in Tabitha's.

Residents kept and shared images of parks being blown away, as Walter and others did. They also resisted these images, as Tabitha, Betty, and Gail all demonstrated. The language around being blown away, and the frequency with which residents used and resisted the phrase, demonstrates that residents both critiqued and accepted popular understandings of their precariousness. The way they returned to the words and images of being blown away speaks to a more generalized unease about their own disappearance, an anxiety over rootedness.

I found this anxiety present in the dozens of parks where I lived and visited, though some of these parks were actively closing and some were not. For instance, Sunny Acres, a park of 60 homes encircled by a chain-link fence and tucked away behind a liquor store near downtown Miami, was open for business. Still, residents there expressed a sense of unease similar to residents in parks where eviction was on the horizon. Walmart had put in a bid to purchase Sunny Acres and the city council had been reviewing their application for well over two years, but to residents this recent development seemed like only another in a long line of potential developments that had threatened the park.[1] Jean, a 70-year-old immigrant from Trinidad and resident of Sunny Acres, explained:

> You hear that from people, right? People keep talking, talking. Yes, no.
> They're going to close down, they're not going to close down. And now
> I notice what they're doing is—the people who have too many people
> living in the trailer, they're breaking it down [evicting them and
> removing the trailer]. So that means they're trying to fix the place
> better for people. I hear for nine years now. And I worry because every
> time I go to them I say, I hear the park closing down. You're hearing,
> you're hearing, you're hearing. For over nine years I'm hearing that.

The neighbor next door to Jean, however, had lived in his mobile home for eight years but had never heard anything about the park closing. Yet three doors down from Jean, Claude, a recent transplant from Port-au-Prince, Haiti, had already begun to worry and search for clues to alleviate that worry. Claude had been living in the park for one year, having moved in with an aunt so that he could attend a technical college in Miami. He tried to make sense of what he saw in the park during that time: "To be honest with you, I really don't know what's going on here, because sometimes I hear people talk about they are planning to close it and then I always see a lot of people come and rent places to live. So I hear people say they will close it but people still come in." Along the streets of Sunny Acres, other residents felt much the same:

> A few streets over from Jean and Claude I speak with a young Latina woman, Stephanie. She lives in an extremely dilapidated, very old looking trailer that has mold growing up the outside of it. Her husband is in the yard next to their singlewide working on their car. She comes out to stand on the porch and talk with me for a bit. When I ask if she's heard news of the park closing, she seems eager to talk about this very point. She goes back and forth on the subject, she tells me as she gives her young child a bath in the kitchen sink.
>
> Stephanie: "I'm not sure. There are rumors that they are going to close. But it has been like that since like two years ago. But they have been moving, see all the places where there used to be mobile homes? I'm not sure if they are moving them because they're closing or if they are moving them to make the park better—like they're dangerous and they're not able to fix them. They haven't told us anything unfortunately."
>
> Stephanie has lived here with her husband for five years. She says that it has been this way for about three years.
>
> Stephanie: "Unfortunately we don't know anything. I wish we would know so we would know what to do. But unfortunately, no."
>
> Esther: "So are you just going to keep living here until they tell you . . ."
>
> Stephanie: "Until they tell us, of course, because, if we had a place to go, and when you have kids, I have four. And unfortunately that's how a lot of people is here, like three kids, two kids. It's a convenience because you have like two rooms, and an office. And that's a big issue, you don't know when they're going to close. They don't tell you. If they could just have, like a meeting and say you have how many months."
>
> Stephanie has her hands full of soap suds as she balances the baby in the sink, so I don't want to bother her longer. She says, "Now you know what to write for your book."

The last residents I spoke with that day in Sunny Acres were two Latina women who appeared to be in their early sixties. They were sitting between their two homes in a lush patio garden paved with paving stones, shaded by a large tree, and heavily landscaped with tropical plants. A small picket fence surrounded the patio garden and enclosed the space between the two homes. I stood in the street and talked to them over the low picket fence:

> The two women are both immigrants from Colombia. Sonia has lived in the park for 12 years, her neighbor Soledad for 13 years. They met in the park and became close friends. Together they built, share, and maintain the flower-filled patio where they both sit.
>
> On the topic of possible closure, the women repeat a conversation they seem to have had a thousand times.
>
> Sonia: "Is it gonna close? We don't know. We don't know. We want to know, but we don't know . . . I've been living over here for the last 12 years and I've been hearing that since I started living here. They're going to close, they're going to close—we're still here. So I don't think so, I don't think they're going to close it."
>
> Esther: "Why don't you think so?"
>
> Sonia: "Because they are trying to fix it up. They tear up the ones that are not good."
>
> Soledad recalls that they have been fixing up the park for the last year and a half. Pulling out the older trailers.
>
> Esther: "I want to know, how does it feel to live in a place for 12 years and they always say it might be closing?"
>
> Sonia: "Oh it feels terrible, of course it does. I'm trying not to worry about it, because the more I worry the more I get upset and depressed. I try to take one day at a time."

SEARCHING FOR SIGNS

In the face of housing insecurity, residents were left to "take one day at a time," in Sonia's words, while at the same time they searched for clues about the possibility of closure. They did so by keeping track and tallying landlord's investments in park properties as a sign of whether their park might close. Similar to Stephanie, Soledad, and Sonia, who all hoped that the removal of older homes signaled they were "fixing" Sunny Acres and less likely to close, Chip explained how he had looked to the maintenance of Silver Sands for signs of closure in the years leading up to his eviction. Chip was no stranger to housing insecurity. He had lived in another mobile home park in upstate New York where the owner "was a son of a bitch and his wife was just like him." The landlord failed to maintain the park and raised the rent "whenever he wanted." In that park when a resident had a problem, the landlord's answer was always, "It's got wheels on it, move."

Because of this past experience, Chip always appreciated landlord Mr. Silver's directness in dealing with residents. Five years before the eviction took place, Mr. Silver began giving new residents a general notice that the property was up for sale. Mr. Silver had long planned to sell the property and retire from operating a mobile home park. Informing residents of his plan was something Mr. Silver did in part out of respect for his father who had run the park for the previous 50 years and in part out of respect for residents, some of whom he had known since he was a child: "You know, an older couple comes in here and they think, we will buy this place and it's their last bit of money. I feel bad and I know my dad would have felt the same way. He would say: 'You need to tell them.' I don't want you to spend your last dime and then be stuck with it [the trailer] and say, I can't get rid of it. So we want to tell them. We want to tell them up front."

Chip had lived in Silver Sands since before Mr. Silver started officially handing out a notice that the park property might sell in the future. Chip saw the explicit warning Mr. Silver gave in the last five years as simply an acknowledgment of the unstated warning he already knew, ever since his days of being told, "It's got wheels on it, move."

Yet, as Avery Gordon (2008) reminds us, life is complicated. Mr. Silver's explicit warning that residents' days were numbered was rare and unique among all landlords in this study. Silver Sands residents knowingly acknowledged this threat and yet they still spoke of their community as a permanent home. On one hand, residents in both states articulated a clear understanding that the land under their homes was the property of the landlord. However, *in practice* they experienced their home and community with an expectation of stability and permanence. Elderly residents often expressed the expectation that they would never again move in their lifetime, despite their formal understanding that they did not have rights to the land under their homes. Hank, an elderly evicted Florida resident, said, "I thought that this would probably be my last home. I thought that I would probably die in this unit." Similarly, Len, a 70-year-old Silver Sands resident, said, "I've lived here most of my life and now I have cancer and I'm going to die. I have two to five years, I thought I was going to die here." Len was evicted shortly before he died of cancer.

Residents' practical understanding of their homes was complicated and clouded by this expectation of permanence. In both states residents cultivated, depended on, and imagined their lots as their own. Residents made additions and improvements to their homes, often expanding the homes on property that they knew did not belong to them. During her eviction, Tabitha had difficulty distinguishing between her home and improvements

FIGURE 5.   A picket fence encloses land that the homeowner
cultivates but does not own. Photo by Edna Ledesma, 2013.

she had made on her rented lot, even after she was informed by a mobile
home relocation company that her porch addition was not part of her home
and could not be relocated with the home:

> So they are like, can't you just live without a porch? And I'm like, if you
> bought a three-bedroom house and then was told that you could only
> have two of the bedrooms, what would you think? How would you
> feel? He said, how often did you sit out there? I said, that's not the
> point, it was part of my house! I bought this place—that was one of the
> reasons that I bought this place, because I liked the house and I liked the
> porch. And I liked the location. Not that it was mine, but I felt it was
> part of the house. I thought it was part of the house. I felt it was part of
> the house. As if it was attached to the house.

Residents' experience of home was complicated. It was complicated by a
clear understanding of their precarious property rights as well as a rejection
of the idea that they could simply be "blown away." It was complicated by
a fear of what a park closure would mean for the roots they established as
well as a desire to prepare themselves for that outcome. Living under the
specter of dislocation for more than 10 years with his wife Kathleen, Chip
learned to pay close attention to any visible sign that might signal the
park's closure, any harbinger of what was coming. In his complicated reaction to news that Silver Sands would finally close, Chip alternately felt

concern for neighbors and found he could not empathize with those who had not prepared themselves in the same way:

> Chip: "So I can't see why—look, we are living where we are for pretty cheap, pretty reasonable [$250 a month], and it's been like that for years. Like I said, everybody that moved in here was told: it's up for sale. You heard rumors that it's up for sale and it is up for sale. So you knew it was just a matter of time."

Chip explains that he knew from having lived in a trailer park previously that one of the hardest things about buying a mobile home is finding a spot to put the mobile home. Parks are full [with few lot vacancies for incoming homes]. So by this logic, parks with filled lots should remain pretty much full. Because of this Chip began to notice when no new homes were coming into the park. He noted over the years every time a lot started to go unfilled and decided then it was "a matter of time."

I point out to Chip that many people's reactions are different from his, that they have explained they felt like the decision to close the park came out of the blue, they felt blindsided. I ask why he thinks this is.

> Chip: "It's like this, Esther, some people don't believe that we put a man on the moon yet. It's as simple as that, see. For instance, we lived here for nine years, 10 years now. So you say apparently he ain't going to sell it. And so you go buy different things for the house and stuff. Then the day comes that it's up for sale and you're stuck. That's what happens, because people are just praying that the time don't come."

Living under the specter of dislocation, "praying that the time don't come," wears on residents. It also distorts their ability to assess whether or not the time is really coming. This is true of any haunting—it distorts one's ability to clearly estimate risk. Residents can live for decades under the specter of dislocation. Residents, like Chip, can spend a decade searching for signs, for unfilled lots. Chip could not empathize with neighbors who did not read the tea leaves the same way. Yet, it is precisely for those living daily in a state of uncertainty, dealing daily with insecurity, that the real state of their insecurity is most unclear.

This state of uncertainty was captured during the week in May 2013 when I first visited most of the parks in Alvin, Texas, including Twin Oaks and Trail's End, looking for a home to rent (before moving into Ramos y Ramos and starting fieldwork there). On these days I made the rounds of every park listed in violation of the city's new ordinance and slated to close. I spoke with anyone I caught outside watering lawns, playing with children, or visiting with neighbors. In each case residents provided different, sometimes conflicting, assessments about whether their park would close or what that would mean. These Texas residents were also searching for signs:

Near the dumpster in the back of Los Alamos Park I meet a man taking out his trash. He's the third resident I meet here who simply does not know the status of the park. Unlike the other two households I've talked with in the park so far he seems more convinced Los Alamos will remain open. He has lived here for seven years. He is actually a fence builder by profession and he knows a bit about what is going on with the improvements to get up to code because the managers of the park have asked him to install a fence around the property, which is one of the criteria laid out in the city's ordinance. He believes that the park is going to get up to compliance because he has seen some upgrades made: the landlords put in fire lanes and put in dumpsters and things like that. This is making him feel confident the park will get up to compliance and remain open. He is relieved.

I continue down the same street in Los Alamos where I meet a young man, Freddie, probably only about 20 years old, standing outside. He lives in a singlewide with his father. I ask if he knows anything about whether the park will be closing or staying open. Freddie says, "I'm not sure, I heard that it's going to take a while before they figure anything out. They say it would probably take another six months to a year. I'm not for sure if they are (closing) or not, I hope not . . . I hope not, because it's on the outskirts of Alvin, because I know they're trying to close down most of the trailer parks inside Alvin."

Later, in Serenity Mobile Home Park I meet an older man in a broad-brimmed hat who is standing outside talking with a younger woman whose three children play around the outside of the house with a small Chihuahua. I inquire about finding rental housing in the park and I ask if the park is going to remain open for the time being or if he knows anything about a possible closure. He tells me that this is exactly what he and his neighbor were just talking about. The young woman is evidently his neighbor. She looks concerned by the conversation they've been having. He tells me that nobody knows; he and his neighbor were just talking about what they will do if the park closes. He asks, "What will I do?" He already has $9,000 invested in his home. He knows it will cost at least $1,700 if he needs to move the home. The neighbors explain that the park across the street is also part of Serenity Mobile Home Park, which is split in two by the road I drove in on. He explains that there used to be a third adjacent park that was part of the same property but that recently closed. He says, "You should have seen it—people were coming in and out, day and night, ripping the metal off of the abandoned mobile homes." The scavenging of this park happened within the view of residents in the two neighboring parks that belong to the same management company. The residents of the other two parks watched it happening "day and night." All of this has made both neighbors worried about what will come to pass on this side of the park.

LIVING UNDER THE SPECTER OF DISLOCATION

It is for those living daily in a state of insecurity that the real state of their insecurity is most unclear. Uncertainty does not always signal a discernible threat or lead to the kind of mental preparation Chip faulted his neighbors for not undertaking. Instead uncertainty can produce complacency as residents reasonably gauge that since it has "always been" this way, it might "always be" this way.[2] This is the confusing and contradictory reality of a life lived under the specter of dislocation. A haunting, in the end, is nothing more than the foreshadowing of risk without the realization of risk. This is the haunting that explains residents conflicted, often contradictory, relationship to their homes and their roots.

In Los Alamos Mobile Home Park on my first visit to Alvin, Texas, a conversation between Pete and Loma, husband and wife, captures the full arc of this contradictory existence and the complex intermingling of fact, fiction, and desire in their experience of home:

> Pete and Loma are a white couple with strong Texas accents. In their 40s, I estimate. They are struggling to get some things from the car into the house.
>
> They take a break to talk. When I mention Alvin's new ordinance and that up to 30 parks are in violation and may close, Loma responds, "News to us."
>
> Pete has a different response: "They say that, but that's been for years, but they say that."
>
> Loma thinks and changes her stance: "They been doing that for years. They been trying to do that, since about five years ago, and it didn't happen. No, they get too much money off this stuff [the mobile homes]."
>
> Esther: "Who is they?"
>
> Loma and Pete at the same time: "The city."
>
> Loma: "They think that mobile home parks, because of the hurricanes and everything, that the parks are the ones who cause damage because the trailers will be rolling. These trailers are tied down, I mean every trailer in this place has to be a Hurricane Rating III.[3] So all these trailers are specifically built for this area. But they think that they are tacky and look tacky and all that stuff."
>
> Pete: "Yeah, pretty much that is their view of it. If they can get rid of these they could build houses like on this other side of the road over

here and over here (pointing). Put housing developments in here and boost their tax rates."

Loma and Pete tell me that there was another park located directly next door to their park that closed last year. Loma says that it was very trashy and it was nothing like their park: "Looks as if the city made them shut it down. There have already been several around town that they have shut down because they were trashy." By trashy she means the mobile homes in them "didn't have no skirting, they had dead cars in the yard, and all that stuff."

This is the second trailer park that Loma has lived in. She and Pete have lived here for five and a half years. She points to her yard and says, "And when we moved here all of this was nothing but a patch of dirt." All along the mobile home a miniature six-inch picket fence lines well-established garden beds filled with assorted flowers. The couple has installed a gardening shed on the lot. Along the side of the shed they've planted their vegetable garden. Large red tomatoes are on the vine.

Esther: "How does it feel—you say you've been living here for five years and for many years they have been telling you we may close—"

Loma: "Not the park manager; the city's been saying it and the paper said that they've been wanting to close down the parks that are not within the city ordinances and all that stuff."

Esther: "So how does that feel for you, living in a park that you know—"

Loma: "I want out of here so bad I can't stand it."

Pete: "You see we own this trailer."

Loma: "We own it outright."

Pete: "So they can't tell me nothing, what I can do with my trailer, I own that."

Loma: "But we would rather be out on our own land."

Pete: "We're gonna do it."

Loma: "One day we're gonna do it no matter what."

Pete: "We want to be able to have whatever we want and then nobody can say: you got to get off. No. We own this, you get off."

Loma: "And what we pay for rent here would be a land note somewhere else . . . If you have your own land it's just better."

Pete: "It's more of accomplishment for yourself—yeah I own my house AND my land AND everything on it."

More than the accomplishment of owning their home and their land, Loma and Pete were looking for security. For Loma news of other park closures produced a singular reaction: "It's a lot of anxiety." Yet Pete consoled himself with the knowledge that parks always seemed to be closing: "They say that, but that's been for years."

In Alvin, the city's ordinance signaled the threat of eviction and set in motion a process that many residents already feared. Similarly in Jupiter, the sale of Silver Sands was the consummation of residents' long-standing fear. Walter and Mattie, who saved the *Jupiter Courier* clipping after Hurricane Jeanne, were no strangers to park closures. The couple had lost their home when a park where they lived was damaged and never reopened after Hurricane Andrew. Their son Sammy, the soft-spoken Vietnam veteran who lived on the lot behind their mobile home, had been evicted from a closing park down the road and moved his RV into Silver Sands about eight years earlier. Mattie described how these events shaped her own assessment of her family's future in Silver Sands:

> Mattie remarks that the RV park Sammy lived in was similar to Silver Sands in size and location, so she long feared Silver Sands would close. Plus she admits, "It [Silver Sands] was always for sale, even way back when the grandkids were going to school." Mattie points out that she was not really surprised when they got the notice about Silver Sands because of the amount of development that has occurred along the main thoroughfare outside the park. "We've been here 20 years and when we came here that was just a two-lane road out here, and then they built the post office. And now it's so built up it ain't Jupiter anymore. As they kept building, we figured, the land was good."

During the city council meetings where the redevelopment of Silver Sands was considered, the lawyer representing the Silver family reinforced the notion that the park could close at any time for any reason. Addressing the city council after the developer, Flagler Inc., had presented their plans for redeveloping the property, the lawyer talked for a bit about the history of the Silver family and their operation of Silver Sands. He explained that both the city and the residents were lucky "that the family has found the right buyer" who planned to work with residents to provide additional information about accessing Florida's state relocation assistance for evicted mobile home park residents. (In actuality, this concession was not a product of magnanimousness; Florida statutes mandate that residents be informed about state relocation assistance when a park closes due to rezoning.) Still, the lawyer highlighted residents' multilevel vulnerability, driving home the point that the park could close for a number of reasons other than rezoning and explaining that residents were fortunate the park was being rezoned because rezoning is the legal requirement needed to trigger Florida's relocation assistance:

> Standing at the podium, the lawyer for the Silver family explains to the city council: "I think you can see from what has come forward . . . that

the family has found the right buyer. And for the tenants this is fortunate too, candidly, because absent someone [Flagler] who could come in and take this, the family really is looking at moving on with their retirement and they have every right to be able to exit the business and close the park and leave the land vacant . . . If this application were denied and the sale were to fall through, all of these tenants who want to take advantage of all the things that have been negotiated—for all the tenants that want to take advantage of that, that would be lost. What the net effect would be is that the park would ultimately close and they would be left with the minimum statutory protections."

———

After the city council meeting I drive home with Walter and Gail in Gail's minivan. They discuss everything they've heard over the last several hours.

Gail summarizes: "I think that they made a very valid point tonight several times. If this sale falls through, if Flagler falls through, and they don't approve the change of the use of the land, or if they do that and Flagler backs out—Mr. Silver can still close the trailer park and nobody is getting any help . . . So I think people better be real careful. I would love to stay where I'm at. I would love to see Mr. Silver not sell the place and city council not approve it and stuff, but I knew going in the game that the property was for sale."

The knowledge that parks could close at any time for any reason made Gail thankful, rather than incensed, that Silver Sands was being sold to be redeveloped into luxury apartments, since this redevelopment would at least entitle her to financial help with her move.

When deciding where to move after the redevelopment was approved, the specter of dislocation was also foremost in residents' minds. Chip believed the possibility of another closure should be a determining factor in his and Kathleen's decision about where to relocate their mobile home. Once the eviction notices were handed out, Chip and Kathleen made a lot reservation at a park half an hour north of Jupiter but were unsure of their decision. They talked with their neighbors frequently about the parks they had chosen. One night Chip and Kathleen debated moving where their neighbor Marty had chosen to move. Both Kathleen and Chip were disabled and their neighbors in the park were their primary support network. However, the fear of another park closure was their most salient concern. The pain of losing neighbors did not trump the risk of being evicted again:

Kathleen tells Chip that the owner of this park [where Marty is moving] is 90 years old and so there is a chance he will be selling the park soon.

FIGURE 6.   A For Sale sign on a mobile home that has been deemed "structurally unsound" for relocation. Next door a home has already been removed. Photo by Edna Ledesma, 2013.

Chip agrees. He points out that there is a possibility that they could move up there and only be there for a month. He sighs and says, "It's a hard decision for anybody to make."

The decision over where to move next, like the decision to move into Silver Sands in the years the landlord began handing out notice that the park might one day sell, was complicated because the threat of eviction was unclear and residents were left to simply guess at their risk. The riskiness of their land tenure and their inability to clearly estimate risk led residents like Chip and Kathleen to choose parks that they only hoped might not close in the future. It also led residents to move to parks located outside the city in the county jurisdiction and hope, like young Freddie, that living on the "outskirts of Alvin" would keep them safe from eviction.

Uncertainty factored into residents' practical decision-making. But more importantly, uncertainty was central to how power operated in closing mobile home parks. The roots of residents' insecurity both as tenants (on rented land in parks) and as citizens (on the losing side of development decisions made by their city councils) was vested in their divided claim to the property under their homes. Within the "American paradigm of prop-ertied citizenship" (Roy 2003), property *is* power. It defines the model ele-ments of "the rights-based relationship between individual and state" (ibid., 464). In this equation, the specter of dislocation is not merely a subjective haunting, but an objective exercise of power. The relational power embedded in evictions is a *relationship of property.* The paradigm of propertied citizenship is central to the production of contemporary urban marginality as it excludes a growing number of individuals (those evicted, homeless, or precariously housed) from the discourse and practice of full citizenship (Purser 2016). Commenting on Roy's work, Blomley (2017: A20) adds:

> Eviction reminds us that property is a state sanctioned power relation, predicated on the violence of law. Eviction itself derives from the Middle French word *evincere,* meaning to overcome or conquer . . . The work of eviction can be connected to the concept of precarity, understood *both* as an outcome of a set of objective conditions (e.g. deregulated labor markets) and the *experience of such situations.* Precarity has a direct connection to property and power. One way to define a precarious situation is one that is liable to be changed or lost at the pleasure or will of another. [emphasis added]

In parks pressured by redevelopment, residents are evicted in the original sense of the word; they are *conquered* by the threat of dislocation, which undermines their emotional investment in their homes, reshapes their relations to their community, and resigns them to the decisions of their public officials.

PASSING BY

The specter of dislocation took shape in the final days of eviction (which the following chapters explore). In these final days in Silver Sands the majority of residents had already relocated. Most of the remaining mobile homes that *could* be relocated were jacked up on their axles, the skirting torn away, and the owners staying elsewhere. The park was spattered with abandoned trailers, the older homes that could not survive a move. The siding was pulled from a few in the hope that the price fetched for scrap aluminum might help defray the costs of moving. The few households that remained in the park were scrambling to find housing elsewhere and vacate before the final day of tenancy.

One evening in the middle of this, I encountered Elizabeth, a woman I had never met in almost a year living in Silver Sands. Elizabeth was roaming the empty streets of the park like a ghost. She looked haunted, walking slowly down the center of the street, her faced turned toward the sky. I approached to ask if she was all right. She told me that she was not; she was searching for a lost bird.

Only one year prior, Elizabeth had moved into the singlewide left to her after her mother's death earlier that year. Before that, Elizabeth lived in a townhouse she had rented nearby for the last 14 years. "I am devastated that I left it, for this," she said, gesturing to the ransacked streets of Silver Sands. Elizabeth was one of few residents who received the informal notice from Mr. Silver when she took over the home. She was told at the time she moved in that the park was up for sale, but she did not clearly understand the risk. After all, she explained, her mother "lived here for 25 years and the park had been for sale all that time."

I ask, "So you moved into her home and inherited it?"

Elizabeth: "If that's what you want to call it. I inherited the headache. The bird is the last straw for me. I just feel so depressed."

Elizabeth's voice sounds completely expressionless and flat as she begins to talk about the bird, telling me that she has had the bird for 15 years and the bird is like her best friend. The bird has never been in the wild. She escaped a cage Elizabeth had borrowed to transport her as she vacated her home, which cannot be moved. The bird flew away. Now Elizabeth has been waking up every morning at 6 a.m. to go look for her bird. She has been looking for four days and put up signs and everything she can think of.

Elizabeth: "I mean, I had everything out of here. I did it by myself. Moved everything. She was the last thing to go, and she had to fly away."

The home Elizabeth inherited cannot be moved; it is too old. She tried to find a rental in the townhouses where she lived one year ago but now none are available. In fact, she has not been able to find a single rental unit she can afford in Jupiter. She is moving down to a neighboring city to live with her brother, who recently had a stroke. She has been his full-time caregiver for the last year.

Elizabeth: "He doesn't speak. He drives me crazy. All he can say is, 'I don't know.' But his place is the only place I have because I haven't been able to get a job because he is so time consuming. I'm the only one who has power of attorney. I'm the only one that has been to every doctor. Like I have been to the doctor already three times today. Since yesterday I have drove 200 miles, just with him. I drive him to his speech class way out, then I come back home for 45 minutes, then I go back to get him, take him to the doctor, take him for x-rays, take him for this and for that—it's so frustrating. And right before this, my mother died. I moved in here, they say that they are closing the park."

I continue to walk with Elizabeth, searching for the lost bird.

Days ago, Elizabeth heard the bird in a tree. Finally she saw her but she was too high to grab so she pulled her car around and stood on the hood of the car to try and grab her up in a higher branch. Exasperated she describes how she lost her balance and fell off the hood of the car while the bird flew away. Because she was lying on the ground she did not see where her bird went. She shakes her head and says, "And then in between these times I have to go and listen to: 'I don't know.' "

Elizabeth seems pushed to the limit. She tells me that she is not leaving the park until she finds her bird. She warned the representatives from Flagler of this, though we are legally mandated to vacate in two days: "I told them already, I'm not leaving until I find her. But it's been almost five days. I think I need to give up, it's too upsetting."

We continue to walk, eyes to the sky.

Elizabeth: "It's so hard to just give up, you know? I know I need to, but I don't want to."

After we search for a while, I part ways with Elizabeth, telling her I will keep my eyes out. As I walk away I wish her luck and say, stay strong. She answers, "I'm trying, but I'm at the end of the rope, it's just a little string now."

Elizabeth could not bring herself to leave, but knew she could not stay. She knew her chances of finding her bird grew increasingly slim, but could not call off the search. She felt increasingly unraveled as she continued, like Chip, to search for signs.

Elizabeth kept up her search in each moment she had away from caring for her disabled brother, who reflected her own conundrum back to her in his constant stroke-induced refrain: "I don't know. I don't know." In the final days before the last residents were evicted from Silver Sands, Elizabeth's loss became a preoccupation not only for her but for a number of other residents remaining in the park. These residents surprised me when in these very last moments, when the eviction was most pressing and their needs were most acute, they spent precious energy worrying about the bird and precious time in the middle of their moves searching for it. Perhaps they saw the lost bird as a symbol of their own loss and uprootedness.

Christy, the resident who 10 months earlier had assured me that residents were "fighting this" and worried months later over the way the eviction "weighs on you," was one of a handful of residents left in the park in the final days before the final eviction date. She felt frazzled trying to plan her move with her bedridden mother. Nonetheless when I went to check in with Christy on her front porch she immediately brought up the bird, asking if I had seen it. She also had never known Elizabeth before she met her out searching for the bird, but she had been keeping up her own search ever since. Just that day she had visited Elizabeth in her home to see if she had found the bird.

Similarly, ever since Josefina found Elizabeth outside searching for the bird she had been taking breaks from her own moving preparations to join the search. Josefina, a Guatemalan immigrant, liked to practice her English when I visited. Looking visibly distressed about the woman and her bird, she explained slowly and thoughtfully in careful English: "I said to my husband, it is sad to know that even though we don't know these people but everyone has their own stories. I said, and so it is like we are setting up a book. Who is going to read that book? If someone writes something about us, who is going to write that book? Who is going to read it? And so I say: we are passing by. I didn't see it this way years ago. But now I say, we are all just passing by." Josefina feared that, like her neighbor's bird and like the community where she had made a home, she was becoming uprooted, "passing by."

This is not to say Josefina had always experienced her park as just passing by, as "a permanently transitional community" in the words of MacTavish, Eley, and Salamon (2006). The "essential restlessness" highlighted by those like Salamon and MacTavish (2017) is not inherent to life in the mobile home park, as Josefina (a longtime park resident) explicitly stated: "I *didn't* see it this way *years ago*." Rather, the specter of dislocation had reshaped Josefina's sense of self.

At the root of Josefina's introspection is a fundamental anxiety over becoming detached: being blown away. Here, Avery Gordon's (2008: 196–97) central claim holds: "It is essential to see the things and the people who are primarily unseen and banished to the periphery of our social graciousness . . . Absent, neglected, ghostly: it is essential to imagine their life worlds . . . [and thus] see that all these ghostly aspects of social life are not aberrations, but are central to modernity itself." In the modern metropolis, displacement has become both a taken-for-granted reality and a vague haunting. In her study of urban renewal—the program of the U. S. government that bulldozed 2,500 primarily Black neighborhoods throughout 993 American cities—Mindy Thompson Fullilove (2005) argues that this upheaval created a lasting syndrome in uprooted residents. The syndrome, which she calls "root shock," is "the traumatic stress reaction to the destruction of all or part of one's emotional ecosystem" (11). She describes root shock as both acute and persistent, as both individual and collective grief that haunts displaced communities like "a dense fog" (4).

Like Josefina who feared "we are all *just passing by*," a resident displaced by urban renewal told Fullilove the bulldozing of his childhood home during urban renewal continued to haunt him into adulthood: "My impression was that we were like a bunch of nomads *always fleeing*, that was the feeling I had" (13; emphasis added). Though the deep and extensive damage wrought by urban renewal on Black communities is unique, root shock is not.[4] Fullilove argues:

> One hundred years ago, the distinguished African American scholar Dr. W. E. B. Du Bois wrote that the problem the twentieth century needed to solve was the problem of the color line . . . I venture to propose that displacement is the problem the twenty-first century must solve. Africans and aborigines, rural peasants and city dwellers have been shunted from one place to another, as progress has demanded, "Land here!" or "People there!" In cutting the roots of so many people, we have destroyed language, culture, dietary traditions, and social bonds. We have lined the oceans with bones and filled the garbage dumps with bricks. (2005: 5)

From those displaced by urban renewal, to those "moved to opportunity" by contemporary projects like Hope VI. From the intergenerational trauma articulated by Native American protesters resisting oil pipelines through their ancestral lands, to the shelter struggles of Chinese villages and Brazilian favelas swept away in the planning for the world's next mega event. From the panhandler told to "move on" and the tarp tent broken down and cleared from Skid Row, to the mobile home resident told "it's got wheels on it, move." In the constant displacement that haunts the lives of those who are poor, marginalized, and abandoned by the state we see displacement as the problem of the twenty-first century. Understanding these shelter struggles not as individual losses and acute crises but rather as collective and intergenerational traumas, allows us to historicize and globalize the contemporary reality that certain people can and likely will be "blown away."

Saskia Sassen understands displacement as an archetypal contemporary global phenomenon, arguing that property dispossessions in the Global South must be understood alongside processes such as mass incarceration in the Global North; together such processes mark the development of a new era of insecurity. This era is "one marked by *expulsions*—from life projects and livelihoods, from membership, from the social contract at the center of liberal democracy. It goes well beyond simply more inequality and more poverty. It is, in my reading, a development not yet fully visible and recognizable . . . It entails a gradual generalizing of extreme conditions that begin at the edges of systems, in microsettings" (Sassen 2014: 29).

In the microsetting of the mobile home park we can see one mechanism through which conditions of insecurity, of expulsion in Sassen's words, become generalized. The specter of dislocation structures a broader subjectivity whereby housing insecurity not only shapes *processes* (dislocation) but also *persons* (the dispossessed). In mobile home parks and in communities facing displacement across the globe, a divided, contested, and insecure relation to place underlies the sense of powerlessness and expendability that haunts residents, reshaping their very understandings of their rights and power to fight for them. Looking beyond the acute trauma of eviction (which the following chapters explore) to examine the specter of dislocation helps us better comprehend how this most fundamental insecurity, the insecurity of place, has become a generalized haunting in the twenty-first century.

4. "We Are Not for Sure Wherever We Are"

For Lupe the eviction was not over. In fact it hadn't really begun. Lupe was one of the lucky ones, but it didn't feel that way. Trail's End Mobile Home Park, where she lived, was one of the parks listed in violation of the City of Alvin's new ordinance. As part of the seemingly arbitrary rules of that new ordinance, the city defined a "mobile home park" as more than three mobile homes on a property. Lupe's landlord could allow three homes to remain, evict all other households, and not be subject to the prohibitive rules of the new ordinance.[1] The landlord chose Lupe's home and two others because they were in relatively better condition than others in the park. So Lupe had not been evicted, but it felt like she had. Everything around her was different. The two homes on either side of her were occupied, but all the others had been pulled out or sat abandoned. On a couple of occasions in the last month, an unrecognized truck drove up the center dirt lane of Trail's End and someone hopped out to pick over an abandoned trailer, harvesting copper wire or aluminum siding that fetched decent resale value on the scrap metal market. From the bay window in her bedroom at the front of her singlewide, Lupe stared out at the picked-over bones of a neighbor's home and the empty concrete pad where her sister's home used to be. She pulled the blinds.

Before that summer, Trail's End had looked much the same for decades. If a sign once marked the entrance to Trail's End, it had long ago been covered by a tangle of bushes and small trees. The park's twelve singlewides sat in two rows facing each other across a center dirt drive riddled with potholes. All the homes were owned by individual households. Residents who moved out easily found friends, relatives, and acquaintances looking to purchase a pre-owned mobile home and move in. The landlord did not get involved; as long as lot rent was paid, residents could rent or sell their home to whomever they wished. The park's central location and affordable lot rent of $300 a month were highly appealing for a core segment of Alvin's population, Latino/a working men and women who staffed the local building industry, rice factory, and seafood processing plant. The park had always been full. But now Lupe's home sat among empty lots of homes that had been moved and abandoned homes that were too old to be moved. The sight of the park made Lupe feel "just sad." She spent time with her young daughter trying to make it look better by picking up pieces of aluminum and debris that had fallen off homes when they were relocated. Even with her neighbors' homes hauled out, she did not want the park to look "trashy."

Physical space functions as a material symbolization of social space (Bourdieu 1999). Lupe attempted to make up the social distance between her and the surrounding community by cleaning up the physical space inside her park. The phenomenological understandings of place that opened this book argue for *emplacing* place, understanding places as sources of identity (Relph 1976), as sources of security (Tuan [1977] 2001), and as sources of roots (Heidegger 1958).[2] Yet, these phenomenological understandings also, problematically, *moralize* place (territorialized in property).[3] This marginalizes individuals (or homes) seen as having weak ties to place and contributes to a "moral geography of mobility" where impermanence is seen as "the assumed threat to the rooted, moral, authentic existence of place" (Cresswell 2001: 14).

This chapter explores the collective emotional framework through which residents experience eviction. Communities are dismantled during eviction piece by piece, home by home, family by family. Lupe watched this from her unique vantage point as the eviction in Trail's End was carried out. We sat together almost daily that summer as she reflected on her experience of home and the dissolution of her community. For Lupe, and many others, the uprooting of her community was experienced through an emotional framework of grief, loss, and indignation. What *happened* during the eviction was important, but also important was how it *felt*. After all, home and community make up a complex emotional ecosystem (Fullilove 2005). The moral exultation of place, home, and roots goes hand in hand with the emotional trauma and indignation of being uprooted. In his classic study of the displacement and trauma following an Appalachian mining town flood, Kai Erikson (1976: 55) argues for the need to "look for scars" not only in individual minds but in the connective tissue of community ties.

While the previous chapter explored the individual subjectivity of insecurity that is catalyzed by living under a specter of dislocation, this chapter explores the collective indignation communities experience as parks close and residents are scattered to wherever they can find housing. This chapter first contextualizes collective indignation through an extended description of Lupe's experience of eviction and her growing conviction that mobile home residents were viewed as "a plague." It then outlines some of the risks and practical challenges faced by residents as they attempted to either break out of the cycle of uncertainty in mobile home parks or salvage their housing investment by relocating their homes to other parks. In both cases residents found that they were not just evicted from parks but from the cities where they had lived. The chapter then turns to the experience of grief and loss that created mental and physical health consequences over and above the many practical challenges residents faced. I understand the mental and physical toll of displacement in terms of the *collective indignation* that became a salient reaction to eviction. I argue, alongside legal scholar Bernadette Atuahene (2014), that property takings must also be understood as "dignity takings" when they involve processes of dehumanization, community destruction (Atuahene 2014, 2016), or socio-spatial stigmatization, in the case of mobile home residents.

A PLAGUE

When I sat with Lupe the first time she invited me into her living room, she was apologetic for the condition of her home: "I know it doesn't look like much but my husband has worked on it to make it nice." She showed me how he made an archway over the hallway that led down to the bathroom and one bedroom. She and her husband Pablo purchased the home for $6,000 four years prior with savings from the Earned Income Tax Credit. When they purchased the home it was infested with fleas from the previous owners' dog. Together they tore out the carpet and put in parquet floors, and since then, she reflected, they hadn't had any problems with the home.

Trail's End had been Lupe's family home for the past 10 years. Her parents and her sister Mara (28) lived in the singlewide next door to her and Pablo, and her other sister Hilda (25) lived with her boyfriend in the singlewide across the center dirt road. The family had moved from a rental apartment in Chicago, where Lupe (22) was born shortly after her mother and father first immigrated from Morelos, Mexico. Lupe's mother had arthritis and the cold Chicago winters were difficult for her, so eventually the family moved to Texas, directly into Trail's End where some of her mother's family already lived. The singlewide they purchased with cash installments was the first home they ever owned in the United States. Eight years later, Lupe's parents and Mara still lived in that home. At 18 years old, Lupe met and married her husband, Pablo, and they had their daughter.

When they began to look for their first home, a mobile home not only seemed like her best option, but it was the only option Lupe could imagine for her small family. Most of her extended family and many of her acquaintances lived in mobile home parks around Alvin. Lupe reflected the cultural imperative for single-family housing felt by most in this study by saying simply, "We're not apartment people."

Staying close to family was also important to Lupe. After she first married Pablo, they rented a mobile home on two acres of land outside the city for $300 a month (for the home and the lot combined). It was affordable, but Lupe did not like being far from her mother and Mara. Finally, Lupe found her own 1972 trailer in Trail's End when she learned that the two women renting the home next to her parents were planning to move. She contacted her landlord to get in touch with the man who owned the trailer. Lupe and Pablo purchased the home, their first home, next door to her parents in Trail's End and she moved back into the community where she had lived since she was 12 years old.

> Esther: "How was it growing up in this park?"
> Lupe: "It's just calm, I loved-loved this trailer park. I call it home. Whenever I go somewhere and then I come back, I don't know, I just feel it's home, because I've been here so long I think. So I love living here and I have never seen gangbangers here like in Chicago. It's not as hectic as it was over there. There, there were gangbangers everywhere."
> Lupe tells me a story of her aunt getting mugged in Chicago; her purse was stolen and during the mugging the perpetrators closed her hand in the car door and dragged her through the street.
> Lupe: "Here it is calm and no one messes with you and you don't see violence and you don't see anything. It's just, everyone's in their own home except for the little kids that play. Everything is great from what I see."
> Still, Lupe later adds, "In the future I would like a home, a real home, a house."

Lupe's comment is not simply an afterthought, a trivial musing about the future. Her comment—"a home, a real home, a house"—cuts to the heart of life in the mobile home park. Trail's End provided generations of Lupe's family stable housing, in a community that she "loved-loved" where her family had an extended kin network of support. Yet Lupe's experience of her own home was also shaped by imagined perceptions of mobile homes and by very real experiences of the risk involved in being a mobile home park resident. That summer, she could see the material outcome of housing risk in the bare concrete pads where the homes of her neighbors had been removed and in the abandoned trailers left by neighbors who lost everything when they learned their home was too old to be relocated. I pressed Lupe on her comment:

> Esther: "So do you see living in a mobile home as something that you wouldn't want to do for the rest of your life?"
>
> Lupe: "I would only want to do it if it was my property and if it was a newer mobile. That would be good. And yeah, people see you as less, like less of a thing when you live in a trailer home."
>
> Esther: "Is that true?"
>
> Lupe: "Yeah. Well to me it is, because we always invite my husband's family to parties but I think it's because we live in a trailer home that they never come to the parties but expect us to come to their parties. And I think it's because they have a house and it makes them feel like more of a person."

She feels the same perception coming from acquaintances she knows who live in a mobile home, but on land that they own.

> Lupe: "The people that live there they've got their own piece of land and they keep telling us, I can't believe you guys are citizens and you guys are not more of a thing than we are—which is the illegal people here. Like we have stuff and you guys don't. Because they have their piece of land already, and they have their trailer."

Lupe says these acquaintances see their own home as "kind of better or moving up."

> Esther: "So when you say, 'that's kind of better or moving up,' do you see a home like a brick home as moving up from a trailer or do you just see it as a home on a piece of property that you own?"
>
> Lupe: "Yeah. Whether it be a doublewide or whatever it is, something that I can call mine and know that I'm not going to be kicked out of there. Because right here, we don't know in a month or two if they are going to say: we changed our minds. And where am I going to go?"

Lupe had been told that her trailer, her mother's trailer, and one other trailer belonging to Mary, a homebound, single, elderly white woman, could remain in Trail's End. Her landlord, Christine, had informed her of her plan to keep three homes on the property. This was based on the city's ruling that a property with three mobile homes or less did not constitute a mobile home park and was not required to meet the requirements of the new ordinance. But still, Lupe felt a nagging sense of insecurity and a fear for the future that continued over the course of that year.

> Lupe: "The future scares me because I have a child and everything, especially starting school. I'm just used to being here so much and moving to another place, I don't know what people are going to be like where I'll live. I mean, I know one day I'll have to move because if I want to buy my own piece of land and everything. I know one day,

whether it's because the city closes this place or because I buy a piece of land, I'll have to. But I hope it's a long time away from now. If I could, I would stay here forever. If I could."

Esther: "Even as a renter?"

Lupe: "Yeah."

Esther: "Even though you said you wanted to one day own your own piece of land?"

Lupe: "I want to own it because we are not for sure wherever we are. Like, I don't know, per se, if I am going to be able to stay here my whole life. That's the reason I want to get my own piece of land because, like I said, we don't know if we're going to be here and I want to take care of my daughter. At least I want her to have a place to live. I want a place for her."

Lupe watched as all of the other households in her park, besides the lucky three, were scattered. She saw firsthand what it meant to be a trailer park resident. She could not escape this sense that "we're not for sure wherever we are." She wanted, for herself and especially for her child, to be for sure.

Lupe had established a relationship with her landlord, Christine, helping her in the park and serving as a translator for residents who did not speak English. Christine, a local schoolteacher, had assured her she would not be evicted. She explained to Lupe and in interviews to me that she intended to continue to operate the park, as her mother and grandmother had done before her. Lupe was savvy. She knew based on previous conversations with Christine that she still had a loan out on the park from a time she had refinanced the property. Lupe assured herself that Christine therefore needed the rents from the remaining three households to pay off that loan. Still, her landlord's financial obligations and personal assurances could not allay the creeping fear Lupe felt.

Lupe had only taken a couple of community college courses before becoming a full-time mom, but she still dreamed of being a lawyer. She had an exacting memory and meticulous attention to detail that led her to scour the internet any time she felt uncertain of a subject. She sometimes scoffed at the naivete of Facebook posts by peers who seemed unable to distinguish real stories from fake ones, or lacked the drive to root out the truth. When Trail's End began to close, she located and read the lengthy original document for the city ordinance in an effort to understand her future. She saw right there in the language of the ordinance that now with only three homes left, Trail's End was not considered an operating mobile home park and was not subject to the rules and regulations being imposed on other parks in the town. Still, looking around at the empty lots and abandoned homes of her displaced neighbors she could not escape this haunted feeling, the specter of dislocation.

The more Lupe scoured the news as the city ordinance was put into effect, the worse she felt. One day when I visited, she greeted me visibly upset. Ushering me inside, she pulled out her phone and brought up a PDF from the local paper, the *Alvin Advertiser*. She asked me to look at an editorial cartoon that characterized the mobile home park evictions occurring at the parks in violation of the city ordinance. The cartoon's banner stated "July 15, 'D' Day for Mobile Homes," referring to the final day landlords had to get their parks up to code or else close and evict residents. The cartoon portrayed a line of trailers being pulled down the highway out of the city as evicted residents inside the trailers sang, "Jus' lookin' for a home. Jus' lookin' for a home." The chorus going up from the long line of trailers was denoted by little musical notes. Lupe found those lyrics strange, so she looked them up. She discovered that the cartoon mobile home residents were singing an early twentieth-century traditional blues song called the "Boll Weevil Song." The song is about the infestation of boll weevil beetles that came from Mexico and caused devastation to U.S. cotton crops in the 1920s. In the song the boll weevils sing the refrain "Jus' lookin' for a home" as they roam from farm to farm looking for more crops to infest:

> Today when I visit Lupe she's angry, more angry than I've ever seen her. She starts discussing the political cartoon right away. Last night she looked up the song the cartoon references and now she is very offended. She plays the whole song for me.
>
> Yesterday when she saw the cartoon, she didn't know if she thought it was offensive but after listening to the song she feels like the cartoon is racist and directed toward the primarily Mexican residents in the city's trailer parks.
>
> Her reasoning is first because the singer first says that the boll weevil's home is "square" and his "whole darn family" lives there. She points out that a mobile home is rectangular and this is the first obvious link between the bugs and mobile home residents.
>
> Plus, as she points out, mainly Mexicans live in trailer parks.
>
> She plays the song, stops it, and points out specific lines, especially ones that characterize the boll weevil as a migratory pest that destroys the land wherever it goes. (In the song the pest is found "wherever cotton grows" and the farmer asks helplessly, "Why'd you pick my farm?" while the boll weevil continues to move in, saying, "Ya better sell your old machines. 'Cause when I'm through with your cotton, you can't even buy gasoline.")
>
> After playing the song on her phone, she looks back at the cartoon.
>
> Lupe: "Now when I hear the song it is offensive . . . I feel like it's condemning about Mexicans because Mexicans come in, they take most of the jobs because either Mexicans charge cheaper or they do jobs that

most other people won't do . . . And the other parts—like the insect, it's kind of like a plague, and kind of like Mexicans because you can't get rid of them even if you put borders—which is kind of like insecticide— they are always gonna be there. It's kind of like saying that we're a plague. And I mean, who else would they be referring to? In many of the trailer parks I've been to there are Americans living there, but I don't think they're referring to them. I know that they are referring to mostly Mexicans. Because every Mexican practically lives in a trailer. When you put one and one together it's two. So it makes me mad."

"So now I'm thinking, is this city closing parking lots because they don't look good in Alvin, or is it because they want to pull Mexicans out of Alvin because it's overpopulated with Mexicans? It used to not be like that, it used to be more white people and people of other races than Mexicans. But as the years transcended, it's more Mexicans than any other people. So they are kind of starting to plague in, or come in, to Alvin. So now I'm thinking, is it really because of that?"

The racialized stigma Lupe felt as she looked at the depiction of her family and neighbors as boll weevils was tied to the place where they made their home. The indignation of being viewed as "a plague" was a collective indignation, marking all park residents equally with an ascribed and stigmatized social status. The experience of witnessing eviction in the park, even though she was not among the evicted, had marked Lupe. Her view of herself as a homeowner had changed. Her view of herself as a citizen of the city had changed. The specter of dislocation had descended. Despite being able to remain in her home in Trail's End, she remained convinced that she and her family were not safe. Her landlord's assurances did nothing to allay this fear, because the park closure had exposed the weakness of her roots.

Lupe: "She said these three trailers can stay, but we don't know if the city in one year or two is going to change their minds and say that we can't stay. It's basically up to the city. She [Christine] said that we can stay and she had a meeting with the city and she said these three trailers can stay but, like with the other trailers, when they decided to evict them, it's up to the city. This is the heart of Alvin, and I think they don't want trailers in Alvin."

Esther: "Why do you think they don't want trailers here?"

Lupe: "Because it makes Alvin look bad or something like that. Because they're not new, they're not new trailers, they're old trailers. It's the heart of Alvin, they want it to look the best it can."

Lupe explains this to me like it's obvious, something everyone should know. The people at city hall don't want trailers in the city. They're not like other houses in the town. She shakes her head. "I feel that one day the city is just going to close this parking lot."

FIGURE 7.   A woman sits on the foundation of her former home. Photo by Edna Ledesma, 2013.

When speaking English, Lupe and others often used this turn of phrase, referring to the trailer park as a "parking lot," as if the homes were just temporarily parked there. When speaking in Spanish they also called the park a *parqueadero,* a car park or parking lot. Residents did so unconsciously, "When they close this *parqueadero...*" they would say. Lupe clearly knew that mobile homes were difficult to move. She witnessed the damage done to neighbors' homes when they were relocated. She saw neighbors lose years of investment when they found out their homes were immobile. She experienced the material impact of outsiders' view that these homes could easily be pulled from their foundations and uprooted. Still, Lupe's language internalized the outlook of the city council whose ordinance treated these homes as if they were mobile and disposable. She internalized the view of the cartoon she found so offensive that depicted migratory residents pulling their homes down the road. She stated, "I loved-loved this trailer park" precisely because "I just feel it's home, because I've been here so long." But she interchangeably called her community a parking lot and a *parqueadero.* The specter of dislocation infected the language she used to describe the community—the parking lot—she called home.

Lupe had long been using that term, *parqueadero*. But she had only recently been feeling this sense of unease, that "we're not for sure wherever we are." She knew full well that "People see you as less, like less of a thing when you live in a trailer home." But this had never bothered her to the extent it did when she saw the cartoon depiction of the plague of mobile home residents trailing their homes looking for the next spot to infest. The very process of becoming evicted drove home the stigma, uncertainty, and powerlessness she felt as a low-income, Mexican American trailer park resident.

THE CYCLE OF UNCERTAINTY

Uncertainty and powerlessness continued to haunt residents as they strategized to relocate their homes or find alternative housing. For the majority of residents who moved their homes to other mobile home parks the sense that "we're not for sure wherever we are" followed them. These residents were able to salvage their housing investment (for most their primary source of wealth) but they continued to rent the land under their homes and live at risk of another eviction. Yet even the residents who attempted to break out of the cycle of uncertainty through alternative forms of housing did so by taking on risk, as the stories of Don, Neto, Magda, and Hilda all show.

In Florida, four months before the final eviction day, Silver Sands resident Don had already made the decision to extract himself from the cycle of mobile home park uncertainty. Don was packing up a U-Haul truck parked outside his house and taking Florida's "abandonment fee" of $1,500 (no similar compensation is offered to Texas residents who abandon their mobile homes). Don was "born and raised a carpenter," and though he was in his late 60s he still worked as a carpenter for small jobs. He had the professional skills to undertake extensive renovations on his home, including new cabinets, new flooring, and a remodeled bathroom. He had lived in Silver Sands for 13 years and in Florida since 1973. But after receiving his eviction notice he was willing to abandon his mobile home, his investment, and the life he had built in Florida because of the risk he now saw as intractable from park life. This was not Don's first time being evicted from a mobile home park:

> Don explains how he moved into Silver Sands after he was evicted from another closing park just streets away in Jupiter many years prior. Unlike Silver Sands that park allowed renters and he was one of a few renter households there. That made him "lucky" when the surprising news of the park closure arrived. He saw the difficulty others had in attempting to move their homes. It was easier for him to just move out;

he stayed with a daughter as he looked for other housing. Rents in Jupiter were already too high at the time for his inconsistent income. He opted to use savings to purchase a used mobile home located inside Silver Sands and fix it up. That was 13 years ago.

Esther: "So you've been through this process before?"

Don: "Sure! Seems to be that's the way it is when the property value gets so high."

Esther: "So that is why parks like this close?"

Don: "That and the town don't really want them here."

Don had lived in the area for four decades and his decision to abandon his home came with serious personal costs:

Don: "I don't want to leave Jupiter. My girls are here, my daughters. But I'm not going to stay here—I'm not going to pay outrageous rent, because I want to retire."

Esther: "Can you tell me a little bit more about your decision to sell the home rather than move it?"

Don: "Well, the decision was that they wanted $600 for lot rent [at surrounding Florida parks where residents from Silver Sands were moving] so I went and bought two and a half acres and a mobile home on it and all for less than that [less than the cost he would pay over time]."

Don explains he purchased two and a half acres in Reedville, Georgia, a town of only 900 people. He decided on the town because he has friends who live there. Don drove up to Georgia and looked at about 20 or 30 pre-owned mobile homes before he decided on one built in 2009. He was able to finance the home for $40,000. He likely did so through seller financing, though when I ask him how he financed the home, he answers, "I'm not telling you that." When I mention that it is often difficult to find financing for the purchase of a mobile home, he answers that perhaps that is the case "down here" but it is not the case up in Georgia.

It was not clear how Don financed the home or the risk he incurred to do so (see chapter 6 on mobile home financing). But it was clear that he was willing to leave the place where he had lived for four decades and the daughters he had moved to Florida to be near in order to remove himself from what he saw as an unfair and exploitative cycle.

In Texas, residents like Neto (a single man in his 30s) and Magda (a 40-something mother of three) attempted to extract themselves from the insecurity of park tenancy by transitioning from one exploitative system of land tenure to another. Magda and Neto, both Trail's End residents, were not able to move their homes into other parks because of the structural condition of their homes. Neither sought out new housing in the county parks around

Alvin where they might purchase a used home for $6,000–$10,000 in cash installments. Instead, both replaced the housing insecurity they experienced in parks with the financial insecurity of purchasing a piece of land through "contract for deed," a risky form of seller financing where the seller retains the deed until the loan is paid off and where missed or late payments can result in eviction and forfeiture of all money paid into the property. Neto, who worked for $22,000 a year as a line cook, purchased both land and a mobile home through contract for deed and moved onto a property that was located just behind the restaurant where he worked. He took on a roommate to ensure he would never miss a payment despite his low income and lack of job security. He felt he understood the risks, explaining by comparison: "In the end they just come and close the park and tell you that you're not going to live there anymore, so I think I have a good deal." For Neto, his new land tenure was not perfect, but at least it was clear. If he never missed a payment and the seller did not skip town, he would own a home and a piece of property in 10 years.

Similarly, Magda and her male partner began self-building a small house on land they were purchasing through contract for deed in the county outside of Alvin. For Magda, the self-building of her house proved difficult. She and her partner started work on the home themselves, while working full time to pay for construction materials. Self-building from scratch, they were forced to live for at least the first year in a rudimentary one-room shelter with no privacy for themselves or their three children. As the property was located on county lands outside of the city, it lacked city water and sewer and the family was using a pit latrine under a hole cut in the floor as their toilet. Still, Magda defended her decision to move to the property. She realized the hazards and endured the hardship because she felt at least she understood the risks and had clarity about her rights.

The insecurity residents felt as their parks began to close led others to see risky transactions as viable options. In Trail's End, Magda encouraged her neighbors, including Lupe and her family, to consult the man who sold her land through contract for deed. This man said he was planning to develop a mobile home park on another plot of land that he owned. The prospect of moving their homes onto this undeveloped plot of land was surprisingly appealing to several households in Trail's End; at least 4 of 12 households gave the man a $200 payment to hold a spot for their mobile home. The prospect appealed to these residents because their households would be able to move together and retain the kin and social networks that had proved both emotionally and practically important over their years living in the park. It also appealed to them because they thought a park located outside city limits might be less likely to close.

The tip about this property owner also came in the weeks when residents began to learn that moving within the city would be nearly impossible. Hilda had called four different parks in Alvin and found none would accept her older model mobile home: "I tried looking all over Alvin but the places were like, you have to buy a new mobile home. It's so hard to move your mobile home in the city limits." Hilda (Lupe's sister) was desperate to find a solution that could keep together the three households of her family that lived in Trail's End: "We actually went up and started looking for land. We thought that maybe we could buy land. Not pay full, but give payments. But they were asking for too much and we had to put sewer and water, that's a lot."

When Hilda heard about the vacant property owned by the man who sold land to Magda, "I was like, maybe we can all move together. It's going to be free space for us, not 'free' but open, like it is going to be a lot of land and so I was excited." Her desire to stay with her family and the allure of having a piece of property, not one that she owned (she had quickly learned that purchasing land was financially out of reach) but one that felt stable, led her to assume a serious risk. She was the first to give the man a $200 deposit for a lot on an undeveloped property and pay $1,400 to have her home moved onto the land. The others were able to learn from her grave error.

At the kitchen table, Hilda begins the story of her relocation as if she is beginning a long saga.

Hilda: "The owner of that property, he said that he would have the place ready in one day. As soon as we put in the mobile home, he would connect everything up. I was like, that sounds good."

Lupe: "He painted a pretty picture. He said I will put the driveway to your house. He said I will do this and I will do that. Rent would be $200 plus the water. Maybe like $230."

Hilda: "He painted it so good. So I actually was the one that said, you know what, I want to live here."

Hilda found a mover through neighbors in the park, "someone else had contacted him and he came by and gave us all quotes." She had to spend a bit of extra money because her home was old; her hitch was in bad shape and needed to be welded. The welding cost $200 and the moving cost was $1,200. The mover was going to charge her $400 to tie the home down [i.e., install "tie downs" that mount the home to the concrete pad] but she explained that she did not have this money and so he told her to contact him when she did and he would come back to tie the house down.

Hilda: "That guy [the property owner] had said it was ready and everything and so I believed him. And then I called the light company because, I mean, we stayed there for one week, there was no light, the guy hadn't connected the sewer, he hadn't connected the water. I mean it was bad."

She and her boyfriend purchased a kerosene camping light and ate their meals out.

Hilda: "I thought that it was going to be for a night. I thought that tomorrow he is going to come and plug everything in and we will just wait on the light and just wait on everything. But no. The second day went by like that. The third day I called and I was like, when are you going to do this? And he was like, I don't know, maybe in a week. And I was like, but we need to go to the bathroom! And we need to get water. He had said that when the home was moved he was going to connect the water and the sewer . . . He said that he could put in a [electrical] post back there. He said that it was going to be okay. But then the fifth day I thought okay let's get the light on at least."

Hilda explains at great length how she began to realize the seriousness of her situation. She called the power company to ask about turning on her electricity. The woman at the power company told her she would need to get a permit to get electricity on the property. She was told to call the city. When she gave the property's address to a woman at the city, she informed Hilda that she could not move a home onto this property because it was under investigation for environmental violations.

Hilda: "And I just remember crying. I was like, Are you serious?! I just paid $1,400 to move in to this place and you're telling me that I can't live here? She said, I'm so sorry, you need to get ahold of the owner. So I called the owner and I asked if he knew that this was going to happen. He just cussed them out. He was like, I guess we'll just have to wait a while. I was like, I can't wait! (She pauses and sighs deeply) I can't wait. A week had went by and I gave him a call and said, you know what, the light company told me that something was going on. That this place was under investigation for environmental violations. And the water company said they couldn't do anything right now, to give a call to the city. Then when I called the city that is when they told me that I cannot do anything because it was under violations."

Hilda was forced to abandon the home. A couple of weeks later, Lupe, Hilda and I went out to see the home still sitting on that piece of property. It was an unsettling sight. We parked on the side of a county road and walked about three hundred feet back to where the home sat in a tangle of razor grass and bramble. Lupe still insisted the home was beautiful, "We painted it. We fixed it up. It's beautiful. But I have to let it go." The abandoned home, Hilda's first home, still sits there today.

Don, Neto, Magda and Hilda all attempted to break out of the cycle of park insecurity, with varying degrees of success. But for most residents, such attempts seemed impossible. The burden of the investments they had already made in their homes, the unforeseen costs of relocation, and the lack of rental options they could afford made moving to another mobile home park the only practical choice for the majority of residents in both Florida and Texas.

In Trail's End, the stigma, uncertainty, and powerlessness that Lupe described after seeing her community depicted as "a plague" in the local paper were reinforced as she helped family and neighbors search for parks that would accept their homes before the looming eviction deadline. After receiving the eviction notice, residents in Trail's End and nearby Twin Oaks learned that the city ordinance prohibited relocated mobile homes from being installed in parks within city limits. Because they were unable to move their homes out of closing parks into any operating park in the city, displaced residents were effectively evicted first from parks and then from the city itself. Most residents were eventually forced to install their homes in parks located in the county, where property was less expensive and regu-lations were more lax. These parks were cheaper than parks in the city, but they were also crowded, poorly maintained, and located miles from city schools, jobs, and amenities. One household evicted from Twin Oaks had moved out of one of these county parks and into Twin Oaks years earlier precisely because of these poor conditions. Five years later, that family was forced to move back into that same county park when they were evicted from Twin Oaks.

The physical fabric of the parks located in the county outside Alvin bore the mark of prior dislocations, visible signs of the cycle of insecurity. Lupe and I went to visit her former neighbor Gloria shortly after she relocated her home from Trail's End to a park far out in the county, which residents referred to only as *el barrio Mexicano,* the Mexican neighborhood. Many of the homes crowded along the streets that made up *el barrio Mexicano* showed traces of prior relocations.

> The park where Gloria has now moved is huge, maybe 20 streets of trailers, but it's in the middle of nowhere. We come onto it after driving for about 20 minutes out of Alvin on a state road past open fields. Despite the seemingly endless open land that sprawls in every direction, once we enter the park we find trailers clustered tightly together, almost as densely as an urban neighborhood.
>
> The trailers here are very dilapidated, more so than any in parks I've seen in town.
>
> The homes tell the stories of past moves. Many have clearly been moved before, parts where additions were torn off for transport are visible.
>
> Some of the trailers have plywood boards tacked on to the sides covering large openings, where extra rooms were removed so the home

could be hauled. The house next to Gloria's has a section of the home where an addition was torn away that is now just open. Not even a plywood board covers the gaping hole, which is probably 5 feet by 4 feet. In place of a wall the residents have set up a tension gate like the ones used to block off a doorway from a baby or dog. The side of the house is open to the outside.

Gloria's home, deconstructed and moved more recently, has two large portions that are covered in plywood: one was an extra room, the other an "outside balcony." Luckily Gloria and her husband had help in Trail's End doing the work of closing these back up. Lupe's own father pitched in. Lupe laughingly says he did the work for beer.

Several residents in Twin Oaks and Trail's End would eventually move to *el barrio Mexicano* and similar mobile home parks in the county. Their housing and neighborhood quality was greatly diminished, as Gloria explained on my first visit: "Here I don't know anyone and I try not to go out a lot because I don't know anyone here and there are no stores close by so I don't go anywhere. I am always here, locked up." Gloria was one of the first to move after residents received notice that Trail's End would close. She felt she had no choice but to move to this park in the county. When I asked if she considered moving to an apartment to remain in Alvin, she explained:

> I didn't think about it because it would be more expensive to live in an apartment because you have to pay all those bills and I only have to pay the $200 and if I had to rent an apartment I wouldn't have enough to send to Mexico and to pay my bills here and also pay for food here. If our daughter was out of school [in Mexico] we would have thought about going back to Mexico. But since my daughter is still in school we felt that we needed to stay here [to pay for school]. We thought about moving to another park that was located within Alvin because that is much closer to my work [at the seafood processing plant] but since my job is only a seasonal job I worried that we would not have enough money if my job put people out of work. I worry that we might not have enough to pay in some other parks because they were charging about $500 plus bills and plus phone and then plus the cost of the car. That is why we found this option and we thought it was best . . . If they are telling you that you have to go, you can't fight, and you just have to go. And plus many of the people in the park, they don't have papers and so that is something that would not help them.

For Gloria and several others, her undocumented status limited her ability to ask questions at city hall and search for other alternatives ("They [undocumented residents] don't want to make a scene and everything. Because they just want to do everything they have to do. Because they are scared.") Gloria's options, already limited by her low income, were further restricted by her fear of becoming too visible if she exercised her rights. The substandard housing in *el barrio Mexicano* seemed like her only option.

Gloria's sense that most residents in Alvin's parks "don't have papers" was similar to Lupe's claim that "only Mexicans live in parks [and] if they are illegal, they're scared." This sense was echoed by other residents in Alvin parks: "It's Latinos [in parks], everyone. No white people. No Black. Only Latinos." This collective Latino/a identity precluded rather than enabled collective action. As Gloria said, "If they are telling you that you have to go, you can't fight, and you just have to go," and as Emilio had reiterated, "The majority of us that live here are Latinos. How can you go against the city and what it says? How can we go to the city and have the city listen to us? The city has all the power and Latinos don't have a voice right now."

Although the fears of Alvin's Latino/a residents were unique because of the undocumented status of many residents, the sense that their collective identity hindered collective action was not. It was echoed in white Florida residents' view that local officials would not listen to them because "We're trailer trash to them." As Mattie summarized: "They think that the people that live in mobile homes are not wealthy enough or do not have enough money or enough income or a good enough job to be average citizens. They think that they don't have any rights or that they can't protest for what they want." In these cases collective identity did not facilitate collective action; rather, it created *collective indignation*—the shared sense that the evictions were impelled by external conceptions of mobile home residents as a marginal and disposable class of citizens.

COLLECTIVE INDIGNATION

Mindy Fullilove's (2005) analysis of African American residents following urban renewal argues for bringing emotions back into the study of human mobility and its demonstrated negative impacts to mental and physical health. Fullilove maintains that the trauma of U.S. urban renewal was due to the destruction of the "emotional ecosystem" of historic Black neighborhoods. For residents of mobile home parks this emotional ecosystem includes the ecology of the home and what it represents, as well as the ecology of the community and what it provides. The complex emotional ecosystem tied to home and community helps explain why collective displacements like urban renewal in the United States (Fried 1966), housing market renewal in the United Kingdom (Allen 2008), and apartheid-era relocations in South Africa (Atuahene 2014) have been described in terms of emotional pain and loss.

The pain experienced by mobile home residents during eviction was tied to the collective indignation they felt over the loss of their communities. Nonetheless, it is important not to romanticize these communities, as many residents themselves did during and after eviction. Gloria's lament from *el barrio Mexicano*—that "everyone knew everyone" back in Trail's End— was often repeated by displaced residents in both states but had also been a source of ire before eviction. In daily life, residents saw their communities as close, at times too close. I witnessed neighbors, even those within the same family, gossip about, fight with, and avoid each other at times. Life was never perfect in these parks, community life was not always smooth. Still, for better or worse, neighbors were there when something serious transpired.

The closeness of neighbors meant the "eyes on the street" that Jane Jacobs famously found in dense urban environments (1961) took on new meaning in parks. I was amused one day while working furiously on a deadline without leaving my mobile home, when my neighbor Walter knocked on my front door, worried since he had not seen me that day, as he always did, that perhaps I "had a fall" in my home. Walter's fear made more sense when later that year a few streets away, Betty heard an audible thump from the trailer next door and was able to call an ambulance after her neighbor fell in his home. The tight spatial and social arrangements found in parks are a product of decades of municipal regulations and planning practice that segregate and seal them off (see chapter 1). In the case of the African American communities displaced by urban renewal, Fullilove (2005: 75) argues that analogous external constraints created an internal closeness that "knitted" segregated Black neighborhoods. In mobile home parks, this knittedness contributed to the pain and loss residents felt as parks closed and communities were treated like an assemblage of parts that could be divided up, hauled out, moved anywhere, or taken apart and salvaged for scraps.

Social life in the parks was not always rosy, but it was ordered in such a way that it also ordered the lives of residents: "Social scientists have established that social loss of that order makes people vulnerable. After a loss, a second blow will hurt more and do its damage more quickly than the first, setting in motion an accelerating downward spiral of collapse. Thus for the displaced citizens, urban renewal sapped resources and depleted strength in a manner that increased the vulnerability of the uprooted not simply for a few years, but for many decades to come" (Fullilove 2005: 99). The knittedness of neighborhoods displaced by urban renewal compounded the trauma of displacement due to the loss of a social order: "the loss of neighbors who 'automatically came' was devastating" (ibid.).

Community destruction is double-faceted in that it involves both individual and collective trauma (Erikson 1976; Adams 2012; Atuahene 2014). Time can heal individual trauma, but it does so more effectively when it works in a setting of communal support (Erikson 1976). The second face of community destruction—collective trauma—dismantles these systems of support and extends the first-order trauma of eviction.

Residents in both states experienced the collective trauma of eviction through a similar emotional framework in which pain and grief were central. Trail's End resident Eunice summarized the experience as she spoke with a neighbor on her front porch:

> Eunice leans against the rail of her porch, talking with her neighbor about the notice they received last month. "On learning the news I was surprised, I didn't expect it," she says.
>
> She has lived in the park for seven years. She remembers that when she first heard the news she felt "a lot of sadness." Neither women talks about the details of the move, the logistics or challenges. Instead, Eunice talks about how her children and her husband were all feeling the same way, sad mainly.
>
> Eunice's neighbor tells her that when she learned that the park would close, she felt similar: "Duele, se Duele." It hurt.

The hurt described by these neighbors became a common refrain in the days leading up to the eviction. So did a sense of grief. The closure felt, as Rachel in Twin Oaks said, "like when something important to you dies." But the experience of pain in these parks was not simply born of loss. As the eviction process began, residents in both states described a pain that spoke to a more fundamental experience of *indignation*.

My Silver Sands neighbor Walter used his characteristic dark humor to express how feelings of hurt and indignation intersected. In the months leading up to the closure of Silver Sands, Walter was increasingly confronted with the indignities of trailer park life. Like Lupe, he was no stranger to the perception of park residents as trailer trash, but the eviction process brought outsiders' demeaning perceptions to his front door.

> Sitting out in his patio garden, Walter is preoccupied with one thing, a conversation he had with an acquaintance he knows from outside the park.
>
> Walter describes offensive language this man used about mobile home park residents. In a conversation the two had after the city council decision to rezone Silver Sands, the man suggested park residents were stupid for living in parks at all and that they must know very little about the ins-and-outs of real estate. Walter details their conversation at length, growing frustrated.

Walter: "And I was feeling so good! Here I am, I thought I was looking so good. I put on a clean shirt every three or four days, change my
socks once in a while and shower here and there. And I thought damn,
I'm pretty high up. Come to find out I ain't nothing."

He laughs. But then he tells me he lay in bed last night thinking.

Walter: "It is funny yeah, but it's also kind of serious too—not that
people say all that stuff about how I should know my level, but it's just
kind of sorry that people think that way. That's the thing that hurts."

The thing that hurt for Walter was the indignation of confronting an
outsider's view that his park was disposable just as the emotional loss of his
community was setting in. Lupe expressed a similar sense of indignation
when she saw her family and neighbors compared to pests and treated as "a
plague." Maria looked face to face at this indignation when she stared up at
her investment parked like refuse in an empty field and said, "We painted
it. We fixed it up. It's beautiful. But I have to let it go." Gloria felt this indignation as she recognized that seeking help from the city might bring scru-
tiny on her undocumented status and understood that "you can't fight, and
you just have to go."

Tabitha experienced this indignation physically in the sense of feeling
unsettled as she watched her home being hauled away. She explained, "This
whole thing is not settling. Watching your home be pulled down the street,
crooked . . . It's unsettling." Indeed, Tabitha was not alone in her indignation at watching the physical removal of her mobile home. When I first
moved in to closing parks, I had anticipated that the moment of receiving
the eviction notice would be most salient for residents. I trained my analytic eye on this moment, waiting to capture its effects. I never anticipated
the primacy that the physical removal of the home would have, until residents told me time and time again how it *unsettled* them. When residents
told me "you don't know how it feels to see your home being hauled down
the road," they were correct. I did not know and could not know how this
felt. Insulated from the emotional experience of uprooting and from the
stigma associated with rootlessness, I failed to imagine how watching their
homes being hitched to semi-trucks and hauled away would crystallize
their collective indignation.

The concept of *dignity takings* (Atuahene 2014) can help us understand
the symbolic hurt and sense of indignation that became a salient feature of
these evictions. In her study of land dispossession during South African
apartheid, Bernadette Atuahene uses the concept of dignity takings to refer
to state actions that deprive persons of property while simultaneously
depriving them of dignity in the form of dehumanization, infantilization,

FIGURE 8.   A home is relocated out of a closing mobile home park. Photo by Esther Sullivan, 2013.

or community destruction (Atuahene 2016). Atuahene's concept delineates specific mechanisms for assessing whether involuntary property loss also entails a dignity taking, and it is useful in its specificity (see Atuahene 2014).[4] Taken more broadly, however, the concept of dignity takings is also useful in expanding conventional legal definitions of property to account for the multiple values property can hold (Atuahene 2016). While legal scholars focus on formal rights of ownership and understand property as the bundle of (primarily economic) rights to possess, use, exclude, and transfer property (Merrill 1998), this narrow definition of property limits our understanding of property loss. Property holds not only economic but also emotional and symbolic values, as is clear in the case of mobile home residents who have no economic claim to the place where they live but still imbue their communities with deep emotional and symbolic value.

Through the lens of dignity takings there are clear parallels between the property loss experienced by park residents who witnessed their homes being hauled out of closing parks and Cape Town residents in Atuahene's study who witnessed the bulldozing of their homes as they were forced into apartheid-era "coloured townships." In these moments, Atuahene argues, residents experienced a loss of dignity that occurred over and above their loss of property. Residents felt "discarded" (Atuahene 2014: 39). As one resident remembered: *"The bulldozer just come. You are still standing* there. You can get mad then they just take that house, in two seconds it is flat" (ibid.; emphasis added).

In mobile home parks, *the trucks just came.* With shocking ease they pulled residents' homes from their foundations. In these moments the full impact of residents' indignation was laid bare. This was what they meant when they insisted, "you don't know how it *feels* to see your home being pulled down the road." Park residents described the experience of seeing their home hauled away as unnerving, demeaning, and painful.

> We've been standing outside Walter's home for the better part of the day, waiting as it is hitched to the truck. Walter's daughter-in-law, Gail, has come to join us. We've stood around most of the day as the crew works. Finally, around 3:00 p.m. Walter's home starts to move. After all the waiting, it happens so fast. The home comes toward us trailing behind the large semi-truck. We are all silent as the truck, the house, and then the escort car drives by with lights flashing and a wide load banner hung across its back. Within minutes the home turns the corner down the main road that leads out of Silver Sands. We silently pile into Gail's minivan, pulling behind the caravan. We go about 30 miles per hour as we drive behind the trailer the whole way. Gail whispers as she concentrates on driving: "Surreal."
>
> Though both Gail's and Walter's households have been packing and disassembling their homes for months, including serious physical labor like removing the large screened-in porch additions that ran the length of both their homes, Walter mentions for the first time how exhausted he feels.
>
> He's surprised by the toll this day has taken on him: "I'm all worn out and I ain't done nothing."
>
> Gail: "That's when Matthew and I started noticing that we were actually tired, was the day our trailer actually got moved."

Within a powerful cultural paradigm that moralizes place, home, and rootedness, the physical sight of one's home being uprooted and hauled like cargo gains powerful symbolic weight.

"Emplacing" place—understanding the phenomenological experience of home as a source of identity and roots—reveals how the "sadness" and "hurt" through which residents framed their eviction was tied to a broader dignity taking, to the dehumanizing process of being treated like "I ain't nothing" in the words of Walter, like "a plague" in the words of Lupe, like "trash" in the words of so many others. Residents' visceral response to seeing their homes hauled away speaks to the indignation produced by the visible sight of their homes torn from their foundations, the material expression of their own disposability. That this became the most salient feature of

FIGURE 9.   A homeowner watches as his doublewide is split and hauled away.
Photo by Esther Sullivan, 2013.

the eviction for some residents demonstrates that beyond the practical and
financial costs of eviction, the loss of dignity was a primary cost.

Lupe circled the park with her young daughter, picking up debris from
homes that had been hauled away, not wanting the park to look "trashy" but
knowing it was seen that way. Traffic flowed freely by Walter's home as he
followed behind it with Gail in the minivan, and Gail whispered, "Surreal."
The movers pulled Tabitha's home off the concrete slab she had edged with
flower beds and she attempted to articulate her discomfort, "It's unsettling."

In the emotional ecosystem of home, the experience of becoming uprooted
has practical implications that extend beyond emotional pain to physical
health. In Tabitha's own estimation the unsettling experience of eviction was
related to her declining health. As the final date of the eviction approached,
she embodied the stress and discomfort of the dislocation: "I told the doctors
that this was causing me too much stress. I'm down to 71 pounds from 80
pounds. So I am on a nutritional supplement now. I'm really stressed, and
don't want to eat, and everything was so chaotic in here [in her home]. It is
not settling. I'm sick every day. Every single day. I have nausea and vomiting
every single day."

Tabitha is just one example of dozens of residents in both states who
experienced impacts to mental and physical health during the eviction
period. Residents documented their physical health, monitoring and sometimes relaying to me their increases in blood pressure, migraines, use of
narcotics, and hospitalizations. Residents also experienced mental health
issues that ranged from depression, anxiety, and insomnia to panic attacks.
Ultimately the health impact of housing insecurity took its most damaging

form in prolonged illnesses, strokes, and even deaths of residents in this study (see chapter 5). In Sawgrass Estates, a South Florida park closing 90 miles from Silver Sands, Luanne described a similar experience to Tabitha and many others:

> We sit inside Luanne's home where everything is boxed up and has been for over one month. Her computer, her mattress, and some kitchen and bathroom items have been left unpacked. She knows she needs to leave but still does not know when. Around her the park is partially empty, about 60 percent of the homes have been removed. Luanne's park is very large; about 1,500 residents lived here when it was at full occupancy. So emptying the community has taken months. During these months Luanne has felt increasingly emotionally and physically unstable. As we talk, a mobile home moving truck drives by on its way to hook up to a home. The engine of the semi-truck is really loud. We need to stop talking as it goes by because we can't hear each other over the noise. Luanne sounds exhausted as she says, "That is all I hear all day."
>
> Luanne: "Going through this whole thing from the start to here was like going through a death. You know? You had to go through all the emotions like someone dying—crying, non-acceptance. You just had to go through the whole thing to come to acceptance. This is what it is. It took me a long time to get here."
>
> Esther: "How were you feeling before?"
>
> Luanne: "Oh I went to the doctor, I had such bad anxiety from it. I couldn't face the day. I couldn't think about what was coming up next—where we were gonna go."
>
> Esther: "Had you ever had problems with anxiety before that?"
>
> Luanne: "Not to this extent, no. Not to be extent that—now I take a pill, every morning. It's my chill pill."
>
> Luanne takes 5 mg of Lorazepam [prescribed for anxiety disorders].
>
> Esther: "Had you ever been on antianxiety medication before?"
>
> Luanne: "No. Now it stays with me. And there are a small percent of people in the world that once you start an antidepressant or an anti-anxiety you can never get off of it. I fall in that 1%."
>
> Esther: "How do you know that you fall in that 1%?"
>
> Luanne: "Well, I'm a retired nurse and I told the doctor that I tried to wean myself off of it and that's when I found out that I really couldn't. I fell into that 1%."
>
> Luanne says that she does not want to take a higher dose because it makes her feel like a zombie all day. However, she says that before she was taking the anxiety drug she could not do anything: "I couldn't get out of my pajamas all day, I was just—just dust me as you are going by, okay? That's how hard it was. It's hard but, you know, there's a lot of other people in the park, there are a lot of them that are far worse off

than I am. Their homes cannot be moved or they have no family. They will stay here till the end and then take something and never wake up, that's what they've told me."

Luanne talks about people she knows, people who have had heart attacks since the eviction process began. I tell her that a close neighbor of mine in my park had a stroke just this week.

She responds by shaking her head and saying simply, "It's real. It's real."

The health impacts of housing insecurity are real. Luanne's experience, living amid the sights and sounds of uprooting and waiting for her own removal, encapsulates the bundle of anxiety, loss, grief, and powerlessness that were rolled into her experience of displacement. In parks across Florida and Texas, the emotional pain of community destruction contributed to material illness. Silver Sands resident Jo had a more embodied experience of this pain:

> As if she's getting it off her chest, Jo tells me that she is now taking 5 mg of Oxycodone in both the morning and evening. This troubles her since, she also explains, regulating her use of the drug has always been important to her. She used to attend a pain management clinic after a back injury, but she cut her ties with the clinic when she felt the doctor was pressuring her to increase her dose. But now, with the eviction coming, she's begun increasing her own doses because she feels "constant pain."
>
> She says, "But with all this, and the pain in my back and in my stomach I am taking two pills in the morning and two at night. Now I took the pill an hour and a half ago and my stomach still hurts. So you can imagine how much it hurt before I took it."

Silver Sands resident Christy also turned to substances to dull the pain she felt, so much so that she ran out of the pain pills she was prescribed for a back injury. She explained that she had never been a big drinker, but without her pain medication she had been taking Aleve or Motrin and drinking a beer or two at night to "at least try and function."

Residents in both states physically embodied the emotional pain of property loss. They felt a loss of control, strength, and well-being that coincided with their loss of place, roots, and dignity. Understanding dismantled neighborhoods as lost emotional ecosystems (Fullilove 2005) helps us account for the physical and psychic trauma that displacement inflicts. Residents' expressions of injury—whether from seeing their neighbors treated as a plague or from seeing their homes treated as cargo—encourage us to think beyond the immediate practical and financial difficulties of eviction, to understand community destruction in mobile home parks as an ongoing dignity taking (Atuahene 2014). In mobile home parks, dignity takings reproduce cultural understandings of mobile home residents as marginal and disposable, serving as a mechanism that structures their housing insecurity from the inside. The following chapters explore how residents' housing insecurity is structured from the outside, by the policies that manage mass eviction differently state by state (chapter 5) and by a mobile home industry that capitalizes on residents' precarious right to their communities (chapter 6).

5. Relocation and the Paradox of State Interventions

On a sweltering hot June day in Alvin, Texas, the Castillo family was evicted from the first home they ever owned. It had been two years since they purchased their mobile home from the previous owner in Twin Oaks Mobile Home Park. They paid cash for the used four-bedroom singlewide and rented their small lot for $200 a month. Standing in their living room where tin foil–covered windows helped block out the Texas heat, 15-year-old Rachel Castillo read aloud the short eviction notice: the Castillo family had 30 days to move both their family of five and their home. We pored over the eviction notice. It was written only in English, even though the majority of households in Twin Oaks spoke only Spanish. Mr. Castillo alternately muttered and shouted, "One month!" Meanwhile Rachel and I marveled that there were no further directions given, no numbers of anyone at the city to call, no contacts for other mobile home parks, for movers, or for anywhere residents could seek help. Even during this traumatic moment of learning his family would have to move to an unknown place at an unknown cost, Mr. Castillo was immediately concerned for his neighbor Señora Reyes, the 87-year-old widow living with a disabled grandson next door: "This is sad for these people. You need time for everything! . . . What will we do? And next door, the old Señora, what will she do? Maybe cry, maybe die."

"THE CITY TELLS YOU TO MOVE, YOU MOVE": NO TIME AND NO HELP IN TEXAS

That same day I visited Señora Reyes at her home in Twin Oaks. Like most of the other parks in Alvin, Twin Oaks was developed several decades earlier, but in an effort to "improve" the housing conditions in the community (at least aesthetically), the city council stated that the park needed to comply with the ordinance's new standards or else close. Local landlords argued that since compliance would cost over $10,000, the town was effectively forcing their mobile home parks to close. However, until that day, households in Twin Oaks had not received eviction notices, leaving them to wonder if their landlord would upgrade their park or shut it down.

Only four days earlier, Señora Reyes had told me that she did not know anything about her park closing or any potential evictions. Now she had a letter in hand, but she did not know what it said. She asked me to translate. Stunned, I realized Señora Reyes did not yet know she was being evicted:

> Esther, translating: "This is to notify you, Ms. Reyes, that the City of Alvin has closed the park. You have 30 days' notice and your tenancy is terminated July 1."
> Señora Reyes whispers: "July 1 . . . We have nowhere to go."

In Alvin, most residents, like Señora Reyes, were blindsided by the eviction notice. All but one of the town's landlords withheld the notice until 30 days before the town's final code compliance deadline. Some of these landlords sincerely thought they would be able to bring their parks up to code in time and remain open, but many others deliberately kept this information from residents to ensure that their tenants continued to pay rent until the park closed. They gave only the bare minimum of 30 days' notice. The result for residents—an initial period of shock—would be the worst period of the relocation as they grappled with their inefficacy in the face of their eviction. Four days after the eviction notice, my field notes capture this inefficacy back in the living room of the Castillo family:

> I ask Mr. Castillo if he will go down to the city offices to talk with them about the eviction but immediately regret the question. He shouts: "How can you go against the city and what it says?! How can we go to the city and have the city listen to us? If we don't move by July 1st, I don't know what the city would do to us. The city doesn't care about us! The city tells you to move, you move."
> Mr. Castillo and Rachel both discuss the apathy of the city toward them. Rachel reiterates; if they have to throw you out, they will. A whole family.
> I ask Rachel how she is feeling right now.
> Rachel: "I think that this is why there is a lot of suicide. I think that is why people do suicide, because right now you are just depressed . . . You want to kill yourself. I mean, it hurts. Oh. I'm gonna cry. It hurts because . . . (Rachel does start to cry, her voice breaking.) We don't have any money right now. My mom is the only one working. Every time she comes home she is all tired. It hurts."

Like others in Alvin parks, the trauma of the Castillo family's forced removal was most keenly felt in this initial period as residents told me they could not believe what was happening, had no idea what they would do, felt "depressed," "*mortificada*," "like when something important to you dies." Yet, despite the shock of their short notice, the lack of state or local resources, and their insistence that they had absolutely no funds to move, the relocation of these Texas residents would unfold quite differently, and with better outcomes, than their counterparts in Florida.

"IT WILL BE . . . GOD KNOWS HOW LONG": ASSISTED RELOCATION AND UNCLEAR AID IN FLORIDA

Although Silver Sands residents received a formal letter that the development company Flagler Inc. was interested in purchasing their park in April 2012, no one would receive Florida's state-required six-month eviction notice until the following October, seven months later, when the application to rezone the park was approved by the city council and their landlord finalized the sale to Flagler. Florida laws require that local city councils hear and approve any rezoning change that results in the closure of a mobile home park. Silver Sands residents waited to see how the process would unfold. During the many months and multiple meetings it took the city council to hear and eventually approve the zoning change (over the summer and into fall of 2012) eviction had become both a daily topic of conversation and a seemingly distant reality.

By August 2012, although we had not received the eviction notice, abandoned homes already dotted the tidy streets of Silver Sands. The few lucky "snowbirds" (northerners temporarily relocating to warmer southern climates in wintertime) had already vacated the park before the summer months, leaving behind the majority of permanent residents at Silver Sands. The snowbirds' mobile homes had allowed them to fulfill a secondary American Dream of homeownership, a retirement home in Florida. But even for the snowbirds, whose incomes were higher than the majority of low-income, year-round residents, the price of lot rent during the unknown period leading up to eviction and the costs of relocation made their budget retirement homes an impossible luxury. Many sold their homes at a financial loss to neighbors who feared their own homes would not survive a relocation. Others cut their losses and abandoned their homes in the park. "For Sale" flyers fluttered on the corkboard in the communal laundry room, but used mobile homes that needed to be removed at the buyer's expense received few interested inquiries. Their owners' equity had evaporated.

In the garden that stretched the length of his mobile home, my neighbor Walter transplanted aloe plants entrusted to him by a snowbird neighbor who abandoned his home and flew back to Michigan. Despite the return migration of the snowbirds, the residents who remained in Silver Sands still had no idea how long they had. October came, and still no one had received an eviction notice, even though everyone was aware that talks continued between the landlord, Flagler, and the city council over the zoning change that would seal the sale of the park. As if defending his choice to replant the aloe in the ground rather than in temporary pots, Walter stopped digging to tell his wife, Mattie, that even the developers who eagerly awaited the zoning approval did not really know when the eviction notice would be given. He pointed out, "It could be two months or it could be twelve months."

That fall, talk of the eviction notice was everywhere. On cool afternoons, Kathleen would prop her front door open and roll her wheelchair out onto her fiberglass steps, hoping to catch a neighbor in conversation. In the grassy space between her home and her neighbor's, Kathleen, Betty, and I stood around one afternoon talking about the eviction. Tabitha, whose mobile home backed up against Kathleen's, joined us and started right in by asking if we had heard anything new about when we would receive the notice. These conversations had become a daily part of life in Silver Sands, as had the constant speculation about how long the process would actually take. Without any new information from the city council or the landlord, many imagined that things were being held up in a bureaucratic municipal process that could take many months. Others optimistically, though falsely, hoped that local media coverage—a newspaper article and a piece on the local nightly news—might have swayed the city council to reconsider rezoning the park. Everyone knew that Florida law gave mobile home residents six months to move from whatever date they eventually received the formal eviction notice. Factoring in the seemingly stalled city council process and the state-mandated eviction period, many repeated the increasingly commonsense refrain that the whole process would take "a year or two." In fact, during these first seven months in Silver Sands I heard this refrain so often that I became convinced of it myself and reorganized my life—a subletter for my apartment back home, a place for my dog, a revised timeline for a grant proposal—according to this collectively invented timeline.

Although this imagined time frame had not changed much in those first seven months, the tone of the conversation surrounding the ever-anticipated eviction notice had begun to transform. This shift colored the conversation outside Kathleen's backdoor that October day. Tabitha greeted us with the usual question about news regarding the eviction date, but went on to speak about the eviction papers without the usual trepidation so many residents exhibited in those initial months. Instead Tabitha now seemed eager, anticipating the day she would finally get the formal eviction notice. Betty agreed, wishing Flagler would hurry up and "get it over with." Tabitha told us, "The thing about it is I just *wish* they would just give us a more *definite* time. It's dragging this stuff out that makes it hard." In the past Tabitha had listed many other aspects of the relocation that would "make it hard" for her, including a lack of savings and a $700 a month fixed income, a physical inability to pack her home since a degenerative disease made it difficult to lift even light objects, and a three-times weekly regiment of dialysis that she would need to reestablish with the public transportation for the disabled that she used to get there. But now, the *waiting* had become most salient for Tabitha. Her neighbors nodded in agreement as she diagnosed this most disruptive feature of the looming eviction. From her wheelchair Kathleen summarized her powerlessness in the face of time, saying, "All you can do is just sit tight."

To "sit tight"—"to wait for everything to come from others" (Bourdieu 2000: 237)—is a key mechanism through which the dominated experience power (Auyero 2012). As Auyero demonstrates through an ethnography of welfare offices and polluted neighborhoods where poor people "sit tight" for state assistance that is rightfully theirs, waiting and delay are "relational practices linking daily state operation with the lives of the subordinate" (5). The days, then weeks, then months that Silver Sands residents waited to receive their eviction notice were not simply the calendar in which this ethnography took place—they were key "temporal processes in and through which political subordination is reproduced" (4). Urban sociology dating back to Gans's study of urban renewal in Boston's West End has shown how resistance to displacement is hampered as residents are confused and made complacent by the drawn out and detached (from them) timeline of urban decision-making, which they experience as "a seemingly purposeless, erratic, and infinite series" (1962: 290).

This chapter explores how waiting and confusion are embedded within contemporary neoliberal housing policies that extend well beyond park landlords and city decision makers. It analyzes different iterations of neoliberal housing policy in which state regulations are replaced with regulation by the market (Brown 2006; Harvey 2005; Peck and Tickell 1994, 2012) and market logics creep into the management of those in need of public-sector services (Collins and Mayer 2010; Hays 2003). Following Bourdieu, Auyero, Gans, and others (Schwartz 1974; Adams 2012), I show how the timing of eviction either mitigated or aggravated the sense of confusion and subordination felt by residents. I extend these analyses by demonstrating how confusion and delay are institutionalized within neoliberal state policies and practices that rely on public-private partnerships to administer the aid to which residents are entitled by law.

In very different ways the state laws of Texas and Florida determined where residents moved, who moved them, and with what effect. By detailing the preparations, strategies, and concerns of residents in the days leading up to and immediately following evictions, this chapter compares the different ways mobile home park evictions are legally and administratively managed under different state policies and then compares the effects. In Texas, the state has taken a traditional laissez-faire approach to park closures, refusing to adopt legislation that would provide advanced notice or relocation assistance. Texas has no state agency that regulates mobile home parks or the mass evictions that occur when they close. Without a system of oversight, Texas's on-the-books eviction policies (which mandate 60 days' notice for nonrenewal of lease and 180 days' notice for a change of land use) go unenforced, and on the ground landlords evict residents with only 30 days' notice, as all except one of Alvin landlords did. In the event of a park closure, Texas residents are required to move their homes at their own expense or be fined. Under this laissez-faire iteration of neoliberalism, park closures were unregulated and evicted residents were left to seek help within a private market of relocation providers. Residents of Twin Oaks and Trail's End scrambled to locate these providers and drained all available resources as they self-financed and self-managed their moves.

In Florida, on the other hand, the state has explicitly intervened in an effort to assist mobile home residents during park closures. Florida laws require a minimum six-month eviction notice period, a stipulation that land use changes on park properties be approved by the local city council, and a state trust that provides relocation assistance in the event of a park closure. In Florida, a state that has been called "a national leader in the pursuit of neoliberal and paternalist reforms" (Soss, Fording, and Schram 2011: 10), relocation aid is administered through a neoliberal model of market-oriented, public-private partnerships that provide relocation services for displaced citizens. The protections enacted by Florida paradoxically produced a more devastating relocation process for evicted residents. Under this system, residents in Silver Sands and Sawgrass Estates became increasingly bewildered by the eviction process as they found themselves at the mercy of multiple private actors who each had a stake in a state-funded, voucherized marketplace of relocation services. Within the public-private partnerships formed by Florida to relocate mobile homes from closing parks, residents experienced a prolonged and disorienting dislocation even once they returned to their homes, a condition—as I have called elsewhere—of being *displaced in place* (Sullivan 2017a). This condition would become a principal characteristic of Florida's management of its citizens' housing needs and a primary way those residents encountered state power.

MANAGING MASS EVICTION

Back in Silver Sands next to Kathleen's fiberglass steps, Tabitha and Betty continued to discuss the unknown delivery date for the eviction notice and the waiting that made their upcoming eviction both emotionally and practically disruptive. As Kathleen reminded her neighbors, all of them were told that in the event of eviction they would be entitled to state funds to help them relocate their homes. But Kathleen also noted that she had called the state agency administering the funds; they told her residents would receive those funds, "but *not until* we get the papers *in our hand* . . . because legally this place has not sold yet." The eviction notice was the legal artifact that set the gears of aid in motion. Indeed, the state mandates that a homeowner must submit a copy of the eviction notice at the time that he or she applies for relocation compensation from the state (Florida Statute 723.0612). Betty sighed and lamented, "We can't *plan* anything. We can't *plan anything at all* not knowing when we're going to get the papers, when it's going to say we can move." From inside the mobile home Kathleen's husband Chip shouted out to us, joining the conversation as if continuing one he had been going over in his head: "When we get the six-month thing [the eviction notice], *then* we can start working. *Then* we can get in touch with the other trailer park—because I know we can't put the [wheelchair] ramp up until the trailer is in. But I want to start getting the lumber up there so that once they put the ramp up they can inspect it. I don't want to wait until the last minute and then she can't get into the trailer!"

While the eviction process seemed stalled to residents, Flagler Inc. (the development company purchasing the park) was hard at work. In their effort to convince the city council to approve the zoning change that would evict 130 elderly residents from Silver Sands, the developer worked to demonstrate that they met the requirements of the Florida Statutes. There are two crucial requirements of the Florida Statutes. The first is that the purchaser of the park inform residents that Florida provides relocation funds in the amount of $3,000 for a singlewide and $6,000 for a doublewide (or a $1,500 abandonment fee if the home cannot be moved). The funds are administered by the Florida Mobile Home Relocation Corporation, which controls a trust fund paid into yearly by a small fee charged to every mobile home park resident in the state and distributes relocation funds from that trust in the event of a park closure. The second requirement is that the purchaser provide residents with six months to move after they receive notice. Flagler convinced the city that they met and exceeded these state requirements by not only informing residents of the state laws, but also by organizing a system to deliver the Florida relocation funds to residents once the eviction process began. Florida provides these relocation funds in the form of a voucher that must be redeemed by a licensed mobile home mover. In city council meetings, Flagler representatives explained that their company would facilitate the distribution of these vouchers and assist residents in redeeming them through a "relocation package" they had put together by partnering with two other privately owned companies: a mobile home mover, "Max Movers," that almost exclusively moves mobile homes out of closing parks and into parks owned by the second company, Lakeshore Communities, which is the largest owner of mobile home parks in Florida.

While Silver Sands residents continued to wonder how the eviction would take place, Flagler Inc. presented a clear plan and streamlined process to city council members who remarked that the company had gone "above and beyond" in considering the relocation of park residents. In the final city council hearing the mayor declared—just before the city council voted unanimously in favor of the zoning change—that she was "glad to see the buyer has been trying to come up with a plan to provide additional facilities . . . So I think that it's going to be quite good!"

While the city seemed impressed with Flagler's system of distributing the state relocation funds and facilitating residents' moves (and while this provided them sufficient justification for evicting 130 of their city's residents), the relocation arrangement presented by Flagler was hardly a novel one. In fact, Flagler was entering into a partnership with Florida companies whose business model was centered on various development companies' efforts to empty closing mobile home parks. Many of the mobile home movers operating in closing Florida parks never hauled new homes from the factory and installed them on site. Instead, movers like Max of Max Movers explained that the displaced homes of residents in closing mobile home parks were their company's bread and butter. Max made a living hauling the homes of evicted mobile home residents. Sitting in the cab of his semi-truck, as we hauled yet another home out of a nearby closing park,

Max laid out clearly how he had made a business out of partnering with companies like Flagler Inc. within a marketplace organized around state mobile home relocation funds:

> Max: "The builders figured out that they can buy these parks and get rid of the people cheaper than they can actually go and buy the land and pull buildings down and stuff. So I got in with the builders, so I've actually been closing these parks for almost 25 years. I didn't even mess with the personal [moves]. I've never competed with any competition. The builder knew the job, I knew what I was going to do . . . They call me and they say, 'Listen, we are going to go close this park,' two or three months before anybody would know. And I would go skate into these parks and I would just ride around quietly and I would check everything out and see what was going on and I would give them an idea of what it was going to cost. And then we'd set up a deal. The state's got a fund which pays money and the park has to pay a little bit to the state, so that they were making money on the deal."
>
> Esther: "Who was?"
>
> Max: "Everybody was! I would go to other park owners [like Lakeshore Communities]—like we are doing for you people now [at Silver Sands]—I would go to the park owners and say, 'Listen, these people are moving.' . . . So say you [at Lakeshore] have 50 empty lots, for every lot that you could fill, your property just gained real value . . . You have a tenant that is paying money on it. So the new park owner would pay the $10,000, plus the state money which turned it into $16,000 [for a doublewide]. I moved the house, everybody's a winner . . . I have the contract. The builder is getting the thing emptied. Everybody is happy!"

In Max's assessment, everybody was happy because these partnerships (a) allowed development companies to efficiently empty parks in preparation for redevelopment and (b) produced profits for both moving companies and receiving parks, a process paid for in part by state funds. However, according to the more benevolent narrative Flagler presented in city council meetings, the development company's alliance with Max Movers and Lakeshore Communities was formed primarily to assist residents in accessing state aid. This benevolent narrative also structured an April 2012 meeting that Flagler held in the Silver Sands rec room to inform residents of the status of the company's purchase of the park. Dan Bloomsten, the primary Flagler representative whom residents referred to simply as "Blooms," outlined Flagler's potential purchase of the property and the state laws that would regulate residents' relocation if the sale were finalized.

The basic structure of these state laws is essential to understanding how the eviction unfolded in Silver Sands. Blooms explained that the state of

Florida provides compensation from its relocation trust fund, which is paid into by all mobile home residents in the state when they register their homes each year, plus a fee paid per lot by a park owner if he or she closes a park. The Florida funds provided $3,000 for a single-section mobile home, $6,000 for a double-section home, or a $1,500 abandonment fee for a mobile home that could not be moved, but Blooms also told residents that the compensation from the state was significantly less than the actual cost of relocating a mobile home. When he gave the estimate of $10,000 as the true cost of relocating a mobile home, residents gasped and whispered nervously to their neighbors nearby. But Blooms assured residents that Flagler Inc. would be able to offer an expanded compensation package because of their partnership with Max Movers and Lakeshore Communities. Together they would cover up to $10,000 in relocation costs. This figure included the $3,000 voucher from the state, which would be recouped by the mover. All other costs would be paid out by Lakeshore; the corporate park company covered relocation costs to get homes into their parks to fill out vacant lots. To Lakeshore, relocated homes were worth this expense because homeowners would be unlikely to ever be able to move their homes again, thus guaranteeing lot rents in perpetuity. Residents would not actually see any of this money and would not receive any direct financial compensation. The $10,000 figure Blooms cited was the cost traded between the various companies working to relocate them. These were the same exact figures that Max cited to me in the cab of his truck. Residents at the meeting were then given a glossy pamphlet of Lakeshore parks within a 50-mile radius (there were no Lakeshore parks within the city). Blooms assured them that not only would they have the entire cost of their relocation covered but that the companies with which Flagler partnered were experts on relocating homes from closing parks: "They've done this before, they understand what needs to be done, and they are able to offer the expertise needed."[1]

DIVERGENT PATHS TO NEW PARKS

In Texas no such system exists. Instead, park closures are governed by a more conventional laissez-faire approach. Without any state system of oversight to enforce its meager on-the-books laws, residents in Texas parks were evicted with only 30 days' notice and were not entitled to any compensation. Texas residents are expected to contract their own relocation services on the private market, where they pay $1,500–$3,000 for private moving companies to move and install their homes. Only one state agency, the Manufactured Housing Division of the Texas Department of Housing and

Community Affairs, regulates manufactured housing, but its role is merely to track the production, licensing, and installation of homes. In an interview with the agency's executive director he lamented that Texas has no system for identifying park closures, no state agency that regulates them, and no public or nonprofit program that provides financial assistance for relocation.

In Florida parks, the indefinite waiting that began even *before* residents received their notice would come to characterize the entire eviction process. Meanwhile in Texas, residents were evicted with little time and little help. Predictably, the lack of relocation aid created a serious financial burden for residents, who drained savings, borrowed from family, and frequently used up sacred stockpiled funds from their Earned Income Tax Credit. Yet, paradoxically, the shortened time frame in Texas seemed to alleviate, rather than aggravate, residents' emotional anxiety during the eviction. From the beginning, residents expressed a desire to "get over with" the move. Using their own resources and self-managing the relocation, they did just that. In Twin Oaks, all residents relocated within three weeks after receiving the eviction letter, in several cases a week before they were required to vacate. In Trail's End, the one Alvin park where residents were given a lengthier four-month notice period by their landlord, five residents relocated their homes in the two months after she gave notice and all remaining homes were gone well before the final date of tenancy. Repeatedly, residents described the palliating effect of beginning the relocation process, which they conducted, as much as possible, according to their own terms and timing, as noted in the following field note:

> It has only been about a week since the Castillo family received their eviction notice. So Rachel surprises me when she says, "Right now we're looking, we are less stressed right now."
> Both she and her father look much less stressed than I've seen them in the days after they received their notice.
> Rachel: "We are just looking at it in a positive way and trying to make it better . . . Like right now we are already packing and stuff."
> The family does not yet know where they will move but they are already preparing to move. The living room is lined with partially packed boxes.
> Rachel: "I mean, the first day was bad for everyone. Second day was just, wow. You know? But then, like now, it's just like—we're trying to see it in a positive way . . . We're not as stressed anymore. We are still a little stressed but we're like: we can do this, we can go. My sister is pitching in for money and my mom is pitching in for money and my dad is trying to get a job and I am trying to get a job too . . . We're already packing."

Back in Florida, residents were not afforded the opportunity to focus their energies on getting prepared for the move. While the developer navigated the approval of the rezoning with the city council, residents were simply left to wait, not knowing when or whether they would receive eviction notices. On October 24, 2012, seven months after Flagler's initial meeting in the Silver Sands rec room and the day after the zoning change was approved, residents finally received this notice. After months of waiting, worrying, and wondering, I found mine unceremoniously tucked in the screen door of my porch.

Residents in Florida's Silver Sands were not surprised by the receipt of the notice like the Texas households were; however, they were bewildered at the ensuing speed with which the eviction then began to unfold. Even though Silver Sands residents had not yet been able to form concrete plans, their general plans hinged on the six-month state-mandated notice period they knew would begin on the date they received the notice. With the exception of two or three households that wished to relocate right away, most planned to live out the full six-month eviction period—that is, to stay until May 1, 2013. They wanted to remain in the park that Walter affectionately called "Paradise" and to take advantage of the cheaper rent at Silver Sands, which was almost half what it would be in the Lakeshore parks. Kathleen summarized the perspectives of her neighbors in these first days after the notice when she told me there was no reason for her not to remain in her home until May: "They can't *force* people to leave when they want them to leave . . . They can't *tell* you when you're going to move."

However, after months of waiting to be evicted, residents were shocked to begin immediately receiving phone calls from the companies involved in the relocation package pressuring them to schedule their moves in the upcoming weeks. Kathleen had not even received all of her copies of the eviction notice when Lakeshore Communities called her to inform her of the date they had schedule her to move—January 11, 2013.[2] She was devastated to know she would have to move over the Christmas holiday, her favorite time of year. But the representative from Lakeshore explained that Max Movers had another big job moving seven hundred homes from another local closing park, Sawgrass Estates, and they needed to get her scheduled. They informed her that some of those homes might be coming to Lakeshore Communities so they could not assure her that her lot would be reserved in the park where she planned to relocate. The same rationale was repeated to all relocating Silver Sands residents. In fact, the representatives from Flagler and Lakeshore officially stated they were not scheduling any homes to be moved after January 2013—months before the end of residents' tenancy.

After Mr. Silver agreed to sell my rental home to me for $1,500 I met with a Lakeshore representative to ask if there was any chance of having the home moved in April 2013. The company representative insisted that they simply could not justify scheduling a single home move in April if households wanted to stay until the final date of our legally mandated tenancy, May 1. He justified this stance by insisting that it would not be safe for me to stay in Silver Sands until May when the majority of the homes had been moved. My November 13 field notes record this visit with the Lakeshore representative:

> The representative explains that some people have said they want to wait until the very end and he simply cannot do this. He insists these households do not want to wait until the end anyway. He says, "Towards the end you're going to start having certain homes left, only a number of them, and people start to come into parks like that and start to do things at night and it's not safe for you to be here and it's not safe for them to be here. When it's a half-empty park and it looks like it's closing and being abandoned, people start coming in and doing bad things." He goes on to say that there are a couple different reasons why he can't schedule the homes to move at the end. He says that first everyone would want to wait until the end because the lot rent is cheaper here. However, he points out, if you wait until the end then there are going to be problems not only with moving but also with vandalism and personal safety. He reiterates that really it is a "safety issue" and he says that most residents do not know what it's like to be in a park with only 20 residents left but he knows what it's like to be in these parks because he has seen it. He says, "I've done this before so I know what happens, is not good to be the last homes in the park. I've seen all types of bad stuff happen."

Within one month after receiving the eviction notice, every resident of Silver Sands was scheduled to move before the end of January, many during the holidays when family members were less able to house them and nearby motels were even further out of their financial reach. Kathleen said, "I cried when I heard it was going to be Christmas," a time when she decorated her mobile home and baked dozens of cookies for her neighbors on the cul-de-sac at the back of Silver Sands. Dejected she shrugged, "That's the way it is. [Max Movers] has a big moving job . . . that's their excuse. The bottom line is . . . get us out of here, get this job done. Over and done."

Residents scrambled and struggled to prepare their homes before their fast-approaching moving dates. But then, because of issues coordinating

FIGURE 10.   A resident works on the exterior of his doublewide in preparation for relocation. Photo by Edna Ledesma, 2013.

permits between Lakeshore, Max Movers, and the counties where the Lakeshore parks were located, these hastily scheduled moving dates were postponed for weeks and then months as residents waited, yet again, in their boxed-up homes to be told when they could be rescheduled. Throughout those winter months, on weekday afternoons, residents would gather outside the former Silver Sands rec room, which had been turned into the Lakeshore "relocation office." A banner affixed to the outside of the relocation office cheerfully read: "Lakeshore Communities—We're Here, For You!" Oftentimes, though, the office sat empty and frustrated residents would leave with unanswered questions.

This experience was not unique to Silver Sands. I witnessed the same prolonged waiting, growing confusion, and crippling anxiety in another Florida park, Sawgrass Estates, where I interviewed and spent time alongside evicted residents. In Sawgrass Estates several different moving companies were receiving the Florida voucher and transporting homes to a completely different set of parks (most not owned by Lakeshore). Despite differences in the particular private actors managing the move, the experiences of Silver Sands and Sawgrass residents were remarkably similar under the same state system of voucherized relocation aid. Reflecting back over the last six months from inside her dismantled Sawgrass home, Luanne described a persistent sense of bewilderment as she waited for the companies managing the move to tell her when she could be relocated. She said that six months prior she felt "horrible, just like I feel today. Because right now, I'm *still waiting* for the company to come and take it apart." The

FIGURE 11. A doublewide is split apart and propped on its axles awaiting relocation. Photo by Edna Ledesma, 2013.

experience of Martin and Mariela is illustrative. In front of their Sawgrass Estates home, which sat for weeks completely stripped, propped on its axles, and readied for transport, I asked the couple when the home would be moved. Demonstrating the unclear and conflicting information each had received, Martin responded assuredly, "Esta semana [this week]" at the same time that Mariela answered, "Este mes [this month]."

While waiting for their homes to be relocated by the network of private actors managing the move, residents were also bewildered by the administration of the aid they were set to receive. They experienced the structure of relocation assistance established by Flagler as yet another constraining factor that limited their options and curtailed their rights:

In the couple's living room, Kathleen and Chip go over what they've been told about the relocation aid.

Chip: "This is the thing. They say it's $10,000 to move the trailer. So if you don't go where they want you to go, if you want to go to another park, then you are going to have to pay the $10,000 and all you're going to get at the most is $3,000 from the state."

Kathleen asks me if I had driven up to Sunshine Estates in Stuart, the Lakeshore Park where they will be relocating. She asks if I've seen the large sign hanging out in front of the park, which advertises: "Lakeshore Communities—We will move your home for FREE." She took a picture of the sign and shows it to me. Kathleen points out that since the state provides $3,000 for evicted mobile homeowners to move, really, as she sees it, the move is *costing* us $3,000 because "that $3,000 should come to us."

Esther: "So is that your understanding? That if it didn't go to Max Movers, you could get it?"

Kathleen: "And we could give it to whoever we wanted to."

Kathleen explains that if everything wasn't already set up for the residents then we would receive a check directly from the state for $3,000 and we would not be obligated to give it to whatever moving company the developer chose. She knows that residents wouldn't be able to keep it and spend it on whatever they wanted but she says, "At least we would see the damn thing. It wouldn't be invisible."

Esther: "So why can't you do that?"

Chip: "Because you don't know much it costs to move it."

Kathleen: "Because it's a package deal . . . we would just have to turn it over to them [Max Movers, Flagler, and Lakeshore] anyway."

Esther: "So do you think you are getting a better deal with them making this deal for you, or do you think you're getting a worse deal?"

Kathleen: "Oh I think we're getting a worse deal."

Chip: "We don't know!"

Kathleen: "We don't know. I think it could be moved cheaper. My problem is that I thought I lived in America. I didn't think I could be dictated to as to who has to move your trailer."

Chip: "And nobody is working on how much a guy would move you for to begin with. It might not even be $3,000 to move you. The other thing is, they say it costs $10,000: $3,000 plus Flagler or Lakeshore is going to put in $7,000—now I've been up there and I've seen the sign that says 'We will move your trailer for FREE.' They would move me in there for free, but now I live in this trailer park and it's going to cost $10,000? Does that sound right to you? It doesn't to me. I don't care. I don't really care about the $3,000. I just don't like somebody telling me that the government is going to give you $3,000, but it costs $10,000 to move the trailer, but we're going to put in $7,000, but you ain't going to see that $7,000, you ain't even going to see that $3,000. So you don't know if it only costs them $1,000 to move you! See what I mean?"

This discrepancy became a fixation for Kathleen and many of her neighbors who constantly wondered over these figures, knowing they would receive no cash compensation. Even the local newspaper used the same figures, which in Kathleen's estimation only further absolved the local community of their responsibility to the evicted residents in the park. Kathleen clipped and saved a *Jupiter Courier* article covering the final city council meeting where the rezoning of Silver Sands was approved. She lent me the clipping, and when I returned it to her she asked me to comment about the statement in the article that evicted residents would be receiving $13,000 in relocation aid. She pointed out that this was completely inaccurate. She became frustrated, arguing that people seemed to think residents would "be handed $13,000." This was not the case: "All that money will be used for moving expenses and to pay the moving companies. The amount of money that we will actually get in hand is *zero.*"

Kathleen remained baffled over these discrepancies:

Today Kathleen asks me if I saw the man yesterday who was in the park handing out flyers for another mobile home park in Okeechobee. She shows me the flyer. It shows a park with ample green space. It has wide lawns and many trees and a central pond. The flyer states that the rent is $275 a month. As a moving bonus, for the first six months residents only pay half-rent and after that they receive a 10% discount. She points out that this would mean a lot rent of $135 (compared to the $600 she will pay in the Lakeshore park). She says the man was a really nice guy and he told her that there are a lot of activities in the park for residents, which she likes.

Max Movers will not move her home to this park since it's not a Lakeshore Community. Her neighbor Hanna has been told that Max Movers would not be able to move her home to a cooperative park where residents own their lots. This park is not one of the Lakeshore Communities. [In the end, Hanna moved her home to this park at her own expense.] Kathleen is frustrated, saying it's ridiculous that residents cannot have their homes moved to communities that are not owned by Lakeshore. She says, "They're dictating to us!"

Kathleen: "I'm sorry but this whole deal is so freaking crooked. I guess the contract is: Max moves the trailers and we get no choice but four Lakeshore Communities . . . Their so-called 'contract.' They're dictating to us. They're telling us where we can go. Isn't that communistic or dictating?"

Like other residents of Silver Sands, Kathleen and Chip debated and debated these phantom moving costs and lack of choices right up to the day they signed over their $3,000 Florida voucher to Flagler and Max Movers moved their home to the Lakeshore park where the sign out front read, "We will move your home for FREE."

When I returned to my own mobile home that evening I called the number listed on the flyer Kathleen had saved:

Later I call the park in Okeechobee from the flyer Kathleen showed me. The man was here yesterday handing out flyers. The number listed is for Mike. I leave a message and he immediately calls back.

I ask if his park is willing to put any money toward the move of the home. He explains that the company who is purchasing the park where I live should pay for the trailer to be moved.

When I ask if his park is a Lakeshore Community, he answers no, but he tells me that the park is located on water, a lake.

It's a privately owned "mom and pop" park. The owner was actually the one who came by Silver Sands yesterday to pass out flyers. Mike is the manager, but still he tells me he doesn't know anything about moving the home, who can move it, who pays, or anything like that. All that would need to be done on my end.

The system set in place in the Florida parks made options like this seem untenable. The number of private actors involved in managing residents' moves conveyed an image of mobile home relocation as a complex and technical process. Few imagined they could complete this process on their own, as the Texas residents quickly learned they could. Plus, the phantom price tag of $13,000 convinced residents they could not afford to move without the help of Flagler, Lakeshore, and Max Movers, who continued, in Kathleen's words, to "dictate" the relocation process.

RETURNING HOME

In both Texas and Florida, residents stressed that the most disruptive part of the move was not this initial notice period, but rather the period in which they were forced to be out of their home while they waited for it to be reinstalled in a new park. In both states, residents emphasized their desire for a timely reinstallation so that they could return home. In Texas, this disruptive period was temporally delimited. Texas residents contracted with local movers whom they located using networks within their parks and workplaces (which often included acquaintances who had previously been evicted from closing parks). Some residents used the same mover, although those who did not communicated with neighbors about relocation costs ($1,500–$3,000) and thus secured competitive rates. As the sole financiers of the transport of their homes, Texas residents had significant leverage in dictating the terms of the move and they benefited from a degree of clarity about what to expect. The private Texas movers moved and installed one or two homes at a time and residents were allowed to enter the same day. The lack of regulation and oversight in Texas meant that some homes were damaged during transport or installed incorrectly in the new parks (creating future consequences and costs). However, during the eviction period, the shortened relocation period drastically reduced the residents' immediate stress, as residents told me the period of waiting to get back into the home was the most traumatic part of the move.

Rachel Castillo surprised me again when she was back in her home just a week after the move from Twin Oaks and said her family was already feeling "more relaxed" or "settling in" in their new park. The experience of the

Castillo family was not unique. Across town Julia, who relocated one month after receiving her eviction notice from Trail's End, explained: "There was stress the first couple of days. Just the first three days, not knowing if the trailer would make it safely . . . But it came out okay." Julia told me that her stress dissipated once the home was moved and she saw that it was safely installed. Likewise, when I saw the Castillos' neighbor Señora Reyes for the first time in her new park, she greeted me with a wide smile and invited me into her living room. I mentally noted damage to her home caused by the relocation (the cracked roof and windows), but Señora Reyes expressed her deep sense of relief at returning home: "It was *great* to get back into my house, because it is *my house*. I wanted to be home already." On the couch next to us her daughter laughed and nodded in agreement: "She told me every day: Take me back, take me back!"

Like other evicted mobile home residents, Señora Reyes's wish to return home was in part based on a desire for independence and a general discomfort with relying on friends or family members (no Texas residents could afford to stay in a motel). However, Señora Reyes's wish to return home was also based on a desire to begin the household work that, for residents in both states, provided an essential means of reestablishing themselves in the home. Although (or perhaps *because*) mobile homes are prefabricated according to a finite set of designs, residents in the communities where I lived and worked took pride in altering or enhancing their homes. Because interstate highway laws limit the width of vehicles and their hauls, only the body of the mobile home is moved during relocation. This meant that residents in both states lost substantial portions of their homes. Rebuilding what they had lost was a main priority for many residents, who would discuss at length their rebuilding plans. Even in cases where large-scale improvements were impossible because of residents' skill sets or disabilities, smaller tasks like cleaning, decorating, or planting were seen as vital to reestablishing themselves in the home. When I asked Señora Reyes why she had been begging her daughter "take me back, take me back," she answered without pause: "So I could start cleaning!"

In Florida, residents' inability to reenter their homes prevented them from beginning such improvements and kept them in a state of perpetual limbo, of being displaced in place. Unlike the Texas movers that transported and installed only one or two homes at a time, the Florida moving companies profited off contracts to move as many as a hundred homes at once. Transporting each home only took about half a day. However, prior to redeeming the Florida relocation voucher the companies needed to organize inspections to get Certificates of Occupancy. These companies bundled inspections for dozens of homes at once because it was more efficient and economical to get several homes road-ready at a time; move several in a day; level, install electric, and lay foundations for several at once; and then contact city inspectors to visit and write Certificates of Occupancy for several at a time. But this practice forced residents out of their homes for long periods while they waited for the Certificate of Occupancy that would allow them to return. Until then, residents were strictly told they could not enter their homes, even to get personal items, because it was a liability for the parks and the moving companies. When I asked residents about the progress of their move, they often answered "permits" as a one-word rejoinder meant to encapsulate the entire stalled process.

For Floridians in both Silver Sands and Sawgrass Estates the most frustrating and confounding aspect of the relocation was the time it took to return home after their mobile homes were transported. As Luanne, a resident of Sawgrass, pointed out: "They tell you four to six weeks but a friend of mine went before me and he's already on the eighth week . . . I just want it *over.* I want to *go home.* I want my own things. I want to get up and do what I want *in my own house.*" In Silver Sands, after waiting to be evicted and then rushed into relocation, all residents were forced to wait a minimum of 45 days— many longer—before returning to their homes. It was during this period of interstitial waiting that the eviction had its most devastating effects.

One of these effects was the breakdown in ties between neighbors, which had been a primary source of support before the relocation began. Strong community ties in Silver Sands led some residents to describe others as "like family." In my initial months in Silver Sands I spent time every day in neighborly conversations such as the one with Betty and Tabitha in front of Kathleen's front porch. Yet during the eviction period neighbors became increasingly insular and preoccupied with their own bewildering concerns about the move. The close friendships that were a hallmark of life in Silver Sands became increasingly strained.

In fact, the very administration of the relocation aid pitted Florida residents against each other. They became rivals in a relocation marketplace, competing for preferred moving days and available spaces in Lakeshore parks. The same residents who had frequently met, talked, and shared information before the eviction notice grew increasingly distanced from each other and would grill me on my visits for any information I had about neighbors' moving days or lot reservations. They frequently worried that their reserved lots in the new parks might be given to someone else from Silver Sands, a fear reinforced by Lakeshore representatives who originally pressured them to move before lots filled up.

FIGURE 12.   Steps to a mobile home that has been removed.
Photo by Edna Ledesma, 2013.

This constant worry led, in residents' own estimations, to the range of health problems that plagued them during this time. The previous chapter described how Sawgrass resident Luanne began taking the anxiety drug Lorazepam in the first months of the eviction process ("I went to the doctor, I had such bad anxiety from it. I couldn't face the day.") and found herself increasingly addicted to the drug. When I visited Luanne one month later, I found her still waiting, increasingly anxious, in her boxed-up home. The park around her had become alien and hostile, contributing to the anxiety she attempted to manage with the drug. She described the trauma of "going from where the streets were lively, even at midnight you'd have someone walking the dog, driving their golf carts around. Now when you open the door there are no lights really except the streetlights. It's eerie . . . it's not

FIGURE 13. Debris from abandoned and relocated homes litter the streets inside Sawgrass Estates, Florida. Photo by Edna Ledesma, 2013.

comfortable at night. And during the day I kind of feel like I'm in a war zone. You look around and it looks like it's been bombed."

In Silver Sands, Kathleen was forced to call an ambulance twice during this period. She told me, "I was addicted to my blood pressure medication. I would wake up in the morning after sleeping . . . My blood pressure was low and my heart rate was high." The second time she called the ambulance her resting heart rate as she sat in her wheelchair was 140 bpm, a rate one might expect on a strenuous run. An ambulance was not an uncommon sight in Silver Sands during these months. I checked on Frank after I saw an ambulance outside his mobile home. Frank was taken to the hospital by the ambulance after briefly losing consciousness in the bathroom. His wife, Betty, had found him and said: "I hate this. They really upset us because we know we've got to move and now they won't hurry up and move us like they're supposed to. No wonder he had problems. It's very stressful. It's very—because you *don't know* what's going on and *they won't tell you anything*. They don't back up what they say. I don't think any of them know what the heck is going on . . . That's why my husband went to the hospital. Stress!"

FIGURE 14.   Mobile homes wait to be relocated and reinstalled. Photo by Esther Sullivan, 2013.

While waiting to move back into their homes, many residents, like Betty and Frank, were forced to stay in the vacated homes of other Silver Sands residents who had taken the $1,500 abandonment fee rather than the relocation funds. Most of these homes were in poor condition, the oldest homes in the park, abandoned because they were deemed "structurally unsound" by the movers and a liability for their company. Since Flagler Inc. chose to provide the abandonment fee from their own funds, the abandoned homes became the property of the developer. Flagler eventually sold every one of these homes to outside buyers, many to Florida's large citrus farms where they were used to house migrant workers. In the interim the abandoned homes had yet another profitable use; the developer rented them out to displaced residents for $15 a day. At $450 a month, the dilapidated rentals cost residents $200 more than most had paid to rent the lots under their own homes at Silver Sands.

Florida residents lived in these abandoned rental mobile homes for months as the companies coordinated the installation of their homes in several different receiving parks scattered throughout neighboring counties. From his abandoned rental mobile home two streets away in Silver Sands, my former neighbor Walter returned daily to visit his old garden despite the jarring sight of the adjacent bare concrete slab where the home he owned with his wife, Mattie, had rested for 20 years. Walter no longer spent as much time out in the garden. He worried too much about being away from Mattie, who found it difficult to navigate the abandoned rental mobile home with her walker and who had been in poor health since they moved over there. Instead, Walter spent much of his day in a single plastic chair that furnished the screened-in porch of the abandoned rental they now occupied. Like other residents Walter described his frequent trips down to the new park to check the progress of the installation of their home. Unfortunately, he told me, there was not much progress: "It just sits there." Mattie lamented that their home was moved over a month ago and Walter continued to check on it every few days.

After returning from a similar visit to check on his and his mother's home, Joseph was also frustrated. He recounted the specific dates that specific contractors were scheduled to be out, but no progress had been made on the installation of the home. He called the office at the new park several times. No one in the office answered. Joseph paced back and forth in the living room of the abandoned "dump" home he rented in Silver Sands, shouting:

> They don't care! They take their time! That how it is . . . I keep calling. They ain't doing nothing! They take their time. What's the sense of me keep calling? Nothing's happening. They ain't telling me nothing. So what's the sense of me calling? They ain't telling me nothing anyways. I ain't heard nothing from nobody. I don't know when we're getting out of here! I do know that the stairs aren't in. I had to get a ladder. I had to get in there with a ladder . . . and it's been like a month today since they moved it!

Like others, part of Joseph's frustration was his inability to get into his home to make some planned improvements, the kind of improvements the Texas residents busied themselves with in the weeks after relocating.

These repairs were seen as essential to the process of resettling in the home. Tabitha badly reinjured a shoulder, on which she had surgery before the eviction, trying to make such repairs. When I visited her after her home was relocated to a new park she showed me where the pins from the surgery were beginning to protrude through her skin. This caused her great pain, but she was more concerned that it kept her from doing things that were left undone in the home. She asked, "How am I supposed to do stuff? I *have* to do stuff." She admitted that she has always been "anal" about her home, but emphasized that it was more a matter of wanting to finally get things finished: "I want it done. I don't want to be *still waiting.*"

Similarly, from his lone plastic chair in their rented temporary home, Walter would list off the improvements he was planning in order to rebuild their home's screened-in porch once he and Mattie were finally able to return. For them the relocation was not the difficult part; after a lifetime career in the U.S. Army and then 19 years living out of the Volkswagen bus, Walter estimated, "we probably moved 100 times in 30 years." Rather, it was the wait to return. Mattie listened from inside, sighing, "It will be a year before we are resettled." Tellingly, Mattie included in this estimate the eviction period, the stalled installation process, *and* the time it would take Walter to rebuild their screened-in porch. She marked the end of their eviction as the anticipated date when they would finish the porch reconstruction. The rebuilding of the screened-in porch was both practical and symbolic. Walter had designed the steps on the front porch to accommodate Mattie's walker and thus it served as her main access to her home. The porch was also the primary place that Mattie could enjoy the outdoors. Walter sat out in "Paradise," his shady patio garden, and Mattie used the porch to practice her beloved hobby, orchid growing, since her disabilities kept her homebound. The porch was the place that several of us had gathered the previous fall to celebrate Walter and Mattie's 70th wedding anniversary, where Mattie reminisced about graduating high school with Walter from a one-room schoolhouse in Maine and Walter joked that in their class of 10, Mattie was valedictorian and he was ranked tenth.

For one month after their home was hauled to a new park in a neighboring county Walter continued to check on the naked home, stripped of its porch and all the minor additions he had made over the last 20 years. He frequently worried over the date he could begin to reconstruct Mattie's porch so that she could enter the home comfortably when they finally got their Certificate of Occupancy. However, during these weeks of waiting Mattie suffered a stroke inside the abandoned trailer the couple rented in Silver Sands. Mattie was taken to the ICU and then spent several more weeks in the hospital with Walter perpetually by her side. She maintained her dry wit in her hospital bed, insisting that no one worry about her and saying, "I'm not sick, I'm just falling apart." Even in the hospital when she and Walter spoke of their home they continued to discuss the progress on rebuilding their screened-in porch. But Walter's plans for the porch were delayed as the moving company took weeks and then months to provide a Certificate of Occupancy. In the end, Mattie would never see the finished work on her porch. She would never enter her mobile home again. Mattie died in the hospital two months after her home was moved. When I picked up Walter from the VA hospital, where he was admitted in the weeks following Mattie's death, we drove back to his own mobile home for the first time since the eviction. He finally entered it, alone.

DISPLACED IN PLACE

In Florida, residents were dislodged from the familiar fabric of their homes as they waited an indeterminate time for the homes to be reinstalled elsewhere. At the same time, they were torn from the social fabric of community bonds as neighbors became competitors in the relocation marketplace. These twin processes unfolded while many residents were forced to wait inside closing parks that had physically and socially transformed around them. Florida residents experienced these twin processes as a bewildering sense of being pushed *out of place* while simultaneously being *displaced in place.* In Texas, residents stressed the hardship imposed on them by the short 30 days' notice they received, but they described the challenges of the eviction primarily as practical and financial. With little time and little help, households drained their entire savings to pay for these moves just across town. The very real financial costs for individuals and families living well below the poverty line underscore the importance of not viewing the Texas residents' experience of relocation as a call for less state involvement, fewer regulations, or a more laissez-faire approach. These moves were deeply traumatic in both states, as the preceding chapters show. Indeed, while the comparative analysis of Florida and Texas demonstrates that Texas residents experienced a shortened, less disruptive relocation process, this is true only for the *immediate* relocation period and only in comparison to the deep dislocation felt by Florida residents. In both states, residents experienced the specter of dislocation (see chapter 3) and the sense of collective indignation (see chapter 4) that continued to haunt them even after their eviction. However, avoiding a dislocation extended over a year, as in Florida, was a significant component of Texas residents' more benign experience of the relocation process. The orbit of their upheaval contracted as Texas residents dictated the *terms* and *timing* of their moves. Many agreed with Julia that the relocation had been a disruptive "couple of days," one that they could put behind them as they began the work of resettling in their homes. They began to discuss the move as if it were an event in the past, even just weeks after they moved into their new communities.

Conversely, Florida residents spoke of the move as an ongoing event, even a full year after they had relocated. Months, even one year, after moving into their new parks, they complained of the time it took to reestablish themselves in their homes and the many structural issues they dealt with upon returning. Despite a more highly regulated relocation process in Florida, homes there were also seriously damaged in the moves. By fall 2013, more than a year had passed since that conversation with Betty, Tabitha, and Kathleen on her front porch when Chip had interjected, "When we get the six-month thing, *then* we can start working . . . I don't want to wait until last minute and then she can't get into the trailer!" But after waiting seven months for that notice and five more months before their home was relocated, Kathleen and Chip were not only out of their home for two months, but Kathleen spent the next three months getting into her house by shifting up the stairs on her backside with one leg while she tried to find a nonprofit to rebuild her wheelchair ramp (the developer had insisted as part of the relocation package that no additions to the homes—sheds, porches, extra rooms, etc.—would be moved and told Kathleen on multiple occasions that this included her wheelchair ramp). While she insisted toughly that she had gotten this system of entering and exiting her house down pat, she blinked back tears when she explained the hardest part was simply not knowing when they would be able to complete her ramp and finally feel resettled in the home.

The ability to exercise control over time is essential to power (Schwartz 1974), and in the case of Silver Sands residents, the inability to control the timing of eviction was linked to their sense of powerlessness. By comparison, Texas residents orchestrated many aspects of their moves. Although they had less control over *where* they moved, they at least determined *when*. Even in Texas where these choices were made within a severely limited time frame of a few weeks, residents expressed a desire to get the move over with, and they did.

Alongside the *unclear timing* of eviction, persistent confusion over *unclear aid* characterized the eviction process in Florida. During their extended relocation period, Silver Sands residents became increasingly confused about who could answer their questions and where they could seek help. The process made Frank "baffled and mad." Gloria pointed out, "It's confusing! Who do I really talk to? Do I talk to Lakeshore? Do I talk to Flagler? Do I talk to the landlord?" Florida residents also became increasingly paranoid about the inscrutable intentions of the various private actors who repeatedly claimed to work in their interest yet frequently ignored, dismissed, or opposed their requests. Gary insisted that the developer *purposefully* "wants everybody so confused and so scared."

Representatives from the private parties contracted to deliver Florida's relocation voucher contributed to this unclear timing and unclear aid as they coordinated primarily among themselves and worked according to timelines that worked for them. They did so while uniformly repeating the slogan that they were "here for" the residents, as the banner outside the empty relocation office announced: "Lakeshore Communities—We're Here, For You!" This process produced the kind of confusion and tension that expressed itself in the arguments that unfolded between residents like Matthew and Gale, husband and wife. One night at a cookout with a few other neighbors, things got heated between the couple when Matthew became frustrated as he recounted their experience: they had been told they could not switch to another Lakeshore park, even though the Lakeshore park they originally chose was experiencing months of permitting delays. Matthew was told they could not switch because Max Movers already filed for most of the moving permits in a bundle and the change would be costly.

> Matthew tells us this whole thing is "bullshit." He points out that he should just fill out the application for the permit online himself.
> Gale: "But I don't think it's just about the permit, I really don't . . . I think they're trying to encourage us . . . Lois [the Lakeshore manager] was very considerate on the phone and I think she wants to see us be able to go where we want to go. Because we chose a certain place to live and they want to do what they can to make sure we can live there."
> Matthew: "At our expense for how long? How long do I gotta wait!?"
> Gale: "But really when it comes right down to it they don't have to answer a damn question or a damned thing—"
> Matthew [sarcastically]: "Because they're giving us a place to live."
> Gale: "Because they are paying to move the trailers. It's not your money. It's not our money."

In their dealings with the network of private actors that profited off delivering the relocation aid, Gale and Matthew lost sight of the fundamental fact that *it was indeed their money*. The relocation voucher comes from the Florida fund that is paid into by all mobile home residents in the state when they register their homes each year, plus the park owner who pays a fee per lot when a park closes. Yet the public origin of this assistance was veiled, removed from residents' view.

The bewildering process through which residents lost sight of this crucial fact did not emerge organically out of the relocation process; it was institutionalized within the administration of the Florida relocation aid. The state trust administers the relocation funds but the state legislature has not increased the amount of the voucher since it instituted the state statutes in 2001. The result is a veritable cottage industry that has sprung up to fill in the gap between the actual cost of relocations and the money the state provides. Although the figure of $10,000 that Flagler representatives quoted to Silver Sands residents was inflated based on my discussions with other local movers, moves do cost more than what the $3,000 voucher covers. As one South Florida Legal Aid attorney put it (mimicking the state shortfall in assistance), "These moves cost a minimum of $5,000, maybe $7,000, upwards of $10,000. Here's your three grand, you figure it out." Because voucherized state funds are available, but are not enough to cover the entire cost of relocation, the Florida Statutes create an institutionalized space for private actors to gain entrée and make themselves indispensable to needy residents, while residents are forced to "figure it out." These public-private partnerships veiled the collective origin of the aid that Florida residents did receive. Many believed that the state funds were coming directly from the constellation of private actors that managed their relocation. Even those who understood that the funds came from the state of Florida never alluded to the actual collective origin of the funds. Because in the case of Silver Sands and Sawgrass Estates, as in many other closing Florida parks, private companies like Lakeshore Communities augmented the Florida funds through partnerships like those described by Max of Max Movers, these companies have an opportunity to take credit for covering the entire cost of residents' relocations while simultaneously profiting off of state aid meant to assist the evicted.

This process—the process by which state-mandated protections are pulled (or delivered) out of the hands of state agencies—has a life and momentum of its own. The state relies on private actors to deliver state aid and the state is pushed into the background as residents haggle with these actors. Yet, private interests also willingly co-opt state aid. They do not merely act as the delivery system for state-sponsored support. They act as though they are the fountain of this aid, its author. This was seen in the simple fact that residents of Silver Sands never called the $1,500 fee they received if they abandoned their home the "abandonment fee," as all my industry contacts did. Instead residents would say, as Ruth did, "The developer *bought my house off me* for $1,500." When Blooms gave 60-year-old Randall the $1,500 abandonment fee from the state of Florida, he told Randall not to "be shy" if he needed anything else and, as if he were giving a child an allowance, said: "If you need any more, just ask."

After Randall quickly spent a portion of the $1,500 acquiring and moving his things from his now-abandoned mobile home into a storage unit and spent the night sleeping in a nearby abandoned building, he returned to Silver Sands not knowing where else to go. He decided to follow up on Blooms's offer. Blooms could easily make back the $1,500 selling off Randall's well-kept but "structurally unsound" trailer, plus Blooms himself suggested that if Randall needed anything else he should "just ask." When Randall did ask, calling Blooms later that same day, Blooms said he had done all he could do. In a day, Randall moved from homeownership to homelessness. Meanwhile, the institutionalized positions of the private actors that filtered state aid to residents allowed them to construct a façade of benevolence, a façade that quickly crumbled after residents were removed from the park.

FIGURE 15.   An American flag hangs on the open door of an abandoned home inside Silver Sands. Photo by Esther Sullivan, 2013.

MARKET-DRIVEN GOVERNANCE AND
THE PRODUCTION OF CRISIS

Although the unclear timing and unclear aid that characterized the Florida eviction were bound up in the practices of the companies that managed the move, representatives from these companies did not have to answer to residents because these companies were not paid by residents, but by the Florida relocation voucher and the Lakeshore / Flagler supplemental funds. The interceding role of these public-private partnerships fundamentally shifted the relationship between citizens and the state. The sociology of disaster has demonstrated how an analogous shift to market-oriented emergency assistance requires that affected citizens become capable consumers of state aid (Adams 2012; Klinenberg 2002). But within Florida's relocation marketplace, residents were not merely demoted from citizens to consumers, as those following the administration of social services in the aftermath of natural disasters have described. Silver Sands residents lacked even the basic *clout* a consumer can mobilize to get things done. Instead they were met with what one resident called "everyone's famous refrain: 'I'll get back to you' " or they were outright ignored.

Sociological studies of natural disasters dating back to Kai Ericson (1976) demonstrate how moments of crisis are crucial for uncovering existing inequalities. Contemporary investigations following natural disasters show how they also reveal broader political economic shifts (Oliver-Smith 1990; Klinenberg 2002; Allen 2007; Brunsma, Overfelt, and Picou 2007; Fassin and Rechtman 2009; Flaherty 2010; Adams 2012). Like natural disasters, human-made crises such as mass evictions in mobile home parks can reveal the conditions and consequences of new approaches to governance that have radically overhauled the administration of aid to citizens in need.

A key characteristic of these contemporary approaches to governance is the preference for private over public control that has become the hallmark of neoliberalism (Centeno and Cohen 2012). Under neoliberal restructuring, the task of providing public sector services has continually devolved to states and states have taken a range of approaches to fulfilling this function. This uneven implementation of state-level governance creates *neoliberal adaptations* that vary greatly from place to place (Peck 2002; Greenhouse 2009; Harvey 2005). The differing state responses in Florida and Texas are a material expression of this changing, variegated landscape of neoliberal governance.

In Texas, evictions were (un)regulated with a conventional laissez-faire approach to neoliberal governance, an approach that produced moments of acute crisis. In Florida, the state-sponsored, privately enacted delivery system of relocation assistance took a form that Margaret Somers (2008) has called "market-oriented governance." Under a market-oriented adaptation of neoliberal governance, Florida relied heavily on private actors to convey state-mandated protections. As these private actors constructed new markets around dismantling communities, evicted residents found themselves at the mercy of multiple interested parties. Private actors that intervened in the distribution of relocation aid became the major players in a relocation marketplace. These actors contributed to the unclear timing of the eviction as they worked according to their own profit-driven timelines. They produced unclear aid as they acted as the authors, rather than the agents, of state-sponsored assistance.

The co-optation of state aid further confused Florida residents, who distrusted the actors involved in the relocation yet felt increasingly reliant on them. This limited their ability to make claims, because they viewed themselves as the beneficiaries rather than the originators of aid. Even though mobile home residents fought to get the Florida legislation passed in the first place and even though they pay into the Florida trust fund collectively each year, they repeatedly expressed anxiety over making too many calls or directing too many questions to the developer or the parks where they were being relocated. They worried that they might upset the representatives of Flagler, Lakeshore Communities, or Max Movers. They did not want to "rock the boat," constantly worrying that they might forfeit their relocation assistance.

The redefinition of state services in ways that commodify and privatize social services has blurred the lines between public, private, for-profit, and nonprofit actors (Katz [2001] 2008). It has created new techniques of managing those in need of social services and new vulnerabilities for citizens (Hays 2003; Wacquant 2009; Collins and Mayer 2010). This requires that individuals become savvy consumers of state services, acting as "smart shoppers" (Klinenberg 2002) and "social entrepreneurs" (Adams 2012), "measured by their capacity for 'self-care'" (Brown 2006: 694). Florida's relocation marketplace expands our understanding of these processes by showing how residents were not merely demoted from citizens to consumers, since within that state's system of reinvented public aid residents lacked the basic clout attributed to market actors. Unable to act as savvy consumers, their available choices and information narrowed as they were filtered through companies that organized their move and acted as custodians of their entitlements. Regulations that mandate and institutionalize this private-sector mediation create markets that rely on the housing insecurity of evicted residents, which further reduce residents from citizens, to consumers, *to forms of currency themselves*. Their homes, their move, their (manufactured) housing insecurity are traded by interested parties within a mobile home park marketplace. The dictates of the Florida marketplace shaped residents' relocations, paid for with voucherized funds generated from residents' own annual contributions. In this way, residents were dispossessed not only of their homes and communities, and demoted not only to consumers of state services: they were dispossessed even of their role as citizens, as the collective producers of the public services they were in a position to call upon.

Housing policies in both states contributed to the trauma of eviction, both under traditional laissez-faire neoliberalism in Texas and market-oriented state support in Florida. Yet, the public-private partnerships structured by Florida's neoliberal housing policies more actively disempowered Florida residents during the relocation process. And the residents' lingering sense of impotence created an indeterminate unsettling, extending the trauma of eviction. This happened as households and homes were reduced to a form of currency, bartered and traded between private actors in a publicly funded mobile home marketplace. Yet in a transforming U.S. economy, households and homes are not the only sites where profit is wrung out of precarity. Today, entire mobile home communities are increasingly a source of financialized capital for eager investors. The following chapter explores how mobile home park *communities* are *currency* by examining how the insecure land tenure in mobile home parks undergirds a multi-billion-dollar industry. As this final chapter shows, the interrelation between poverty and profit, which Desmond (2016) argues is central in structuring eviction at the neighborhood level, shapes mobile home park life not only during moments of mass eviction and not only inside closing parks. Indeed, an entire national industry has arisen to extract surplus value out of this otherwise devalued housing form.

6. Communities as Currency within the Mobile Home Empire

The Balboa Bay Resort sits on a coveted parcel of waterfront property in Newport Beach, California. The hotel's white and cream lobby is sprinkled with marine-colored accents that play off the view of the Pacific Ocean seen through floor to ceiling windows. One weekend in February 2017, the lobby bustled with eager entrepreneurs who drove in from various parts of Southern California or flew in from across the country to take a three-day immersion course on mobile home park investing called the Mobile Home Park Investors Boot Camp. Over the next three days we would study the basics of profiting off poverty housing.

At the resort reception desk, a friendly young woman sitting near a floral arrangement of three-dozen white orchids directed me down the hall to a large, well-appointed ballroom that served as the conference room for the weekend. A row of French doors opened onto the resort's pool area, ventilating the heat of many bodies crowded along tables oriented toward a podium and display screen at the front. I arrived a couple of minutes late and took one of only two unoccupied seats. Would-be mobile home park investors sat almost shoulder to shoulder, looking to learn the secrets of "mobile home park investment guru" Frank Rolfe's business model.

Frank Rolfe and his business partner Dave Reynolds have established a $500 million mobile home park portfolio that attracts outside investors with proven yields. The partners are reported to be the fifth-largest owners of mobile home parks in the United States. The boot camp is a side gig for gregarious Frank; managing the portfolio is his primary work. He told me he runs the boot camp because he enjoys teaching potential investors about the profit contained in an otherwise devalued form of housing. Many in the room that weekend were already in the business of real estate, but few knew anything about mobile home parks beyond the stigma.

Frank looked out at the room from the podium at the front. The attend-ees were about 70 percent male, largely white, although there were several Black, Latino/a, and Asian attendees. Many were from California where this particular boot camp was located (the course is offered several times a year across the United States). Others I spoke with hailed from Arizona, Colorado, Florida, Idaho, Louisiana, New York, Texas, and Washington. Many attendees appeared to be in their 50s and 60s, though about a quarter looked to be in their 30s and 40s. There were quite a few couples taking the course together. Frank asked for a show of hands from those who already owned a mobile home park. Out of about 120 attendees only eight people raised their hands. The rest were looking to break into the business; but this meant confronting the stigma of trailer life. Frank patiently explained, "You have to recalibrate your brain. When I started, I had to make a saying for myself: This is a trailer park, not Highland Park [a wealthy neighbor-hood in Dallas] . . . It's okay to be shitty."

Frank began the boot camp by going over the mobile home park inves-tor's mantra: "Affordable Housing is the hottest arena in commercial real estate right now. With over 20 percent of Americans trying to live on $20,000 per year or less, the demand for mobile homes has never been higher—and the big winners are the owners of the mobile home parks in which those customers reside."[1] In this world of winners and losers, the growing divide between two classes of people meant one thing: profit. The profitability of mobile home park investing rests on a simple axiom: demand is growing and supply is stagnant. The slides Frank projected on the big screen at the front of the ballroom contained facts that might be used in a university course on poverty. They read:

> Why Invest in Affordable Housing? 20% of all U.S. Households earn $19,178 or less. That's 60,000,000 Americans living on $10.00 per hour or less.

> Why Invest in Affordable Housing? Based on 28% to 33% of income towards housing [the HUD recommendations], American's earning $10.00 per hour can afford $485–$572 per month.

> Why Invest in Affordable Housing? The U.S. average for a 2-bedroom apartment in 2013 is $1,109.73.

The slides laid out a context of poverty wages and rising housing costs that could open a discussion on the affordable housing crisis in a college course. The similarity ended there, however. At the front of the ballroom, Frank proceeded to paint growing poverty as unequivocally good news for mobile home park investors, because poverty was increasingly affecting a larger and more diverse group of Americans than attendees might imagine and this meant stable returns for investors. Highlighting both the stigma of the mobile home park and the robustness of its target clientele—the growing class of American working poor—he explained: "You cannot build a business model around poor white trash. It won't work; you need poor but paying tenants."

Like the other people crowded into the conference room, I had paid $2,000 to take the mobile home park boot camp. For attendees, this was a small price to pay for the chance to capitalize on an untapped market. This chapter traces the broader contours of the mobile home park market to explore how the experiences of eviction outlined in the previous chapters are structured by market forces operating well beyond the confines of individual parks, cities, or states like Texas and Florida. Panning out from life inside closing parks, I explore the mobile home park marketplace at multiple scales: from the barter and trade in individual abandoned mobile homes; to local businesses profiting off relocating the homes of the evicted; to larger investment portfolios like the one run by Frank Rolfe; to, finally, the mobile home–backed mutual funds of billionaire real estate investors like Sam Zell and the "mobile home empire" of the nation's second-richest citizen, Warren Buffet (Wagner and Baker 2015a).

In his study of evicted Milwaukee renters, Desmond (2016: 306) followed urban landlords and desperate tenants to expose a gap in current poverty debates, which "have overlooked a fact that landlords never have: there is a lot of money to be made off the poor." As urban landlords in his study explain: "The 'hood *is* good" (ibid.). Yet, profits are wrung out of housing insecurity not only in the 'hood, by individual players, or at the local level. The extraction of surplus value from housing insecurity occurs at a national scale and supports entire industries. Only by zooming out from closing parks to capture a picture of the mobile home park empire can we fully understand the intersection of poverty and profit in the broader U.S. affordable housing market.

Over three days at the Balboa Bay Resort, boot camp attendees seeking to break into this industry were exposed to a world many had never thought of, but all were excited about. The man who sat next to me on the first day was taking the course for the second time. When he learned it was my first time at boot camp, he told me, "Soak it in, it's a mind-blowing course." At lunch break that first day, attendees filtered out to one of several restaurants at the resort. Many socialized, asking each other whether they owned a park or were looking for one. They grabbed spots at outdoor tables along the sun-filled marina that ran the length of the hotel. The

Pacific Ocean glistened just beyond the million-dollar yachts parked along the deck.

I sat in the lobby near the cascading arrangement of white orchids, look-ing out at the tables of mobile home park investors flanking the marina of luxury yachts. The yachts, the hotel, the $2,000 check I handed over to take the boot camp all made me think of a very different time and place. They made me think of Kathleen, the Florida resident whose story opened this book. Housing insecurity had structured Kathleen's life in Silver Sands, a life lived under the specter of dislocation. But here in the resort, housing insecurity undergirded the business model that made mobile home park investing so lucrative and exciting. Back when Silver Sands closed, Kathleen had attempted to make up for the insecurity and indignation she felt during her eviction by constructing her own resort experience, using a $2,000 check she received from Flagler Inc. to splurge on a motel room while she waited to resettle in her home. Kathleen's experience, worlds away from the genu-ine resort experience enjoyed by the boot camp investors, contextualizes the human costs of the insecure housing at the center of a mobile home empire.

KATHLEEN

As the final date of the eviction in Silver Sands approached, Kathleen had tried to assert her rights and preserve her pride by refusing to rent one of the abandoned homes in Silver Sands during the weeks it would take to install her old home in a new and unfamiliar park. With little savings and fewer affordable options nearby, other Silver Sands residents had already begun to pay Flagler Inc. (the company redeveloping Silver Sands) to rent the homes of others who had been forced to abandon their homes. These abandoned rentals were the oldest and most dilapidated homes in the park, the ones that could not be moved. Kathleen remained steadfast. She not only did not *want* to move into a stranger's abandoned home but she also *could* not, since these homes were not wheelchair accessible and she was confined to a wheelchair after the amputation of her leg. After months of phone calls and emails to Flagler Inc., she forced the company to provide her a $2,000 check she could use to rent a wheelchair-accessible motel room while her home was transported and reinstalled (she was the only resident in either state to receive any additional financial support).

Kathleen imagined herself a fighter. For her, the housing conditions res-idents were expected to endure gained symbolic importance. She was incensed that during the extended period it took for the network of private actors to relocate and reinstall the homes in Silver Sands, residents like

Walter and Mattie or Joseph and his mother (see chapter 5) were forced to pay the developer $15 a day to rent the structurally unsound homes of others who had abandoned in the park. Kathleen was infuriated by this: "Living in somebody's abandoned trailer for more rent than we are paying now? They are putting people in abandoned trailers and charging them more than we were paying in rent for our homes in the park!" Her husband, Chip, also took issue with the idea that mobile homes were interchangeable and mobile home residents would accept living in any mobile home: "I think that it's illegal to rent out an abandoned trailer. Because first of all there is a *reason* why the trailer is abandoned. And yet they're renting them out!"

Kathleen had battled to extend her moving date and lost. She had battled to get her wheelchair ramp relocated with her home and lost. She dug her heels in over this last battle. She stated that she had "never used ADA [the Americans with Disabilities Act] to help me get anything." But she also insisted, "I'm being forced out of a handicap-accessible house. That's the bottom line. I'm being forced out, I'm not moving on my own." She called local nonprofits, Legal Aid of South Florida and the Coalition for Independent Living. Both Kathleen and representatives from these nonprofits spent months contacting Flagler Inc. When Flagler finally offered her a $2,000 check and a list of nearby motel rooms, she took it because she just "wanted to be done with the whole thing."

During this process Kathleen's understanding of her rights as a homeowner and as a citizen of her city changed. Like residents in both states, she experienced the eviction as a "dignity taking" (Atuahene 2016). In the face of this indignation, Kathleen tried to salvage her dignity by reframing the $2,000 check and the opportunity to stay in a motel as symbolic deliverance from the stigma and powerlessness she felt. She reimagined the promise of a motel room as a Caribbean cruise, insisting:

> After everything that's been going on and my nerves, I am actually looking forward to staying in the motel ... I just told my son today when he was here, I said, I am going on my cruise next week. Because I've been dying to go on a cruise. Just relaxation. I said, if the wind is blowing and the water in that pool kind of ripples and I'll be glad to be in a lounge chair. Just like a cruise, you know?

She set herself to work finding a room that had a handicap-accessible bathroom and cost no more than $55 a night. Finally satisfied with her search in the week before her move, she revealed her top pick, a small motel near the park where she would relocate. She proudly showed me the full list of motel amenities, reading aloud: a full (not continental) breakfast every morning and a pool. She planned to stay in the motel for four weeks because that was exactly what she could afford with the $2,000 she had been given by Flagler Inc.

Kathleen looked forward to this simple luxury. She and Chip drove up and visited the motel to prepare to move in. They stopped at the McDonald's across the street even though, Kathleen explained, the couple rarely visited McDonald's because they never "go out." While they were there Kathleen had a ranch chicken wrap that cost $1.49. She included this into her careful budgeting for the time she was forced out of her home. She planned to eat the McDonald's chicken wrap every day during the month she stayed at the motel and that way she could eat for the whole month for only about $40. When I asked if a single chicken wrap was enough to sustain her all day, she responded that she had a very small appetite. So this was her plan: "Every day. Healthy, cheap." She had her days in the motel planned out to the dollar. She figured that at $365 a week for four weeks, plus her other costs, she would have $148 left to spend on restocking her pantry when she was finally able to return home.

Kathleen insisted on hosting me for a visit to her motel room once she moved in. I drove up to the motel, about 45 minutes north of Silver Sands. It sat across a busy four-lane thoroughfare from the McDonald's where Kathleen planned to eat every day. It was an average-looking, 1960s two-story motel, the kind that numbers in the hundreds along South Florida thoroughfares. The parking lot next door was under construction. I found Kathleen waiting outside the door to her room. She invited me in and gave me a tour, pointing out the handicap-accessible shower that was large and comfortable for her. She also pointed out a mini-refrigerator and microwave on a small table sprawled with the grocery items she and Chip were using to prepare meals in the motel room. After three weeks, she found this option cheaper than the McDonald's plan of "going out."

Chip stayed in the room watching TV and Kathleen took me for a short tour of the motel grounds. I complimented the landscaping, which was lush with Florida plants. "Why do you need to go to the Bahamas?" she asked, saying it felt like she was there when she sat out by the motel pool. We took seats in plastic chairs just outside the metal gate that enclosed the pool. I asked Kathleen if she still felt like she was on a cruise, and she answered only that she was trying to stay positive.

> Kathleen: "Yeah, I'm bored but it's a good bored. I can sit out front, watch the traffic, watch the airplanes, say a few prayers, whatever I want to do, I'm okay."
> Esther: "Do you feel more relaxed?"

Kathleen: "I'm looking down the road, unfortunately . . . the repairs, the door [broken during the relocation], unpacking."

When I ask her how that is making her feel, she responds by stating only that she has been smoking a lot, about a pack a day lately. She's preoccupied with this and talks about her smoking at length. She's been smoking "four times as much as usual, easy." She worries over her increased smoking. She feels it is related to some other recent health problems and "blockages" that need to be looked at by a doctor. When I ask when she plans to visit the doctor she says simply, "After."

At that time Kathleen was almost three weeks into her "cruise" and with careful budgeting she had spent $1,000 of the $2,000 check she was given. Still, she planned to leave the motel that coming Saturday. The installation of her home was being delayed and she had begun to seriously worry about the cost of repairing damage that she could already tell had occurred to the home during the move. If she left that Saturday she could spend three weeks in the motel and three weeks at her son's house, saving the remaining money for repairs when she returned home.

The $2,000 that the developer paid Kathleen for the motel was covered by additional money Flagler Inc. had made by selling off deserted and abandoned mobile homes in Silver Sands (after they had rented them out to displaced residents). The money Kathleen received was made possible by the surplus value wrung out of mobile home park residents as their homes and their relocations were traded like currency. In Florida many of the abandoned homes that had been deemed "structurally unsound" for relocation were then bought in bulk and relocated by the state's citrus growers who used them to house migrant workers. Likewise in Texas, homes that were deemed too costly or expensive to move were also bought by second- and thirdhand mobile home dealers who hauled them out of closing parks and sold them in some of the poorest counties in the state, especially in the Lower Rio Grande Valley along the U.S.-Mexico border.

Just as mobile home residents were traded like currency in the contracts made between mobile home movers and mobile home parks seeking to fill lot vacancies, mobile homes were sold off to be reused elsewhere. Kathleen and Chip were shocked as they watched their old powder-blue mobile home with the white wooden shutters (the one they were forced to abandon when they learned it could not be moved) being hitched to the back of a semi-truck to be sold off. The home had been sitting in a back area of Silver Sands for months. During those months Chip had explained, "Nobody wants to tear it down because there is no money in it. They are probably just gonna leave it there and bury it." Instead Kathleen and Chip watched in shock as their old home was purchased from Flagler Inc. and hauled away to some unknown place.

Kathleen and Chip were wrong about the powder-blue trailer, just as I was about the home I rented in Silver Sands. I was certain the home would be torn apart and tossed away in the demolition of Silver Sands. I had been through the process of attempting to relocate the home using the Florida voucher. Representatives from Max Movers and AJ Hirsh (the two moving companies hauling homes from Silver Sands) had been over to assess the home and told me it could not be moved and must be abandoned. On the last day of our tenancy at Silver Sands I ran into a representative for Flagler Inc. and asked about the fate of the home, thinking about the belongings of its former owners I would leave behind—the collection of seashells in the screened-in porch, the calendar with the VA appointments still penciled in. I asked the Flagler representative if the home was going to the dump. The representative surprised me when he stated that he hoped it would be "used as a home" and that "as many of them as possible in here will be used as a home as well." He explained that Riverstone, a corporate mobile home park company that owns over 70 parks in 12 states, was purchasing many of these abandoned homes from Flagler Inc. They would use them to fill up vacant lots in their parks and sell or rent them out as "handyman specials" to attract new park residents. Somehow, Flagler and Riverstone had determined that my home could be relocated (contrary to what its former owners and I had both been told). This likely meant that Flagler would make back each of the $1,500 "abandonment fees" given to residents who abandoned their homes in Silver Sands. Still, the Flagler representative presented the exchange more charitably. He said his philosophy was that he would rather have the trailer used as a home than taking up space in a landfill.

Flagler sold off the abandoned homes of residents like Randall, who fixed his front door, moved his belongings and his mother's ashes into self-storage, and left behind the first home he had ever owned. The Flagler representative claimed to sell Randall's home in the self-professed hope that "as many [homes] as possible in here will be used as a home," while—four years later at the time of this writing—Randall continues to sleep on the streets. In both states, landlords and developers made additional profits selling off the homes of residents who had been told the homes were too difficult or too costly to move. In Trail's End, Lupe's landlord Christine received counsel from the City of Alvin on how to lawfully take possession of abandoned trailers so that she could sell them to Repo Depot, the used mobile home dealer just outside of town. These trades are just one small way value is pulled out of an otherwise devalued housing form. They offer a glimpse into the broader market in mobile home park insecurity, but in the bigger picture they are only small change.

Within this bigger picture, mobile homes represent an economic adjustment being made by millions of Americans who are facing new socioeconomic realities. A 2017 *Time* article highlights these undercurrents in the growth in mobile home living: "The queasy-making economic reality of most U.S. households is almost too dire to face. Social Security is good for only so much. Pensions are nearly a thing of the past. And left to themselves to provide for their retirement, most Americans have proved unequal to the task ... But all is not lost. About 60% of U.S. households own a home. And the sale of a home opens the door to the possibility of trailer-park life."[2] This *Time* article explores the widespread phenomena of downsizing into a mobile home, pointing out what Kathleen and Chip already knew: the mobile home is a material expression of readjustments being made by poor and working-class citizens in times of economic insecurity. The article portrays these readjustments as necessary "accommodations to the inevitable," reflecting: "In a series of accommodations to the inevitable, the mobile home may be just one, albeit the kind that actually keeps a roof over our head."

Dating back to its inception, the *techno-social modularity* at the heart of the mobile home has made the housing invention uniquely adaptive to new market realities (see chapter 1). As Kelly (1952: 44) writes concerning the first period of the mobile home's proliferation: "[The Great] Depression made mobility for employment central to residential choice at the same time that it led industries to scramble for new market opportunities in a deeply changed economy." Contemporary economic readjustments have catalyzed analogous shifts not only in the choices of mobile home residents, making "accommodations to the inevitable," but in the network of players capitalizing on these choices at different corners of the mobile home industry. In an era of economic uncertainty, an entire market has adapted to offer trade in one readily available currency: poverty and insecurity.

THE MOBILITY MARKETPLACE

In the experience of evicted park residents, the mobile home park industry is made up of the landlords who own their property, the moving companies that organize their relocation, and the receiving parks that provide rental lots where they can reinstall their homes. In the world of manufactured housing, these local markets are only a microcosm of a larger mobility marketplace. Nonetheless, the orbit of these local players is the scale at which most park residents encounter the broader barter and trade in manufactured housing.

Max, the heavy-set Italian American truck driver and owner of Max Mobile Home Movers, was one of the local players that structured evicted residents' experience of the mobile home park marketplace. Now in his late 40s, Max was only 14 years old when he took off with the carnival and began operating carnival rides. With characteristic frankness, he explained that this decision came about because his mother died when he was nine and his father was a jackass, so it was time to go. Max had been on his own making a living for himself since that time. He toured with the carnival for six years throughout the United States and Canada. That was where he learned to drive a truck.

Max told me his story on the days I accompanied him and his work crew relocating homes out of Silver Sands and other closing South Florida parks. He seemed to appreciate the company in the cab of his moving truck. On long moving days, much of his job entailed waiting in the truck for his work crew to complete the physical labor of readying homes for transport; only then could he hitch them up and haul them out. From the driver's seat of his truck, Max talked easily about the ins and outs of the mobile home relocation business. In his estimation, it was a competitive field involving a network of players with different stakes.

At one time Max had five trucks working for him and two operating on the road at most times. He was running a half-million-dollar-a-year business, exclusively hauling homes out of closing mobile home parks in Florida. When I asked if that was stressful he sighed and said, "Very." In fact, he said, this is why he had developed cardiopulmonary disease and was downsizing his company. He listed off his expenses at the height of his business. He had to have a Class A license to drive his truck. He paid $500 for the permit covering him for the year to move anything up to 14 feet wide, plus more for all homes over 14 feet wide (more common with newer models). With the number of employees he had on the payroll plus fuel bills of about $65,000 a year, he needed to pull in $5,000 a day just to break even. This meant he had to move as many as four or five homes in a day.

One early morning, I met up with Max and his crew to relocate some homes out of Sawgrass Estates, the closing park about 90 miles south of Silver Sands. We met at Max's "workshop," which was really just a gated parking lot filled with large pieces of machinery, scrap metal, several trucks and trailers, and an old RV. Before leaving the shop for Sawgrass Estates, Max's crew loaded up extra axles to bring with us. The metal chassis that is the base of a mobile home has hangers that hold the axles. Wheels are placed on the axles so the home can become mobile. Max explained that most mobile homes do not still have axles underneath and only rest on their chassis; mobile home installers get money back from the factory if they keep these axles because they can be reused. While Max talked about an acquaintance who made a living buying used axles from installers to sell back to factories, I realized even the individual components of mobile homes—the axles—are a form of currency. Meanwhile, the practice of removing the axles from homes and reselling them contributes to the de facto *immobility* of mobile homes. The crew used a large machine to load axles of appropriate sizes onto a flatbed trailer. They also brought their own wheels. Most homes lacked these as well; they had long been immobile.

Once inside Sawgrass Estates the crew worked underneath and around the perimeter of a doublewide to ready the two sections for Max to hook up. This was the real work of relocation. The crew removed siding and scrambled along the sides, roof, and interior of the home to split the two sections of the doublewide. They hydraulically lifted one section at a time and worked for hours to remove years of accumulated debris underneath.

Max oversaw the work from the cab of his truck. He mentioned casually, as part of another story, a time when he moved his own mobile home after he was displaced from a park that closed. It turned out Max himself had been evicted from a mobile home park. This was over a decade ago; still, I was shocked that Max had never mentioned this part of his story in the months I had been shadowing him relocating the homes of others. He laughed at my surprise, saying it simply slipped his mind. He explained that he had been living in a South Florida park for 13 years at the time. He was already working for a mobile home mover. In his park the landlord had undertaken an informal eviction, pushing residents out by being "nasty" and making life difficult for them.[3] Max was never served with a formal eviction notice or told about his rights to Florida's relocation assistance. Nobody in the park received any compensation or assistance with moving. Because of Max's knowledge of the industry he sold his home to another park with vacant lots and they paid him to move his home and install it himself. With the money he saved over years of living in the mobile home and with the extra money from the sale of the home, he was able to buy his first site-built house, where he still lived.

Max went on to outline how he grew his business by providing contract work for a larger mobile home moving company owned by AJ Hirsh. Max partnered with AJ Hirsh and the two in turn contracted with (1) various Florida development companies who needed to empty closing parks and (2) corporate park companies who wanted to receive relocated homes to fill out

FIGURE 16.   A crew works to split and move a doublewide. Photo by Esther Sullivan, 2013.

vacant lots. This constellation of private actors operated only in one small corner of the mobile home park empire, but nonetheless generated sizable profits. Max explained how he and AJ Hirsh worked together to create a system for moving many homes at once more efficiently by subcontracting out different jobs to different work crews. "It takes the pressure off of everybody. I don't have to clean the lot, I don't have to worry about getting the skirting off right now. My guys are going to come in, they're going to split the top, split the bottom, hang the axles, split the house open, and basically that's my job—get it to the other end."

Like movers in Texas, Max's actual charge for "getting it to the other end" was more in the range of $2,000–$3,000. But the system he had developed with AJ Hirsh had various levels of hidden cost that made the relocations in Florida parks much more expensive than the relocations in Texas parks. For instance, Max estimated 80 percent of his work was moving homes out of closing parks and 20 percent of his work came from one-off jobs moving homes purchased on the mainland of Florida down to parks in the Florida Keys. These were much longer, more difficult moves down a single highway that stretches about 150 miles and across a two-lane, seven-mile bridge; yet, without the additional subcontracting commitments common in closing parks like Silver Sands these moves costs homeowners only

$3,500 for a doublewide and much less for a singlewide. I asked Max about this discrepancy:

> Esther: "So if you say that when you move a home down the Keys you get $3,500 for a doublewide, then how can they tell us that moving one of these homes [in Silver Sands and Sawgrass Estates] costs $10,000?"
>
> Max: "Because you have everybody that's involved—your mechanical, the air-conditioning guy, the inspector are making $1,800. The electrician is making another $1,800. I am making $3,000. And AJ [Hirsh] would be making another $6,000 or $4,000 or whatever it is. AJ would be on the set-up side. We all have our little niches. That is why we are so efficient."

Max believed the contract arrangements made by those like himself and AJ Hirsh created a streamlined and efficient system, but I thought back to the Silver Sands residents who had waited months to get a clear assessment on whether their homes could be relocated and many more months before they were able to return home.

Max continued to explain why relocated homes were so valuable to corporate park owners like Lakeshore, who were willing to pay Max and AJ Hirsh thousands of dollars to relocate homes out of closing parks:

> If you have an old park that is full of old trailers, you cannot realistically expect somebody to come in and throw money into your park, unless you're actually doing it yourself. And most park owners are from the old school, the old days, they are not going to put their money into the park. They are not going to put brand new houses in and try to sell them. You need older houses to fill the [vacant] spaces. So it is a win-win for everyone . . . This is what we found out about these niches: what that space was really worth to the owner of a park, down to a dollar value for them. You say, I am going to bring you 40 trailers times $55,000 [that the park owner would make off a lot with a home versus a vacant lot] and you may have to pay out $10,000. So for every $10,000 that you invest you are making $55,000 worth of equity on your park. It is a no-brainer.

This broader capital-producing scheme on the part of corporate mobile home park companies like Lakeshore was integral to the business model of smaller business owners like Max who hauled homes out of closing parks and into parks that used the relocated homes to fill vacant lots. Similar incentives for filling vacant lots exist in Texas, although without state relocation funds, the relocation transactions were more often between movers and homeowners.

The "no-brainer" model Max described was further elucidated by AJ Hirsh, who subcontracted Max and sometimes appeared at a worksite to oversee the work. Unlike Max, AJ no longer drove a moving truck; instead he rolled into the site in a tinted SUV that Max and I hopped into for a break from the heat. AJ's mobile home relocation work was increasingly administrative. In addition to running his own moving company and subcontracting with movers like Max, AJ served on the board of directors for Florida's Mobile Home Relocation Corporation, which distributes the state relocation funds and is equally balanced between representatives from the manufactured housing industry and representatives of the statewide mobile homeowners association. Like Max, AJ insisted he provided a useful service to evicted mobile home park residents and defended his business by saying "I'm not a carpetbagger."

Still, AJ acknowledged that mobile home parks were a twofold site of capital production that extended far beyond the profits he made relocating homes. He suggested it was small-time thinking to imagine that profits were only made locally off relocations out of closing parks or new rents generated by filling lot vacancies. He explained that the real surplus value squeezed out of displaced mobile homes was in the increased capitalization of the receiving parks. He further illuminated the reason parks are willing to pay to get evicted homeowners into their parks. He used the national corporate mobile home park company, Lakeshore, as an example:

> AJ talks at length about his dealings with Mr. Wolf, who owns Lakeshore. He seems to resent that Wolf hasn't been adequately thankful for the increased value [in the form of relocated mobile homes] AJ brings into Lakeshore parks.
>
> "I'm gonna tell you a story, Joe Wolf who owns Lakeshore. This was when we closed Three Palms—400 to 500 homes. I moved 150 homes for him and another 50 or so for another person. I was very busy back then. In his one park Wolf says: 'You realize I paid you 380K? I've paid you a hell of a lot of money, son.'"
>
> In a tone of resentment AJ continues "I say, I put in a 150 houses and now your park is worth 60K a space more for each of those residents I put in there. You made 6.7 million dollars. And you know what he said to me? 'You're pretty smart, aren't you.' This is the thing—a vacant lot in a mobile home park is worth bubkis; it is worth nothing to the bottom line. With a resident and a house there it is worth $60,000 to the bottom line of that park or its net worth. And these guys re-hock all the time. They hock the parks."

AJ explained that the increase to the net worth of the park occurs because the owner will "re-hock" the park, meaning the owner will continuously refinance the park to pull out equity. The more occupied lots there are, the more equity the park owner can pull out. This way, he claimed, park companies are able to get a 10 percent return for investors. This was the same capitalization rate I would hear thrown around years later by excited would-be investors at the mobile home park boot camp. "They are making that much money?" I asked AJ. "Off of the people that can't afford to make money," he responded.

The "people that can't afford to make money" have increasingly turned to mobile home living as an adjustment to new economic realities, as Kathleen and Chip did when they downsized into a mobile home in their retirement. But these new economic realities are reshaping life for those all along the income scale. As a dwindling share of income is based on labor and an increasing share is generated from returns on capital (Piketty 2014), the people who *can* "afford to make money" are doing so less through work (like Max) and more through financialized capital and new financial instruments (like Lakeshore's method of refinancing parks to generate 10 percent returns). Mobile home park investing of the sort we learned at the mobile home park boot camp is one example of this shift. The attendees crowded into the boot camp ballroom were eager to learn what returns could be generated in an uncharted corner of the real estate market. They were eager to become new marketeers.

THE NEW MARKETEERS

From the front of the ballroom at the mobile home park boot camp, Frank projected pictures that confirmed the image many in the room likely already had of mobile home parks— dilapidated mobile homes, aging and sagging trailers in serious disrepair: "If this jars you, you're in trouble." Profiting from an untapped market requires stomaching the sight of poverty. It also requires understanding, as Frank continued: "This is affordable housing— I'm trying to get you in the mindset: This is not your house . . . You have to understand the difference between an affordable house and your house."

Frank advocated both a shift in the *object* of investing (from standard forms of real estate like multifamily housing to mobile home parks) and in the *attitude* of investing ("I'm trying to get you in the mindset: this is not your house—this is affordable housing"). In this resort ballroom and in hotel ballrooms all over the world, similar courses train attendees in both the skills and attitudes required to adjust to new economic realities. As Fridman's (2017) study of financial self-help groups shows, similar seminars train attendees to readjust to a new era of financial capitalism by disregarding work as a source of earnings and focusing instead on "passive income" generated by financial assets and investments.

Macroeconomic readjustments require new economic rationalities (Fridman 2017). The attendees at the boot camp were making these readjustments. The man who sat next to me the first two days, the one who told me the boot camp was "a mind-blowing course," was transitioning from a three-decade career in traditional investing. When I took a seat next to him on the second day of the boot camp, I jokingly asked him if he collected university sweatshirts. The day before he had worn a worn gray Columbia sweatshirt, today he sported a faded black Princeton hoodie. He didn't crack a smile but quipped back that he simply had "been to too many of those places." We were in a completely different classroom now as we listened to a former graduate of the boot camp and fledgling mobile home park owner advise us all to "get comfortable being uncomfortable."

In the hard-nosed world of real estate investing, blatant stereotypes of trailer trash do not scare off investors. In fact, they seem to lure them in with the promise of big returns, unexploited markets, and a captive and growing class of needy low-income residents who keep parks operating at full capacity. A 2014 *Bloomberg* article on mobile home park investing begins:

> When Dan Weissman worked at Goldman Sachs Group Inc. and, later, at a hedge fund, he didn't have to worry about methamphetamine addicts chasing his employees with metal pipes. Or SWAT teams barging into his workplace looking for arsonists.
> Both things have happened since he left Wall Street and bought five mobile home parks: four in Texas and one in Indiana . . .
> With more of the U.S. middle class sliding into poverty and many towns banning new trailer parks, enterprising owners are getting rich renting the concrete pads and surrounding dirt on which residents park their homes.
> "The greatest part of the business is that we go to sleep at night not ever worrying about demand for our product," Weissman, 34, says. "It's the best decision I've ever made." (Effinger and Burton 2014)

The article claims that traditional investors, Wall Street bankers, and private equity firms are now "jostling for position in an unlikely asset class: trailer parks." The readership of *Bloomberg* might be surprised to learn, as the article reveals, that billionaire Sam Zell is the biggest investor in this "hot asset class." The article also profiles smaller investors just breaking into the market, those like Weissman, 34, and his business partner David Shlachter, 32, who has a master's degree in development economics from Harvard's Kennedy School of Government. Shlachter explains the allure of the mobile home park is the escape from the crowded field of investors trying to make it rich in the finance and tech industries: "You've got a lot of really smart people trying to come up with a better way to put a calendar on an iPhone. We'd rather sit at a different poker table, where none of those people dare to go because it doesn't sound good at a cocktail party."

Investors face less competition and reap greater rewards by venturing "where none of those people dare to go." Boot camp attendees did so literally by piling into four charter buses for a tour of Southern California mobile home parks. They hoped to catch a close-up look at what they all hoped to own and operate from a distance. As the buses entered the first park on the tour, Frank Rolfe's pre-recorded voice piped in from the bus speakers, encouraging attendees to look past the veil of poverty to see the opportunities for profit: "Remember, you don't have to live here." This kind of peeking at poverty, without having to bear full witness to its consequences, seemed to be an enjoyable experience for those social worlds apart from residents in mobile home parks. The experience might even help to explain some of the allure of mobile home park investing. The 2014 *Bloomberg* article claims that for investors like Weissman and Shlachter, "owning trailer parks has taught them what it's like to be poor in America." How deep this lesson permeated is unclear, as Shlachter describes life on the other side of the poverty divide this way: "It's hairy, and it's colorful, and it's sometimes scary."

Attendees at the boot camp also told me the mediated experience of life at the other side of the income scale was part of the appeal. Miles, who sat next to me on the bus that transported us from park to park, explained how he appreciated that being a low-income landlord allowed him to "see a whole other walk of life." Another well-dressed man in his 30s told me he was attending the boot camp inspired by a friend who recently retired from Goldman Sachs after buying two mobile home parks. The man explained that while his friend owns the park from a different state, employs a resident park manager, and hires workers to maintain the park, a major appeal of park ownership has been that "they get to work outside and work with their hands." Another attendee, a resident of Orange County, California, who had purchased parks in Nebraska and Iowa, pulled out his phone unprompted during our conversation to show me pictures of his parks. He then gazed at his phone as he showed me a video, a panning shot of a train rolling in front of his 85-lot mobile home park, and murmured, "Magical." Frank himself demonstrated a genuine enthusiasm for mobile homes (he could date their year of production by their differing rooflines) and for mobile home park ownership ("For me there has been nothing better than rolling up my sleeves and going to parks and going to small towns").

These attendees were all attracted by a mediated experience of a life far different from their own, but a more common motivation among attendees was the search for an investment vehicle to produce passive income— income gained through investments rather than work—which was a buzzword at the boot camp. Indeed many attendees said they learned about the boot camp through passive income podcasts or passive income networking groups. The focus of attendees on passive income shows how they were strategizing their own adjustments to macroeconomic shifts, transforming their financial behaviors to better fit with neoliberal market realities (Fridman 2017). Miles, an attendee who left a corporate sales job at Comcast, was passionate about making such an adjustment. He had attended passive income seminars across the United States, then cashed in his 401K to invest in mobile home parks. Blake, the man who attended because his friend at Goldman Sachs liked to "work outside," told me his own reason for attending the course was to leave his job as a corporate attorney and find something "cash flow friendly" that enabled him to generate passive income. Marie and Joe, a married couple in their 30s from Washington state, explained over lunch that they were looking into some opportunities to produce passive income. Joe was a dentist and Marie ran the dental office. They wanted to work less and generate more income from investing in real estate with high and steady returns. Samuel, who sat near us, chimed in to agree, asking the young couple if they had also looked into self-storage. "It's a really good asset class," he told them. He echoed another attendee who had told me he had not yet bought a mobile home park but boasted, "I have self-storage and that's where the real money is." While I thought about the number of mobile home park residents I knew who moved their belongings into self-storage after their eviction, Samuel continued to laud the benefits of self-storage as a real estate asset class and investment on par with mobile home parks. He said after 25 years of real estate investing he knew that the trouble with real estate is the 3Ts—tenants, toilets, and trash—and the mobile home park removes all that because the residents own the homes.

Frank drove this point home in his presentation, cautioning attendees against purchasing parks with rental units. "Parks always work best when every resident is a homeowner. That makes them a stakeholder in the business." Plus, it makes the passive income more passive as landlords are required to do less to maintain the property, passing much of this responsibility on to residents (thus further encouraging their emotional, financial, and practical investment in their homes—both the house and the lot—which so complicated the experience of eviction for the residents in this study). Frank continued to recommend that park owners leave much of the maintenance to homeowning residents while doing just enough to keep tenants happy; he suggested filling potholes and maintaining an attractive entry: "People want to be proud of where they live. I don't know anyone that wants to live in a dump." But at the same time, he cautioned against investing in states with minimum maintenance laws, pointing out these requirements directly affect a park owner's bottom line. He highlighted Texas as a favorite state with "a very low bar for minimum habitability, one of the lowest." Frank bought his first park in Texas and owns many there today.

For Frank and his business partner, operating parks rather than redeveloping them is where profits lie. The parks they own reportedly generate over $30 million in revenue, about half of which is profit (Rivlin 2014). Frank acknowledged that redevelopment can provide opportunities for large one-time profits, and remained neutral and pragmatic about the possibility of closing parks and evicting residents: "You're in the real estate business, you have to displace people. That's just the business. This hotel [the resort where the boot camp was held] used to be something else. It's just natural." He advised attendees to take the same long view: "You always have to look at the future and consider your exit strategy." However, he noted that he was not a land speculator and was not in the business of closing parks: "We haven't had to do that in the portfolio at all." For him the beauty of mobile home parks was not their potential for redevelopment but their capacity to generate sizable returns with little continual investment. The business model is simple. He spelled it out: new parks seldom open up while demand for affordable housing is increasing. To explain this Frank noted the same socio-spatial stigma described in the first chapter of this book: "hostile" city councils actively "zone out" mobile home parks, "not to mention all the neighbors hate 'em too."

In the corner of the mobile home empire where Frank Rolfe has built his fortune, the ebbs and flows of real estate are "just natural" and displacement is part of this ever-evolving cycle. In the understanding of this cycle he disseminated to the rapt audience of boot camp attendees, hostile city councils and surrounding communities that "hate" the mobile home park are simply hurdles to jump over on the way to generating passive income from parks. But for mobile home park residents, these same hurdles present major crises. The cycle of real estate development, the decisions of city councils, and the views of surrounding communities all play a role in removing them from their homes.

THE MOGULS

Mobile homes represent one of the most devalued forms of housing. Yet mobile home parks provide value and a source of wealth for some of the richest individuals in the United States. Dominating their own corner of the mobile home empire are billionaires Sam Zell and Warren Buffett—two of the largest real estate investors in the world, among the richest individuals in the United States, and primary profiteers off of the mobile home park model.

Sam Zell is a standard on the Forbes 400, which lists the world's top billionaires. His investment portfolio consists of assets in hospitality, energy, transportation, finance, healthcare, and communications (*Forbes* 2017a). Zell has been nicknamed the Grave Dancer for "his ability to profit from distressed-asset investing" (*Forbes* 2017a). Less showy and more profitable than his investments in the Chicago Cubs and the *Los Angeles Times* is one major pillar of his wealth, the mobile home park. One third of Zell's real estate investment arm is Equity LifeStyle Properties, which exclusively owns mobile home parks and has claim to more than 140,000 lots in 32 states and British Columbia.[4]

Similarly, the mobile home undergirds the wealth of Warren Buffett, who is the second richest man in the United States with a net worth of $78.5 billion as of March 2017 (*Forbes* 2017a). Buffett is the chairman and largest shareholder of the fourth-largest public company in the world, Berkshire Hathaway, which is renowned for its long-standing performance for shareholders (with an annual growth in book value of 19 percent for the 52 years leading up to 2017).[5] Much of this growth comes from Berkshire Hathaway's diversified interests in energy, manufacturing, and finance, including companies like American Express, Coca-Cola, and Wells Fargo. Less known but no less important to the company's portfolio is its ownership of Clayton Homes, the largest builder and financier of manufactured housing in the United States.

Clayton was purchased by Berkshire Hathaway in 2003. As Warren Buffett boasted in his 2016 letter to shareholders, "Last year, Clayton became America's largest home builder, delivering 42,075 units that accounted for 5% of all new American homes."[6] Put another way, the largest single supplier of homes in the United States is a manufactured home builder. Banking on the synergy between poverty and profit, Buffett explained his vision behind catering to the poorest subset of Americans looking to purchase a home: "Clayton's focus will always be manufactured homes, which account for about 70% of new American homes costing less than $150,000. Clayton manufactures close to one-half of the total."[7]

But manufacturing homes for low-income Americans is only half of what Clayton does. The company also retails mobile homes and the bulk of the company's earnings come from its large mobile home mortgage portfolio. The first chapter of this book explored the barriers to financing a mobile home with a traditional bank mortgage. Along with restrictive zoning, the discriminatory financing of mobile homes as "chattel" has grounded the socio-spatial stigma found in the mobile home park over the last century. Yet restricted access to traditional lending for mobile homes has also created opportunities for companies like Clayton. With growing demand and a restricted supply of affordable housing, Buffett made a sure bet on Clayton's manufacturing capabilities. Without routes to traditional financing for mobile homes, he took a longer shot at expanding Clayton's in-house financing for the risky, low-income borrowers that are the main market for Clayton's homes. The wager paid off, as Buffett points out in his annual letter to shareholders: "This company receives most of its revenue from the sale of manufactured homes, but derives the bulk of its *earnings* from its large mortgage portfolio."[8] What Buffett is explaining to shareholders is that building mobile homes is a good business; lending on them is a better one.

The lessons the new marketeers learned at the mobile home park boot camp centered around passive income generation, as if capital flows freely out of mobile home parks once they are correctly tapped. But the moguls of the mobile home marketplace more actively wring profits from mobile home owners (both those in parks and those who install their homes on private land). Clayton Homes exemplifies the abuses that have become bound up in the pursuit of big yields from one of the largest sources of poverty housing.

Clayton Homes was the target of a joint investigation by the Center for Public Integrity (CPI) and the *Seattle Times* in 2015. The practices the investigation uncovered are likely widespread in the underregulated world of manufactured housing, but the report focuses solely on Clayton Homes. The CPI report examined more than 100 Clayton home sales through interviews and reviews of loan documents from 41 states. Buyers in the CPI report described a range of deceptive practices perpetrated by Clayton, including: interest rates of over 15 percent (over 12 percentage points higher than the average prime fixed rate for 2013),[9] hidden fees that added thousands of dollars to borrower's loans, pressure to take on high payments with the promise that the borrower could refinance in the future, and Clayton dealers that steered buyers to finance through Clayton's own high-interest lenders. These loans saddle residents with enormous risk and monthly housing burdens, but the risk for Clayton's lenders is low. When residents default, their home is repossessed and easily sold again, as the Florida and Texas marketplaces in abandoned mobile homes clearly show. Indeed, the dealerships in the CPI study were much like the Clayton-owned dealerships (operating under different names) that lined the highway outside of Alvin, Texas. Large signs there advertised "New, Used, and Repossessed Homes."

The CPI report begins with the stories of mobile home residents like Carol Carroll, who had been paying down her mobile home for more than a decade and still owed almost 90 percent of the sales price and more than twice what the home is worth. The report's authors found other residents faced similar experiences. Each acquired their mobile home through different dealers and lenders—companies named Luv Homes, TruValue Homes, Vanderbilt, 21st Mortgage—but the loans they used to purchase them all originated with Clayton, which operates related companies under at least 18 names (Wagner and Baker 2015a). Clayton is described as "a many-headed hydra" operating under so many names that buyers falsely believe they are shopping around for the best deal (ibid.). But Clayton's reach is hard to escape. In 2013 the company provided 39 percent of all new mobile home loans (ibid.). The next largest lender, which provided only 6 percent of loans, was Wells Fargo, whose biggest shareholder is in turn Berkshire Hathaway.[10]

Additionally, park landlords themselves sometimes become dealers for Clayton. At the mobile home boot camp Frank Rolfe explained the importance of filling out lots. It was the same story Max had told me as I drove with him in the cab of his truck. The same story AJ Hirsh had told me when we sat in his SUV watching a crew disassemble a doublewide. "For each space you fill, your park just gained real value," AJ had said. Frank was candid in telling attendees that he preferred to do this at the owner's expense by finding a homeowner wishing to move in their mobile home (either one purchased new or one displaced from a closing park). If that is not possible, Frank explained, there are programs designed to assist park owners in filling out lots at the buyer's expense—even rewarding landlords with a small fee if the mobile home is sold quickly. Frank announced a guest speaker who came to give boot camp attendees the details of the program. The speaker was a lending agent at 21st Mortgage, a subsidiary of Clayton Homes.

The representative from 21st Mortgage explained to boot camp attendees the benefits of using 21st Mortgage to place model homes (manufactured by Clayton) in their parks and sell them to new mobile homeowners through 21st Mortgages (a Clayton subsidiary). Frank had invited the 21st Mortgage representative but, he told attendees later, he had never himself used their services because the bar is so low for becoming a mobile home dealer yourself. To sell homes in parks, he explained, you only need to acquire a dealer's license. He continued: "Here's how I got to be a Texas licensed dealer: I went to Austin for two days, stayed in a hotel and took a class for two days, all I had to do I say 'here' four times. 'Here' at 9 in the morning and 'here' at 1 p.m. No test. You could bring anything you want to class—a computer, iPad, a pillow, whatever."

For new marketeers like the boot camp attendees, the loosely regulated world of mobile home dealership is a route to filling lot vacancies in their parks. But for mobile home moguls like Warren Buffet and Clayton homes, it is the basis of an industry that capitalizes on predatory lending practices. The CPI report found that Clayton homes are both initially overpriced and depreciate so quickly that they are often worth less than what the borrower owes even after years of monthly payments. For instance, one disabled, elderly Washington resident in the study purchased a Clayton home for $65,000 with $40,000 from her inheritance. One year later when she attempted to sell the home to help her daughter through college, the appraisal valued the home at $35,000. Indeed in cases where Clayton lender Vanderbilt was required to obtain appraisals before finalizing a loan, the home was determined to be worth less than the sales price about 30 percent of the time (Wagner and Baker 2015a).

These practices negatively impact mobile homeowners both inside parks and on private land. However, the unique nature of divided land tenure in mobile home parks tacks on additional risks. For instance, appraisals are central for transparency and consumer protection and a primary way to guard against risks like those outlined above. In a response to the CPI report, Clayton Homes published a statement in the *Omaha World-Herald* (also owned by Berkshire Hathaway) defending itself by stating: "Appraisals are ordered from an unaffiliated third party on all loans *secured by land* that we finance, and a copy is provided to the customer prior to closing of the loan" (emphasis added).[11] However, the majority of Clayton's loans (65 percent of loans in 2014) are *not* secured by land, likely because they are located *in mobile home parks* where the land is not part of the equation. These loans would not require an appraisal or disclosure to buyers (Wagner and Baker 2015b). Without the security of land, park residents lack collateral for better terms and more transparent lending practices. Even in a system where all mobile home residents are at a disadvantage, mobile home residents in parks likely fare much worse.

CAPITALIZING ON INSECURITY

It is not only moguls like Sam Zell and Warren Buffet who are pulling profit from mobile home parks. Individual investors can do the same through investment opportunities that might seem far removed from the inside of a mobile home park. Yet, investment tools such as commercial mortgage-backed securities (CMBSs) and real estate investment trusts (REITs) capitalize on the need for affordable housing that mobile home parks fill.

The mortgages of mobile home park owners are repackaged into bundles of loans sold as a CMBS (similar to the mortgage-backed securities that were central in the U.S. housing market crash). At the mobile home park boot camp, would-be mobile home moguls learned this is one reason why mortgages are so easily available to them (unlike the residents living in their parks). Loans on parks are "seen as reasonably stable," a capital markets consultant who specializes in mobile home park lending told me. He explained that the need for affordable housing means banks are confident of park owners' ability to repay loans "because of their price points [in parks], they have high occupancy and they just don't stay empty for long." Loans for park owners are often "conduit loans," meaning they are subsequently bundled and sold on the market as a security. This creates third- and fourthhand opportunities for mobile home park investment. At boot camp, Frank Rolfe claimed that since the default rates on loans for mobile home parks and self-storage are "so incredibly low," CMBSs are often eager to include mobile home parks within these bundles of loans, "like the flavor crystals sprinkled on top of the big meaty pie." He advised boot camp attendees that banks "might even seek you out" because they want to include the park owner's loan in a CMBS.

Manufactured housing real estate investment trusts (REITs) are another tool that allows investors to generate value from the otherwise devalued housing found in mobile home parks. Publicly traded REITs are companies that own and typically operate real estate assets, which may include office buildings, shopping malls, apartments, hotels, and self-storage facilities (U.S. Securities and Exchange Commission 2017). REITs allow individuals to invest in large-scale, income-producing real estate by purchasing shares of the REIT on major stock exchanges.[12] Unlike other real estate companies, a REIT does not develop or sell real estate properties. Instead, a REIT buys properties primarily to operate them as part of an investment portfolio.

Currently, manufactured housing REITs, bundles of mobile home parks, are some of the best performing REITs on the market, generating the highest returns of any class of REIT. In 2016, manufactured housing REITs posted a total return of 28.5 percent, compared with total returns of 18.2 percent for apartment REITs and 14.2 percent for the REIT sector overall (Borchersen-Keto 2017; Hoya Capital Real Estate 2016). Real estate analysts interviewed for an investing article on manufactured housing REITs explained: "Nowhere else in real estate do we see this complete lack of new supply and the favorable demand dynamics" (cited in Borchersen-Keto 2017). There is no shortage of finance articles lauding the stable and sizable returns of manufactured housing REITs compared to other forms of real estate: "Over the past three years, manufactured housing REITs have surged nearly 100% and have outperformed the broader REIT index over the prior one and two years as well" (Hoya Capital Real Estate 2016).

The irony of the mobile home investment world is that, while insecurity is a central feature of life inside mobile home parks, investors value mobile home parks precisely because of the *security* they inject into financial products like CMBSs and REITs. As one investment article explains: "Because of the high cost to move manufactured homes, turnover is low, creating stability of income and occupancy for the REITs" (Persin 2015). An investment website's overview of all REIT categories, including manufactured housing, summarizes some of the very themes of this book in its assessment of mobile home park investing:

> MH homes are, in most cases, the cheapest non-subsidized housing options available. To be crass, there is often nowhere else to go, providing some degree of protection on the downside during recessions . . . One of the distinct features of the MH sector is the complete lack of new supply expected to be constructed. With essentially zero net supply coming online for the foreseeable future, manufactured housing is relatively immune from the oversupply fears that encumber other REIT sectors. Across the country, zoning commissions continue to have a sharply unfavorable view of manufactured housing communities. Getting approval for a new development is nearly impossible.
>
> Never underestimate the simple economics of supply and demand in the REIT space. While much of the investing public still holds misconceptions about the manufactured housing sector, the investors that looked past the public portrayal have achieved tremendous performance over the past five years. (Hoya Capital Real Estate 2016)

Both manufactured housing REITs and CMBSs view parks as stabilizing factors. As in other corners of the mobile home park marketplace, these stable profits are deeply entwined with the instability experienced by residents. To generate returns for investors, REITs must either expand parks (difficult for the reasons outlined in chapter 1) or increase the rents of existing households. The latter is the go-to strategy. One investment article assures potential investors that returns will remain stable because "REITs will continue to push through rent increases to existing tenants . . . annual increases have been around the 3 percent range" (Borchersen-Keto 2017). The result for investors is steady returns. The result for mobile home park residents is rising rents and housing precarity.

Insecurity and investment opportunities are ever more closely intertwined under contemporary economic transformations that extend beyond the mobile home park, beyond Texas and Florida, and even beyond the borders of the United States. Similar global economic transformations characterize a "complex and elusive reality of impoverishment in the making" that "goes well beyond simply more poverty and inequality" and gives rise to a new global political economy that is "marked by *expulsions*" (Sassen 2014: 29). Chapter 3 characterized the experience of life under the specter of dislocation, which produces a haunted subjectivity marked by the threat of expulsion. This final chapter probes the internal logics of the economic transactions that profit off conditions that make the specter of dislocation a daily lived reality. From the economic transactions within the mobile home empire to the local urban policies that undergird socio-spatial stigma and sanction park redevelopment, the mobile home park serves as a microcosm of Sassen's proposition (2014: 13–14) that the current phase of development in the global political economy marks a new "era of expulsions":

> My thesis is that we are seeing the making not so much of predatory elites but of predatory "formations," a mix of elites and capacities with finance as a key enabler, that push toward acute concentration . . . Rich individuals and global firms by themselves could not have achieved such extreme concentration of the world's wealth. They need what we might think of as systemic help . . . Such systemic capacities are a variable mix of technical, market, and financial innovations plus government enablement. They constitute a partly global condition, though one that often functions through the specifics of countries, their political economies, their laws, and their governments. They include enormous capacities for intermediation that functions as a kind of haze, impairing our ability to see what is happening—but unlike a century ago, we would not find cigar-smoking moguls in this haze.

We might not find mobile home moguls in this haze either. The spread of the mobile home empire into conventional investment instruments like CMBSs and REITs demonstrates that one need not be part of the global elite, like Warren Buffett, or work inside of closing parks, like Max, to capitalize on the housing insecurity found there. Despite its devalued image, the mobile home park proves profitable for a range of players, from everyday individual investors to small businesses moving evicted home-owners to national corporations selling to low-income buyers getting their first taste of a manufactured American Dream. A political economy of poverty operates within these various corners of the mobile home park empire, where the needs of residents and the insecurity of their housing tenure offer sites for interested parties to extract surplus value.

Conclusion

When I returned from the field, the field followed me. As testament to the lack of data on mobile home park closures and the absence of places that evicted residents can turn, I have been and to this day still am continually contacted by residents of closing parks who have located my work online and are desperately searching for any help they can find. Their stories could be pulled directly from the pages of my field notes. The problems and paradoxes that emerged from Silver Sands, Sawgrass Estates, Trail's End, and Twin Oaks structure the stories of evicted park residents across the United States. The same stigma and invisibility lead them to call and email me. The same specter of dislocation overshadows their lives if they are waiting to be evicted. The same slow-motion trauma ensnares them if their eviction has already begun.

In San Antonio, Texas, for instance, I was pulled back into the field in 2014 as Mission Trails Mobile Home Park became the target of plans by a local real estate developer to rezone and redevelop the 21-acre mobile home park to make way for a 600-unit luxury apartment complex along a portion of the San Antonio River. The area, home to some of the city's historic colonial missions and aging mobile home parks, had been long forgotten by the city council. But in 2014, this portion of the river became the site of a multi-million-dollar taxpayer-funded revitalization project. The developers designed the apartments according to a "Mission theme" and named the development Mission Escondida, the "Hidden Mission."

Of course the hidden mission was really Mission Trails Mobile Home Park, which the San Antonio city council approved for closure to make way for this redevelopment. As outlined in the first chapters of this book, a century of planning and zoning law has codified the invisibility of mobile home parks into law. A century of local planning regulation has segregated mobile homes into nonresidential zones and isolated mobile home parks as a land use. Along with ordinances requiring the visual separation (walls, fences, landscaping) between parks and surrounding land uses, these regulations have made mobile home parks some of the most invisible communities in the United States. When urban growth occurs—as was the case in Jupiter, Alvin, and now San Antonio—the same zoning codes make mobile home parks some of the country's most vulnerable communities.

FROM SILVER SANDS TO MISSION TRAILS

Mission Trails, the parks in this book, and the mobile home parks currently closing across the country are a product of these overt policies and the socio-spatial stigma that undergirds them. The ground for the redevelopment of Mission Trails was laid in 2010 when San Antonio's Inner City Reinvestment Infill Policy identified large areas of the city for publicly subsidized redevelopment (Barajas 2017). The reinvestment map contained Mission Trails and many of the city's lowest-income neighborhoods. In 2012, the council approved a new Center City Housing Incentive Program (CCHIP) to encourage condo and apartment construction through grants, fee waivers, and a streamlined redevelopment process in areas of the central city seen as ripe for redevelopment. The developer that evicted the three hundred residents of Mission Trails is slated to receive some $1.8 million in CCHIP assistance to redevelop the community (Barajas 2017).

In 2014, as first news of the park redevelopment spread, I met with and interviewed residents of Mission Trails and the civil rights lawyer who represented them pro bono. I listened to hours of their recorded testimony in front of the San Antonio city council, then headed by Mayor Julian Castro who would announce his appointment as U.S. Secretary of Housing and Urban Development (HUD) the day after his council voted to close Mission Trails. From a different time and place, the challenges and concerns of Mission Trails residents echoed the challenges and concerns I had documented in Florida and Texas over the previous two years.

Then in May 2017, two years after the final resident left Mission Trails, the group Vecinos de Mission Trails published a report that picked up where I left off, interviewing residents during the eviction process and documenting the ongoing trauma that mass eviction produced. Underscoring the themes of this book, the report (Cortez et al. 2017) is aptly titled: "Making Displacement Visible: A Case Study Analysis of the 'Mission Trail of Tears.'" The thorough research project was designed and implemented by residents themselves in conjunction with local community activists who believe: "The people who went through displacement are the experts on displacement" (quoted in Barajas 2017). Their report is drawn from interviews with 51 (out of 106) Mission Trails households, accounting for 178 residents of about 300 residents, approximately half of those displaced, and some of the same households I interviewed in 2014.

The human toll of housing loss described in the preceding chapters and the "impacts" outlined in the Vecinos de Mission Trails report are painfully consistent. I conclude this book with the findings of these resident-researchers who documented the toll of eviction in their own community and who found, in a different time and place, a very similar set of concerns. Putting their findings in conversation with my own crystallizes the primary impacts of mobile home park closures. The residents of Mission Trails found, much the same as the residents in the parks where I lived and worked, that displacement and relocation had four primary impacts: (1) on housing security; (2) on health; (3) on economic security; and (4) on social well-being.

Housing Security

A cycle of housing insecurity is perhaps the greatest social cost of eviction. Evictions were not one-time events and often resulted in multiple moves. Residents in both Florida and Texas transitioned to lower-quality and often risky housing situations in the wake of park closures. For Silver Sands residents Lois and Stephen this meant abandoning their mobile home and squatting in their old foreclosed and condemned home, where the walls were infested with bees. For Trail's End resident Hilda it meant moving her mobile home onto an undeveloped lot that lacked electricity and running water. For Randall it meant years of sleeping behind the day labor agency where he worked. All viewed their situations as temporary until they could access more stable shelter. Similarly, in Mission Trails more than two of five households interviewed had moved more than once at the time of the study.

One reason for these multiple moves is the shortage of quality affordable housing. The Vecinos de Mission Trails report found that although "many may have ended up in another mobile home park or an apartment or a house, they often did not move directly there. Often there were several moves or a period of homelessness before they located more permanent housing" (Cortez et al. 2017: 43). For mobile home residents, eviction is complicated by the need to also move the home, which quickly becomes a major liability rather than a primary asset. In Mission Trails 51.4 percent of residents were able to keep and live in their homes after the eviction (ibid., 46). In the parks where I lived, about two thirds of residents were able to relocate their homes. The roughly one third of residents forced to abandon their homes in Texas and Florida fought and sometimes failed to find other forms of housing they could afford.

The cycle of housing insecurity also diminished the *housing quality* of residents who were able to keep their homes. After relocation, residents most often greeted me by providing a tour of the damage wrought by relocation, which included uneven leveling of the home; cracked doors, walls, and floors; broken windows; and issues with plumbing, electrical, wiring, and/or siding. The Vecinos de Mission Trails report revealed that 56.7 percent of households encountered these same issues (ibid., 50). The costs of eviction followed low-income residents into new parks, where they paid out of pocket to fix damage and return homes to their pre-relocation condition.

Health

The impact of insecure housing extends beyond shelter and shapes the mental and physical health of residents during and after the eviction period. Residents in this study expressed this in their experiences of depression, anxiety, insomnia, panic attacks, and feeling—as Christy put it—like "a basket case." Residents documented these health impacts by monitoring and relaying to me their increases in blood pressure, migraines, use of narcotics, and hospitalizations. Ultimately the health impacts of housing insecurity took the most damaging form in prolonged illnesses, strokes, and even deaths of residents in this study. The Vecinos de Mission Trails report also found that in the two years after their eviction, 3 out of 5 residents experienced impacts on mental health (most frequently depression, anxiety, and "psychosomatic pain"); 1 out of 3 residents experienced a worsening of chronic conditions (most often diabetes and hypertension); 1 in 5 residents experienced life-threatening health impacts requiring hospitalization (most often complications from diabetes and stroke); and three residents died in the post-eviction period (one committed suicide) (Cortez et al. 2017: 60).

Housing insecurity also affected residents' ability to address the negative health consequences of eviction. In both Florida and Texas health providers were farther away or residents were required to change health providers because the nature of mobile home park closures forced them to move outside the county where they had lived. This was especially complicated for the many residents who relied on Medicare and Medicaid, plans that require the primary care doctor be within a person's county of residence.

Economic Security

Housing insecurity is not only socially but also financially costly, especially for already low-income residents. The main financial costs associated with mobile home park evictions were the increased cost of new housing and the out-of-pocket expenses during the move. The soaring cost of rental housing as well as the cultural value residents attached to single-family homeownership (as Lupe said, "We're not apartment people") meant that most residents—even those who could not move their home—found housing in other mobile home parks, even if this meant purchasing second- and third-hand mobile homes. These new parks, while affordable compared to rental apartments in both states, charged lot rates much higher than the grandfathered rents residents had paid in parks where many had lived for years and even decades. In Lakeshore parks, former Silver Sands residents saw their rent double and even triple. Residents' relocation from one land-lease park to another and the additional costs of living in these parks ensured a cycle of both housing and economic insecurity for already low-income and housing burdened residents. The Vecinos de Mission Trails report found that before eviction 52.4 percent of residents surveyed were housing cost burdened (paying more than 30 percent of their monthly income for housing), while after eviction 71.4 percent of residents were housing cost burdened.

This additional housing burden occurred alongside depleted savings and increased debt incurred to pay for out-of-pocket expenses during the relocation and increased housing and transportation costs after the move. In absence of state aid in Texas, the cost of relocation depleted residents' entire savings, forced them to take on debt, and required that they suspend remittances to family in other countries. The cost of mobile home relocation is so expensive that even in Florida where the state provides some financial assistance ($3,000 for a singlewide) residents still spent thousands of dollars out of pocket. These costs included: the cost of motel stays, new park / apartment deposits, utilities reconnections, food during the move, restocking the home once residents returned, and the expense of repairing damage and reinstalling lost parts of the home.

Residents were eager to make some of these repairs, things like replacing lost porches and wheelchair ramps. Others were required by the bylaws of the parks where they moved, things like replacing skirting and making aesthetic upgrades. Residents of Mission Trails (unlike residents of Texas parks in this study) did receive relocation assistance due to a deal struck with the developer and the San Antonio city council (the developer provided $7,200 in relocation assistance). However 91.3 percent (42 out of 46 relocating households) stated that the relocation assistance they received was not sufficient and they incurred out-of-pocket costs averaging $4,250 for all households surveyed.

Social Impacts

Because of the unique source of owner-occupied affordable housing that mobile home parks provide, they are exceptional spaces where multiple generations of the same family can find units together, as many intergenerational families in this study did. The affordable housing crunch has made this kind of multigenerational housing rare; it is hard enough to find an affordable unit for one household let alone multiple households of the same family. Yet mobile home parks provide a space for multiple and intergenerational households of the same family to not only find affordable housing, but purchase and occupy homes only feet or streets away from each other. Mobile home park evictions dismantled these spatial kin arrangements and forced families to find available lots wherever they could. In both Florida and Texas this resulted in families that had lived feet away from each other now living counties away. For the many households that had family members living in their park (especially the case in Texas) this was the bitterest consequence of the eviction.

Yet parks provided robust networks of social support even for those who did not have family living in the park. The spatial segregation and isolation of parks that is codified in local planning ordinances creates internal community cohesion. The economic and racial homogeneity of these communities (and the age restrictions in Florida's seniors-only parks) has been shown to create additional community cohesiveness (Kusenbach 2009). In these parks, neighbors relied on neighbors, which I witnessed day after day as the evictions unfolded. Neighbors offered and received support in countless ways, small and large, from moving a heavy box to visiting in the emergency room. These vital networks of social support are dismantled during eviction; the Vecinos de Mission Trails report found that three in four households (76.0 percent) experienced disruptions to friendships, social networks, and sense of community. Echoing the words of Kathleen that opened this book ("I'm not happy . . . I don't know anybody. Down there everybody knew everybody"), one Mission Trails resident reported the feeling that "Everyone that we knew [was] now scattered everywhere" (Cortez et al. 2017: 83).

THE INDIVIDUAL COSTS OF COLLECTIVE INDIGNATION

Beyond these quantifiable social, financial, and health effects, mobile home evictions demonstrate that housing, when it is secure, is a powerful locus of social stability. When housing is insecure, it is a site of deep and pervasive vulnerability. The loss of home and community must be understood in terms of the emotional and psychological impact that housing insecurity has on residents' sense of dignity and place in their broader communities. The collective stories documented here argue for bringing emotions back into the study of place, and especially of displacement. Understanding the "emotional ecosystem" of home (Fullilove 2004) not only helps us better understand the effects of housing insecurity, but might also expand the sociological study of other inequalities, such as health disparities as they relate to place.

For mobile home residents in this study, eviction was experienced through a framework of indignation over the loss of home, community, and one's place in the world. Residents lost their sense of themselves as homeowners and, due to an "American paradigm of propertied citizenship" that equates personhood with property rights (Roy 2003), they also lost their place as full citizens. The understandings—that "we're not for sure wherever we are" in the words of Lupe, that "the city doesn't care about us" in the words of Mr. Castillo, that "we are just passing by" in the words of Josefina, that "I come to find out I ain't nothing" in the words of Walter, that "we are trailer trash to them" in the words of Sammy—reveal how mobile home residents' personal sense of marginality and disposability is tied to a community identity that is actively zoned out and swept away in the interest of urban progress. This is why residents experienced their eviction as a deep and "unsettling" collective indignation.

Years after I had concluded this fieldwork and as I wrote this book's final chapter, the Vecinos de Mission Trails released their report and, in their own words, came to a strikingly similar conclusion:

> Another "biggest impact" frequently expressed by residents (10.4% of households or 5/48) . . . was the realization that "none of us mattered to any of the people on the council . . . even people crying, babies." While this was closely related to feelings of betrayal by the city [1 in 5 households said the biggest impact was feeling betrayed or not listened to by city leaders], it rent a deeper and more intimate wound . . . This brings us, then, to the realm of the unquantifiable and irretrievable—what we would call the "intimate impacts" of trauma. Beyond mental health, these were the subtle, hidden, and deeply internal effects of displacement on residents' sense of identity, dignity, self-worth, and core feelings of stability and security. (Cortez et al. 2017: 90)

These resident-researchers had uncovered the same effect of housing insecurity that I had. Although we named it differently, at its core, the outcome was the same: a diminished sense of one's own dignity and full personhood.

Then once again in the summer of 2017, I was called back into a closing park, this time in Denver, Colorado. Residents asked me to accompany them as they sat down with their city mayor to express their concerns over the upcoming closure of their 350-resident mobile home park, Denver Meadows. The practical problems they presented were the same as those I have outlined, as was the emotional toll. Catalina, a Mexican immigrant and mother of three, looked steadfastly at her mayor as she spoke through a translator and said: "We are not asking you for anything but our *dignity*. My children, they are citizens of this country. They think they have a *right* to their home. That is all we ask, for *a dignified home.*"

The words of Kathleen that opened this book are echoed in the words of the Vecinos de Mission Trails and in the words of Catalina. They articulate the human toll of housing instability.

MANUFACTURED INSECURITY

Mobile homes provide the largest source of unsubsidized affordable housing in the United States (CFED 2016). The ubiquity of the mobile home park in the American landscape and the insecurity of life for residents living there begs a fundamental question: How have we allowed one of the country's largest sources of affordable housing to also be one of the most risky?

The answer lies in the interrelation of poverty and profit that has been shown to structure eviction at the neighborhood level (Desmond 2016). From the trade in residents and homes during moments of mass eviction to the financial transactions occurring within various corners of the mobile home park empire, markets have arisen to extract profit from poverty. In times of heightened income inequality and shrinking social supports, poverty is touted as an ever-growing asset class and entire industries have arisen to capitalize on a growing population of low-income residents.

Mobile home parks are a prototypical example of why the four-decades-long shift to the private provision of affordable housing "works" for investors who can claim it "works" for residents, since residents are able to access shelter they otherwise could not afford. Yet the outcome is a system in which housing insecurity becomes a primary feature of housing affordability. Mobile home parks are an evocative site to explore the production and consequences of housing insecurity because the risk is rooted in the very land where residents live. Yet chronic insecurities arising from the private-market provision of affordable housing have been shown to be central in the rental housing market as well (Desmond 2016). Thus the lessons learned in mobile home parks can guide broader approaches to addressing affordable housing needs and providing low-income housing security.

While the problem of mobile home park eviction encapsulates the crisis of affordability and insecurity in the U.S. housing stock, the problems in parks are not born only of this contemporary affordable housing crisis. Mobile home park evictions cannot be uncoupled from over a century of socio-spatial isolation and stigmatization that contributes to the housing insecurity of mobile home park residents. As the opening chapters of this book show, the historic placement of mobile home parks in nonresidential areas, as well as the historic regulatory treatment of mobile home parks which have been effectively "zoned-out" (Levine 2006) of urban civic life, creates spatial stigma that ossifies the social stigma of "trailer trash." The president of Prosperity Now, a leading nonprofit working for manufactured housing reform, calls the stigma against mobile home residents "the last acceptable prejudice in America" (cited in Vick 2017).

For housing advocates, and for social scientists and legal scholars as well, the mobile home park demonstrates that how we regulate translates into how we perceive. The "last acceptable prejudice in America" is undergirded by a century of spatial othering born of regulations that exclude parks from residential areas while requiring that even the sight of parks be visually screened from view. This spatial relegation contributes to the removal of "trailer trash" from the moral universe of those who do not live in mobile homes. "Out of sight, out of mind" or, as Bourdieu et al. (1999) contend, recognition is central to the production of power. The denial of recognition to certain social groups is essential to "othering" and subordination through stereotype (Fraser and Honneth 2003). Parks serve as a reminder of the important, though often ignored, *spatial qualities* of (mis)recognition, which Bourdieu et al. (1999: 102–5) originally highlighted by examining how material resources are withheld to certain persons *because of their address.*

Understanding the spatial roots of social stigma is important not only sociologically but practically. Interrogating how spatial relegation reinforces stigmatization can help to dispel some of the cultural mythmaking that has manufactured the derided image of the mobile home park. Addressing social stigma necessitates combatting the spatial invisibility that has long shrouded these communities. Much of this work can be done on the part of localities to bring mobile home parks into the fabric of cities and towns by removing historic ordinances and regulations that prohibit or restrict mobile homes. The inequities found in mobile home parks also serve as a call for social scientists to study the technologies of governance—regulations, ordinances, land use codes, city plans—that serve to legitimize, naturalize, and inscribe social stigma into physical space.

Regulations might also be used to address the negative impacts of invisibility, especially through the systematic collection of data. This is vital in mobile home parks where invisibility contributes to stigma and where a substantial undocumented population is likely at risk of displacement. Requiring the collection of data at the local and national levels can serve as one form of official recognition and can help to document the extent and nature of this problem. To this end, Doug Ryan of the nonprofit Prosperity Now has argued: "HUD should require that jurisdictions, as part of their comprehensive planning process for CDBG, HOME and other federal funds, track the closure and redevelopment of, as well as the resident evictions from, manufactured and mobile home communities. Why? These actions directly impact a community's ability to preserve affordable housing, which, in the age of declining federal support, is the most tangible affordable housing strategy many communities have" (cited in Denvir 2015). Beyond providing an inventory of the existing mobile home stock and tracking the communities lost through closure, more systematic data collection on mobile home communities would help to identify means of assisting residents during the mass evictions that occur when mobile home parks close. As the cases recounted in this book show, this assistance is necessary to disrupt the cycle of housing instability that follows eviction.

The traumatic upheavals that occurred in Twin Oaks, Trail's End, Silver Sands, and the other parks in this book demonstrate that displacement is not a bounded moment, but rather a long and complicated experience of becoming evicted. As chapters 3 and 4 explored, the threat of eviction shaped residents' lives well outside the eviction process. Eviction operates as a specter of dislocation in the lives of the housing insecure and shapes a broader subjectivity of insecurity, the feeling that "We're not for sure wherever we are."

Although mobile home park residents grapple with a unique form of housing insecurity, their deeply felt loss of home and community is not unique. The same loss has been described in cases of urban renewal (Gans 1962; Fried 1966; Fullilove 2005), gentrification (Goetz 2011), and natural disaster (Erikson 1976; Adams 2012). In various ways, these studies all describe the psychic trauma caused by displacement. As Desmond (2016: 296) summarizes: "Residential stability begets a kind of psychological stability, which allows people to invest in their home and social relationships. It begets school stability, which increases the chances that children will excel and graduate. And it begets community stability, which encourages neighbors to form strong bonds and take care of their block. But poor families enjoy little of that because they are evicted at such high rates." As the experiences of mobile home park residents show, housing insecurity not only shapes processes (eviction) but also persons (the dispossessed). It does so in ways that haunt residents before eviction unfolds and long after it is complete.

Those living under the specter of dislocation might include a growing number of Americans as housing costs soar and incomes remain stagnant. The problems found in mobile home parks, though they uniquely impact lower-income *homeowners* who make up about 80 percent of mobile home park residents, are tied to the *rental* affordability crisis in the United States. These are two sides of the same coin, as Kathleen found when she discovered there was no way to leave the mobile home park where she paid $200 a month and secure a rental two-bedroom apartment in South Florida at the going rate of $1,200.

Kathleen's predicament is reflected in stories of evicted mobile home residents across the country. In Shady Brook Mobile Home Park, Central Washington University students and faculty worked with their university museum to record the stories from just one closing park. There a resident identified only as a Latino man asked:

> I have lived in Shady Brook since 2001, in four trailers in that place. In 2009 I had the opportunity to buy the trailer where I live now. I had to make the repay on the loan, and pay rent for the lot. We can't buy a $250,000 home. I believe that you all have houses and your children sleep peacefully and you sleep well, but when I get home my children ask, where are we going? Will we be sleeping under a bridge? We pay 325 dollars per lot rent. Looking online I see that to the equivalent house we'd have to pay $1200 to $1800. Where will I get that money from? Would I take away clothing and food from my children?

This man's story, echoed by so many others in this book, illustrates the interrelation between the affordable rental crisis and the eviction epidemic found in mobile home parks. In the center of this crisis, mobile homes provide a shelter safety net for those like Chip who asked, "Where else can you go in Florida? Here the rent is cheap."

The choices residents make to live in land-lease mobile home parks, where they face the risk of eviction and the limited housing options they have when they are displaced from these parks, should be understood as an outcome of a broader affordable housing crisis in the United States. Currently, there is no state in the nation where someone working full time at the federal minimum wage can afford a fair market one-bedroom rental unit.[1] Meanwhile, more than 9.9 million extremely low-income renter households, 5 million very low-income renter households, 4.2 million low-income renter households, and 900,000 middle-income renter households are cost-burdened (paying more that 30 percent of their income in housing costs) (Aurand et al. 2017).[2]

Because the issue of eviction in mobile home parks cannot be separated from issues of overall affordable housing scarcity in the United States, this concluding chapter applies the lessons learned in the mobile home park to the challenges posed by the affordability crisis. Sociologists have established the wide range of negative impacts associated with residential relocation. Moving is associated with poor academic achievement (Pribesh and Downey 1999) and dropping out for children (Coleman 1988). It is associated with lower-earning jobs (Hagan, MacMillan, and Wheaton 1996), violence (Haynie and South 2005), drug and alcohol abuse (Hoffman and Johnson 1998), emotional and behavioral problems (Tucker, Marx, and Long 1998), and low self-esteem (Gutman and Midgley 2000) for adolescents. And finally, residential relocation is associated with personal and marital stress, family violence, alcohol abuse, and increased incidence of illness (Sluzki 1992) for adults.

Based on what we know about the millions of Americans who are severely housing burdened, we must recognize that beyond bounded moments of relocation, housing insecurity likely operates as a haunting in the lives of many lower-income Americans. The specter of dislocation likely shapes many different facets of their lives, from how they plan for the future, to how they view their children's education, to how they take care of pressing issues like health and other concerns. The experience of mobile home park residents highlights the toll the threat of eviction has on individuals and whole communities and drives home the importance of addressing housing insecurity well before this threat becomes a reality.

LESSONS FROM THE MOBILE HOME PARK

The mobile home park offers a dramatic and singular example of housing insecurity, but one that sheds light on the broader state of housing (in)stability in the United States. Mobile home park closures offer lessons *for* mobile home parks specifically but also lessons *from* mobile home parks, which might inform equitable approaches to housing more generally.

Lessons for Parks

In addition to the sociological insights outlined above, the practical and policy lessons learned during mobile home park relocations highlight the importance of autonomy, rapidity, and simplicity for minimizing the trauma of eviction. Policy prescriptions for closing parks should be directed toward the following goals to improve the relocation process for evicted mobile home park residents:

Increasing transparency around park residents' rights would affirm residents' stake in their own communities and lessen the feeling that they live "at the whim of property owners" (Consumers Union 2001a: 1). Residents sought, but most frequently did not find, help in understanding their rights when a park closure was on the horizon. Even in parks where an eviction was not actively occurring, residents were often unclear about how (or if) they could address issues such as: lack of maintenance, rent increases, arbitrary fees, and unanticipated rule changes, all of which are commonly reported in mobile home parks. The Washington State Legislature found that "many tenants who experienced violations of [Washington's] manufactured / mobile home landlord-tenant act were often left without protections or access to legal remedies."[3] To address residents' lack of clarity about their rights, in 2007 Washington instituted an Alternative Dispute Resolution Program (RCW 59.30) through the state attorney general's office. The program is funded by a simple $10 per lot annual fee paid by the park owner, who can collect $5 from each resident. The program generates about $750,000 a year, which allows the AG's office to provide advice, dispute resolution, investigation, and compliance measures for all cases, which can easily be reported via the AG's website or by mail.[4]

Establishing a minimum six-month eviction notice and directing residents to state-managed relocation support should be a primary focus of regulation in states where such laws do not exist. Many states simply lack provisions regarding eviction notice periods or notices for a change of land use (Carter et al. 2004). Evictions in these states can take place with as little as 30 days' notice (Jewell 2001), an impossibly short eviction period given the complicated relocation process these evictions entail. Yet, as I found in Texas, even in states with slightly longer notice policies, lack of oversight from regulatory agencies may preclude residents from exercising their legal rights. Texas had no regulatory system to enforce its minimum 60-day notice policy, and in practice residents were evicted with only 30 days' notice. Both enforcing and extending state eviction notice policies will benefit park residents across the United States.

Yet the comparative case of Florida highlights how a longer notice period and protective regulations alone may not mitigate (and indeed may aggravate) the trauma of eviction. Under Florida's market-oriented relocation policy, the state's voucherized relocation assistance supported a market where mobile home movers and receiving parks generated significant profit, but their actions disoriented and disempowered residents. This does not mean that state regulation alone produces negative effects, or that the laissez-faire approach of states like Texas is preferable. Rather, it demonstrates that the structure of state regulation is key. State regulation of mobile home park closures has been highly effective in states such as Oregon, which passed legislation requiring a 365-day eviction notice and relocation fees of $5,000, $7,000, or $9,000 (for an abandoned home, a singlewide, and a doublewide, respectively) paid *directly* to tenants. Most importantly, Oregon laws set up a statewide mobile home park resource center that provides "confidential and neutral" technical assistance, dispute resolution, training, and park closure assistance (Oregon.gov 2017). In addition to publications, a website, a hotline, and a directory of operating parks, Oregon's resource center administers one-on-one counseling for tenants to discuss laws and rights around park closures and provides referrals for tenants' relocation needs. Similar policies would help meet residents' primary request during the eviction process, to better understand (and trust) what was happening to their homes.

Implementing a mandatory and streamlined inspections process is another key area of policy intervention. The cursory inspection process in Texas resulted in structural damage and faulty installations, creating future consequences and costs for residents. The lengthy inspection process in Florida (due to movers' profit-driven practice of bundling inspections for multiple homes) greatly extended residents' dislocation. Furthermore, Florida's lengthy process did not ensure high-quality installations. Residents in both states frequently reported structural issues in their homes after relocation, although homes in Florida did fare better than those in Texas, where serious structural damage was more common. Proper installation is essential to the continued life of a mobile home (Apgar et al. 2002). Thus, future regulations should be geared toward strengthening the inspection process for mobile home reinstallation while also streamlining it by requiring timely post-move inspections so that residents can begin to resettle in their homes.

Regulating the marketplace in mobile home relocation aid is a key final area of policy intervention. Florida's relocation assistance relied heavily on public-private partnerships to convey state-mandated protections. Florida's relocation policy is an example of contemporary adaptations of neoliberal governance in which public-private partnerships arise as the state buttresses the functioning of private markets (Greenhouse 2009; Peck and Tickell 2012). Under these models, the needs of citizens in crisis grease the wheels of the markets providing relief, repositioning the needy as sites for the production of capital (Klein 2007; Adams 2012). Despite Florida's expressed intent of providing state assistance to displaced residents, the state's market-oriented delivery of relocation aid produced devastating effects. The profit-driven timelines of companies that capitalized on the eviction in Silver Sands greatly extended the eviction process.

The public-private partnerships organized to deliver relocation aid in Silver Sands are indicative of broader shifts in Florida's poverty management programs, which has led some to identify Florida as "a national leader in the pursuit of neoliberal reforms" (Soss, Fording, and Schram 2012). Thus, understanding how the private-market administration of state-funded assistance extended the trauma of eviction in Silver Sands is important not only for mobile home parks. These findings have implications for a range of other reinvented social service programs, from education to health care, that are currently being delivered with an increasing and adaptive reliance on the private sector. Neoliberal restructuring in the administration of state aid not only produces "new commitments" (Somers 2008) between the state and private actors, but also new market opportunities and new profits to be wrung out of social insecurity (Klein 2007). These arrangements produce second-order confusion and duress for individuals attempting to access relief from first-order disasters (Adams 2012).

In Florida, these arrangements mean private companies augmented state funds to cover the full cost of relocation and formed a new marketplace of relocation services. As the major players in these markets, companies like Max Movers dictated the terms and timing of residents' moves. The comparative case of Texas, where residents contracted their choice of mover and were able to enter their homes the same week they were relocated, demonstrates that these residents experienced a more satisfactory move. The implication for policy is clear: states should avoid public-private partnerships and ensure direct state assistance in proportion to the actual cost of relocation. This would increase transparency within the marketplace of mobile home relocation services and lessen the power of private actors who administer state aid.

However, the most powerful policy prescription in mobile home parks would target the source of residents' insecure housing tenure rather than its consequence—eviction. Doing so would require remediating mobile homeowners' halfway homeownership while maintaining the affordability provided by park arrangements. Policies that focus only on relocating residents from private park to private park facilitate the mobile home marketplace and fortify the market-oriented underpinnings of current affordable housing policy.

Targeting the roots of mobile home residents' housing insecurity requires imagining new forms of land tenure that move away from the hegemonic model of private property ownership. Collective land ownership can be promoted through alternative land holdings, such as cooperative parks, community land trusts, or public ownership. The mobile home park is an excellent place to test such models, as has been demonstrated in over two hundred parks across the United States where nonprofit groups have assisted residents in securing loans to purchase the land under their homes so they can collectively own and manage their communities.

National nonprofit groups like ROC (Resident Owned Communities) USA work with residents to secure loans that allow them to purchase their parks and convert them to collective ownership, thus guaranteeing the land cannot be sold out from under them. Here again, state law is key. Some states mandate a resident right of first refusal so that residents have the opportunity to organize and secure funding to purchase the property in the event their park is offered for sale. Other states have proposed alternative models, such as amending their state tax codes to provide park owners with tax incentives to sell to residents rather than developers.[5]

Whatever the route to getting there, resident ownership of parks has proven to have a stabilizing effect. Converting parks to resident ownership has not only been effective in the *product* (park properties stabilized through cooperative long-term ownership of the land) but also in the *process*. Residents describe how the very process of converting their park into resident ownership is empowering. For instance, a resident in a Minnesota ROC USA park described feeling "very scared" before the process began. Another resident worried, "We're common folk, where are we gonna come up with $4.3 million [to purchase the park]?" After receiving loan counseling, forming a co-op, undergoing training to manage finances, and learning Robert's Rules of Order to manage park projects, residents no longer approached collaborative park management with fear; instead they felt empowered: "Everybody has a voice, you own a little piece of where you live."[6] Converting private poverty housing models like mobile home parks to collective affordable housing through cooperative ownership is just one example of how attention to community-wide process can mediate the haunting of housing insecurity while answering Ana's request: "We want a dignified home."

Lessons from *Parks*

Ultimately, the eviction and deeply felt dislocation of the residents described here calls for more than mere policy prescriptions. It calls for a better understanding of the central role of housing in the production of well-being and the reproduction of inequalities. It calls for a response to the question that opened this chapter: how can we tolerate the extreme level of housing risk that has become an intractable component of housing affordability? Alternatively, how can we create solutions that promote both housing security and housing affordability?

Doing so first means *extending access*, by increasing investment in the production of affordable housing and investing more in programs designed to assist low-income residents nationwide. A brutal irony at the heart of the affordable housing crisis is that the majority of U.S. housing subsidy is actually directed toward high-income households. The cultural value placed on the American Dream has led to tax policies that create and sustain massive housing inequalities. Currently, higher-income homeowners receive a significantly greater share of federal housing expenditures through the mortgage interest deduction (MID), the program that allows homeowners to subtract the interest paid on their mortgage from their federal taxable income if they itemize their deductions rather than claim the standard deduction (Fischer and Sard 2016).

The MID has long been seen as a primary mechanism for encouraging homeownership in the United States. However, half of all homeowners with mortgages—mostly middle- and lower-income households—receive no benefit from the deduction (Fischer and Huang 2013). It mainly benefits the wealthiest homeowners, the one third of tax filers who itemize their deductions (most low- and middle-income households do not itemize and instead take the standard deduction).[7] The MID is a federal tax expenditure of more than $65 billion per year, 84 percent of which goes to households with annual income greater than $100,000 (Joint Committee on Taxation 2017). By comparison, less than $38 billion was spent on the entire budget of HUD and housing programs for low-income households in 2014 (Fischer and Sard 2016).[8]

For decades, housing scholars have pushed for reforming this single program to fund expanding access to affordable housing. Housing groups have calculated that small changes in the MID would free up $213 billion over the next 10 years that could be used to develop new programs that would provide real benefits at multiple income levels (National Low Income Housing Coalition 2016). On the production side of the affordable housing crisis, reforms to the MID program cannot be overstated. Revenue from reforming the MID could be used to extend housing vouchers, develop and rehabilitate public housing, and support the newly created national Housing Trust Fund.

Yet the problem with many proposed solutions to the affordable housing crisis is one of focus as much as finance. Existing solutions primarily target the supply side of the affordable housing crisis, focusing on *production* and ignoring the vital importance of *preservation*. To truly address our current affordable housing crisis, we must look beyond the production of affordable housing to address the preservation of the existing affordable housing stock. We simply cannot build our way out of the affordable housing crisis. We must preserve the affordable housing we already have. And we must recognize that a large portion of this housing exists in places like mobile home parks.

Here again, the mobile home park can offer some solutions. The adaptable history of the mobile home over the last century, the techno-social modularity outlined in chapter 1, has proven the housing model's ability to respond to changing social needs. Contemporary cooperative parks offer a model of affordability *and* preservation by unsettling the hegemonic paradigm of private property ownership. The collective land ownership that is being tried in resident-owned mobile home parks is just one incarnation of collective property ownership that dates back to Neolithic villages and Native American cultures. Collective land ownership models have been used to preserve other forms of affordable housing, including rental housing, by stabilizing land values, the primary source of rising housing costs. Affordable rental and owner-occupied housing is most often lost as land values rise. Other forms of collective ownership in the form of community land trusts (CLTs) have proven effective in stabilizing site-built rental and owner-occupied housing by removing rising land values from the equation. In a CLT, land (often bundles of properties) is owned by a nonprofit community organization, the land trust. Individual homes are rented or owned through lifetime or 99-year leases on the land. Similarly to resident-owned mobile home parks, residents own the structure while the land is owned by a larger entity (the public or nonprofit trust). Like resident-owned parks, the model promotes stability and permanent affordability because land ownership is nonspeculative (Stone 2006). The land trust is committed to permanent affordability and allows residents to own or rent a structure on the property and even sell or pass on the unit to kin. Through the nonspeculative transfer of land the CLT can offer permanent affordable homeownership or stabilize the existing affordable rental stock in cities and regions.

Resident-owned mobile home parks and community land trusts are just two possible models of alternative land tenure. But both show that affordability and stability is possible if we break from hegemonic understandings of property and envision new, collective ownership models. Giving equal weight to affordability and stability is crucial because, as the stories of residents recounted in this book demonstrate, there are far-reaching consequences of housing insecurity. The trajectories of evicted mobile home park residents reveal how housing insecurity drains resident's wealth, negatively impacts their physical and mental health, and shatters the systems of community support that provide a vital safety net for those with fewer other resources. These residents' stories are first and foremost a call for a better understanding of housing's role in generating broader inequalities. Housing can be a powerful site of stability, while housing insecurity generates widespread social ills.

The far-reaching effects of housing insecurity argue for equally far-reaching solutions. While individual policy approaches should be multifaceted in order to address a crisis that is equally complex, there is one solution that is far simpler: the recognition of housing as a basic human right. The United Nations affirms a human right to shelter in its Universal Declaration of Human Rights and most developed nations recognize (and have policies that support) housing as a human right. Yet, the United States is the only developed nation in the world that does not guarantee a human right to housing (Bratt, Stone, and Hartman 2006). The implications for our housing policy are immense.

Recognizing housing as a human right would restructure our social and political understanding of housing insecurity. This would require enacting legislation and shifting budgetary priorities, which in recent years has seemed like an insurmountable task. But over the last century, the United States has made analogous legislative shifts to ensure fundamental human rights as the needs of society have evolved. As late as 1990 we ensured the basic right for all people, including those with a disability, to enter a standard doorway and into a home. The housing measures within the Americans with Disabilities Act codify that right into law. As a result of this paradigm shift, we reshaped both our built environment and our understanding of that environment. Today a wheelchair ramp and a widened doorway are part of our common building vernacular.

Affirming that housing is a human right would be a paradigm shift in addressing the affordable housing crisis and would create the political will to institute some of the policy approaches listed above. That kind of paradigm shift in how we view housing might even allow us to imagine new forms of land tenure that stabilize residents' rights to their home. In the end, mobile home parks not only show us the value of housing stability for individuals and broader regions; they also show us that we can envision more than one way to grow our housing stock and preserve existing communities.

Methodological Appendix

I never set out to study mobile homes or the destruction of mobile home communities. Like many Americans, I thought the mobile home occupied some niche sector of U.S. housing: an artifact from a former heyday, an architectural oddity, a collector's item to some, a backwoods shelter for the most desperate. Despite my primary research interest in poverty housing, I was unaware that manufactured housing provides the single largest unsubsidized source of affordable housing in the United States. I never knew that 18 million Americans lived in mobile homes.

My interest in manufactured housing began when I literally stumbled upon the skeleton of a mobile home park where hundreds of homes had been removed and hundreds of households evicted. That discovery, one day in 2010, happened as I was in the field on a different project focused on low-income communities in the exurbs of Texas metropolitan areas. The principal investigator on that project had noticed a nearby mobile home park and lauded it as an alternate form of low-income housing in the same area. We were surveying low-income, self-built housing nearby, documenting serious structural and infrastructural problems in this housing stock. In contrast he described the park, Deer Wood, as a "model" source of low-income housing, a bustling community on a well-maintained property complete with playgrounds, a recreation center, and a pool: The ideal of homeownership at a fraction of the cost. On a trip back from interviewing nearby, we stopped to see the community.

What we found shocked me and began the next five years of research that forms the heart of this book. Arriving at the gates of Deer Wood Mobile Home Park, I did not see a well-maintained, established community of affordable mobile homes, but rather a vast empty field enclosed within a low wall where the sign still read "Deer Wood, Slow Children at Play." The

FIGURE 17.   The utilities for homes stick out along an
abandoned street inside Deer Wood Mobile Home Park. Photo by
Esther Sullivan, 2010.

community center was there, the playground still visible, but there was not
a single home in sight. Where hundreds of mobile homes had once neatly
lined a series of streets, there was now only a massive expanse of tall grass
baking under the Texas sun.

I couldn't get the image of Deer Wood out of my mind. I returned to
photograph it, sneaking in between the bars of the large front gate that now
enclosed the empty field of grass. Inside, I saw for the first time what I
would later come to know as the telltale skeleton of an eviscerated mobile
home park. Throughout the sea of grass, PVC hookups, plumbing, electric,
and gas lines—all the guts of the homes that had been removed—stuck up
at regular intervals. The concrete foundations of former homes stood out
like wounds in the rustling landscape. In the open-air recreation center I
found and photographed residents' pinned-up ads to sell or dispose of their
homes, their handwritten notes and solicitations for information and help.
I wondered: Where did they go? What did they do? How did they accomplish this unforeseen exodus?

Discovering the shell of Deer Wood, standing amid acres of community
returned to grass, and reading the sunbaked and wind-beaten solicitations
of its former residents sparked my interest in the questions that make up
this book and began my own years of living in and being evicted from
mobile home parks to document the experiences of park residents and
answer these questions.

GETTING IN

In the months that followed, I tracked down the series of economic transactions that ended with the eviction of every resident of Deer Wood. A California housing development company bought the site to develop single-family homes. The mobile homes were cleared so that redevelopment could begin. State laws facilitated this redevelopment, allowing residents only 60 days' notice and providing no avenue for recourse or source of support. Over the next two years I began to document similar instances of park closures.

To study mobile home park closures, to answer the questions the empty fields at Deer Wood asked, I first needed to understand the scope of the problem. There is currently no systematic data on the frequency and location of mobile home park closures, meaning there is no documentation of the mass evictions these closures produce and no record of the countless individuals and families that are forced from their homes. I began to create a record using Geographic Information Systems (GIS) technology. Using GIS, I formulated a methodology to track and map individual parcels (lots) where park closures had occurred in the case study region of Houston and the surrounding Harris County (see Sullivan 2017b). I chose Harris County because the detail contained in parcel-level spatial data requires that geospatial analysis be conducted within a constrained boundary, such as a county. Harris County contains the largest share of manufactured housing in Texas, which is the state with the largest total number of mobile home residents. I tracked park closures over a decade in Harris County (2002–11) by spatially joining and then mapping parcel-level land use data for all 1.2 million individual parcels listed in the Harris County tax records. This methodology allowed me to locate and spatially analyze where mobile home parks were located and where they disappeared from the years 2002–11.

Some of the results of this analysis and accompanying maps are included in chapter 2. The full results and a detailed, step-by-step methodology (which can be replicated in any jurisdiction where county tax records are available) are published in Sullivan 2017b. For this reason, I do not enumerate those methodological steps here. Mapping the macro-level contours and socio-spatial patterns of where mobile home park closures occur was my first initiation into the scope of this problem. It also informed the selection of study sites (see below). But ultimately, geospatial mapping only generated more questions that macro-level analysis could not resolve.

The questions remained, about Deer Wood and the hundreds of other closing parks my work was turning up: Where do these residents go? How do they move both themselves and their homes? What are the costs and consequences? What does this tell us about the state of housing insecurity in the United States? I realized the only way to answer these questions was to explore the geography of displacement at the micro level, within closing parks and inside the homes of the displaced. I knew I needed to live in and be forced out of closing mobile home parks alongside evicted residents and to follow them in the wake of their eviction. But to do this I needed to find parks before they closed.

To locate potentially closing parks, I began by formally interviewing key players in the field of manufactured housing, including manufactured housing industry representatives, agency officials, mobile home park brokers (real estate agents that exclusively buy and sell mobile home parks), and mobile home park owners in four states (Florida, Texas, Colorado, and Michigan). I interviewed 11 of these key informants during this initial stage (although over the course of fieldwork I spoke with countless others). I identified key informants using a snowball sample. I conducted interviews over the phone and in person; most lasted 1 to 1.5 hours. I found these individuals surprisingly candid and happy to talk about their work. Many were amused that I was writing a book on this topic.

As most mobile home parks are never publicly listed for sale but are sold through private arrangements between buyers, brokers, and property owners, I used tips from this network of key informants to track unlisted mobile home park sales in Texas and Florida, the two states with the largest mobile home populations. I created lists of parks that were (a) offered for sale by the property owner with the knowledge of the residents, (b) beginning final sales negotiations with a buyer, and (c) if sold, soon to enter the legally defined period in which residents are given "Notice to Vacate" (this way residents would be aware of the upcoming eviction and I would not have information they did not). I used the geospatial analysis conducted in the first phase of the project to compare the spatial characteristics of For Sale park properties to the spatial characteristics of previously closed park properties and then made informed judgments about which parks were most likely to close. Using this method, I eventually selected sites that allowed me to establish myself within the community before eviction took place (five months before the eviction notice in Silver Sands, one month before the eviction notice in Twin Oaks and Trail's End).

This was easier said than done. In fact, this was the most arduous and frustrating period of the research—trying to find a place to move in. I contacted one mobile home park broker after another. I scoured online listings of For Sale mobile home parks. I asked industry representatives and manufactured housing advocates for tips. I contacted park after park. But even if

I found one with available rental housing that was up for sale, I was unsure if the seller would ever find a buyer and actually close the park. I worried I might lose months collecting data in a park where an eviction never occurred. At the same time I worried uncomfortably that the very parameters I needed to set to conduct this research rested on the certainty of eviction for entire communities. The following field note registers the frustration and uncertainty of this year-long period:

> Today I was feeling so defeated after spending all of yesterday (hours) on the phone calling for sale MHPs and leaving messages, not talking to anyone, not getting any calls back, finding no rental housing, and having the woman from the Seattle Manufactured Homeowners Association tell me I was "looking for a needle in a haystack."

Eventually I found a For Sale Florida park where residents had received a notice that their city council was considering an application to rezone the park. When I contacted the landlord he told me he was renting out a couple of mobile homes that he had "inherited" from owners who chose to abandon their home rather than continuing to pay rent to a landlord who was in the process of selling the park. I convinced him to rent one of these abandoned mobile homes to me on a month-to-month basis, saying I was in the area temporarily and would not need housing long term. He answered, "Good, we won't be here much longer." This is the park I call Silver Sands.

In May of 2012, I packed my car full of enough essentials to last me through an indeterminate eviction period and drove to Jupiter, Florida. Jupiter is a South Florida city of 55,000 residents located at the northernmost end of the coastal megalopolis that runs down to Fort Lauderdale and Miami. Markedly less diverse than the rest of this region, Jupiter is 83 percent non-Hispanic White, 12 percent Hispanic/Latino, and less than 2 percent Black. Silver Sands was initially opened in 1954 by James Silver and the property was owned and maintained by his son, Ron Silver, the man I spoke to on the phone.

Almost invariably, residents of Silver Sands called their community a lovely place to live, pointing out how well the homes and grounds were maintained and describing their proximity to many practical needs and recreational opportunities nearby. Indeed, Silver Sands was located only three miles inland from the beaches of the Atlantic Ocean, along which runs Jupiter Island, a barrier island with the second-highest per capita income of any inhabited place in the United States.[1] Silver Sands was a seniors 55 and older park. The 29-acre fenced-in property housed 130 residents along nine streets of about 100 mainly singlewide mobile homes that surrounded a large undeveloped green space. All but about five residents (including myself) in the park were over 55 years old and many were in their 70s and 80s (residents mused that Mr. Silver had gotten lax about the age requirement in recent years since he was selling the park). Although some residents still worked as housecleaners or handymen, most were retired, many were disabled, and some were completely homebound. Most lived on fixed incomes as low as $600 a month from Social Security and/or federal disability and described themselves similarly to Gary, a retired engineer, who said, "I'm kinda living on the edge now, from Social Security check to Social Security check." Almost all Silver Sands residents were white except for one Filipino couple and one Guatemalan couple (see Table 1).

I moved into Silver Sands five months before we received an eviction notice. I was an anomaly, a woman in her 30s living alone, one of very few residents under 55 years of age. But during this period, residents had received the notice that an application for a potential rezoning of the property would be considered by their city council, so it was a time when many things were changing in the park. Residents seemed to see me moving in as one of those changes. At the time I took up residence, they fully understood both the potential that Silver Sands would close and my reason for moving into the park.

During my 11 months living in Silver Sands, several other well-publicized park closures occurred in South Florida, which also helped to explain my presence in the park. By the time of my arrival, it was widely publicized that 11 Department of Corrections facilities were closing in the state, which meant that "staff housing" (mobile home parks that house correctional officers on prison grounds) were also closing and evicting residents. Four of these correctional facilities were within a 150-mile radius of Silver Sands and I traveled to them several times in my first months living there to interview relocating correctional officers. I did not have the space to include the experiences of the evicted corrections officers in this book, although their challenges with respect to moving were much the same as the other parks where I lived and worked.

During that same period, three other South Florida mobile home parks also began to close. I call these parks Sawgrass Estates, Sunny Acres, and Ocean Breeze.[2] I conducted days of ethnography and over two dozen formal interviews in these parks over the 11 months I lived at Silver Sands. While each of these parks is mentioned briefly in various chapters of this book, in the end the data from these parks is used primarily to compare and validate what I found in Silver Sands, Twin Oaks, and Trail's End. Because of my work in these seven surrounding closing Florida parks, my neighbors seemed to see me as a researcher investigating relocations throughout the

TABLE 1. Characteristics of Mobile Home Residents

Panel A. Characteristics of mobile home residents in United States, Texas, and Florida*

	National	Texas	Florida
Number of households	6,918,004	592,414	624,882
Located in urban area (%)	49.0	59.7	78.0
Race/ethnicity (%)			
Non-Hispanic White	77.4	58.6	83.8
Non-Hispanic Black	7.8	4.9	4.4
Hispanic	11.7	34.6	10.1
Age 55 or older (%)	41.4	34.3	59.0
Living alone (%)	29.6	21.8	33.6
Non-citizen (%)	6.6	16.5	7.2
Poverty (%)	22.6	23.7	19.8

Demographic characteristics for United States, Texas, and Florida are calculated for primary householder for the years 2007–2011. Urban/rural status for 13% of households could not be identified compared to 16% in Texas and 2% in Florida. *Source*: American Community Survey Public-Use Microdata 2007–2011 five-year sample (Ruggles et al. 2010).

*The American Community Survey and U.S. Census provide data for *all mobile homes*. Thus, the data they provide *do not distinguish* between mobile homes placed *on private land* and mobile homes placed *in mobile home parks*.

Panel B. Characteristics of mobile home residents in study sites**

	Silver Sands	Twin Oaks	Trail's End
Number of households (Total residents)	99 (130)	11 (29)	12 (32)
Singlewide	92	11	12
Doublewide	4	0	0
RV	3	0	0
Located in urban area (%)	100	100	100
Race/ethnicity (%)			
Non-Hispanic White	96.9	6.9	0
Non-Hispanic Black	0	0	0
Hispanic	1.5	93.1	100
Age 55 or older (%)	96.9	13.8	15.6
Living alone (%)	60.6	6.9	1.0

SOURCE: Author's elaboration based on interviews with residents in all parks combined with a survey of all lots conducted by one resident in Silver Sands for submission to the South Florida Legal Aid Society.

** No survey was conducted of the approximately 1,500 residents of Sawgrass Estates, which was located on reservation land of the Seminole Tribe of Florida where access was severely restricted due to the highly publicized eviction of its tenants.

area who had a keen interest in the fate of Silver Sands, rather than as someone living in the park, waiting to investigate their looming eviction.

During my 11 months living in Silver Sands I kept in touch with my network of mobile home park brokers and industry insiders. One alerted me—through an email that he asked me to keep strictly confidential—to a Texas town named Alvin that was slated to close 32 mobile home parks that were in violation of a newly instituted mobile home ordinance. During the course of a week in March 2013, I traveled from Jupiter to Alvin and interviewed residents and some landlords in each one of the 24 parks in violation of the city's new ordinance (others of the 32 originally listed had already made changes to get up to code and out of violation). Most residents were aware of the ordinance but had little information concerning the violations in their communities and were uncertain about the closure; my own observations and conversations with landlords convinced me that several parks on this list would be unable to complete the required renovations and would close and evict residents as a result.

By May 2013, I found a rental mobile home in one of the parks listed in violation of the new ordinance. On May 30, the last day of our tenancy at Silver Sands, 11 months after I moved in and six months after I received an eviction notice, I moved directly from Florida into my new home in Ramos y Ramos Mobile Home Park in Alvin, Texas. Ramos y Ramos was a much smaller park of 10 mobile homes, similar in size to other parks in Alvin. It was owned by brothers Bernie and Miguel Ramos. The park was all ages. Next door to me lived a single man, an immigrant from Mexico, who worked two jobs and was seldom home. On my other side lived a Mexican American family of four, their kids aged 6 and 2. Behind me lived a young Latino/a couple, a boyfriend and girlfriend in their early 20s.

Like Silver Sands, Ramos y Ramos was demonstrative of urban growth pressures that play a key role in mobile home park closures. The town of Alvin, Texas, was once surrounded by rice fields, but now sits at the edge of the large Houston-Woodlands–Sugar Land megalopolis. Located 30 miles outside the Houston city center and just inside the limits of adjacent Brazoria County, Alvin maintains a small-town feel. The town has a population of 24,000 and only one high school, whose athletic fields form the community's epicenter where crowds gather even for practice scrimmages of the high school football team. The lights of the games could be seen from my trailer on autumn Friday nights.

Yet Alvin, like Jupiter, is rapidly changing. The U.S. Census Bureau ranked Harris County as the fastest-growing county in the United States for both 2011 and 2012 and much of that growth occurred in the suburban metro area, which includes Alvin. Alvin itself grew between 2000 and 2010 by about 2,800 residents and 98% of that growth was due to an influx of 2,776 new Mexican American residents, bringing the total Hispanic / Latino population up from 28% to 36% of the total population (and the total Mexican American population up from 21% to 31%).

At the time I moved in to Ramos y Ramos, the park was still listed in violation of Alvin's Mobile Home Park Ordinance and slated to close. Eventually, a week before the code enforcement deadline my landlords, Bernie Ramos and his brother Miguel, completed all the required upgrades on our park and the park remained open, as did several of the other parks that were listed in violation. However, two parks located blocks from my own did close, Twin Oaks and Trail's End. Trail's End was a park of a dozen homes that faced each other across a center dead-end lane, the "Trail's End." Twin Oaks was a park developed around one city block, where 11 homes were lined along the perimeter of the block and the center space was left open and mainly unused. Both parks were very similar demographically to Ramos y Ramos; they were home to families, elderly households, and single working men. Residents in both parks were almost entirely Latino / a, primarily of Mexican descent (see Table 1).

My daily fieldwork included days and nights spent primarily in Twin Oaks and Trail's End and in the homes of residents once they relocated. My complete fieldwork in Texas included time spent inside all 24 parks at risk of closure as well as interviews with residents and landlords there. Notice periods are shorter in Texas, only 60 days. I lived in Ramos y Ramos from May to November 2013, before eviction notices were delivered in June, during the period in which residents scrambled to move by the town's July 15 deadline, and for four months afterward as they settled into their new homes.

Altogether, my ethnographic fieldwork consists of two years in closing parks and in residents' new communities. Of these two years, 17 intensive consecutive months were spent inside closing parks, where I lived in my own rented mobile home full time, 24 hours a day, seven days a week. Afterward, I kept in contact with residents through phone calls, texts, and letters and I conducted several follow-up visits in both states over the ensuing six months until June 2014.

BEING THERE

Anthropologist Clifford Geertz presents ethnography as a task of "being there," a task that poses the following challenge: "Finding somewhere to stand in a text that is supposed to be at one and the same time an intimate view and a cool assessment is almost as much of a challenge as gaining the view and making the assessment in the first place" (1988: 10). Geertz maintains that this is a task of authorship as much as fieldwork. He calls on ethnographers to replace the illusion of fieldwork as the sorting of "strange and irregular" field data into orderly categories with a written picture of "being there" (2–3). Being there is not gauged by the tally of months spent in the field, it is acknowledged through "explicit representations of authorial presence" (16), so I adopted Geertz's stance both in the park and on the page. At the same time, researching, historicizing, and writing about the deep stigma of trailer park life led me to hone a similar approach to other ethnographers of marginalized groups and to deliberately adopt an analytic stance that eschews voyeuristic ethnography (Hoang 2015). Thus I chose to place the words, experiences, and insights of park residents at the heart of the analysis and at the center of this book, while still including myself on the page to make my own interactions with residents visible. I have left deeper discussion of my experience living in and leaving from these parks to this appendix. I hope that I have struck this difficult balance.

Parks are spatially bound communities and a frequent refrain is that everybody knows everybody's business in the park. I found this to be true as residents came up to introduce themselves shortly after I arrived and then began to inform their neighbors that someone new had moved into the community. The potential closure of the parks was forefront in residents' minds and they often questioned me about my knowledge of the closure and my own plans for relocating, even immediately upon meeting me. This was a fortunate turn of fieldwork events, which allowed me to immediately establish who I was, why I was there, and to begin the conversation about the possibility of eviction.

In both Florida and Texas, I got to know park residents shortly after my arrival and those I met first often helped set up meetings and interviews with others I had not yet met. This was important in Florida where some residents were homebound due to age and disability, so it was impossible to meet them out in the park. In Texas, this was especially important as residents' busy work schedules did not allow for the impromptu meetings that were more common in Florida. Also residents in the Alvin parks were almost exclusively Latino / a and many were undocumented immigrants, so some initially avoided or spoke only briefly with me, a white woman. Fortunately, my own residence in a nearby mobile home and my ability to converse in Spanish soon lessened those residents' suspicion of me.

Some Alvin residents remembered me from my first trip to Alvin in March, as did Lupe, a resident of Trail's End and a stay-at-home mom close to my age who became my very regular companion. Lupe admitted that the first time she saw me at her neighbor's house she thought I worked for social services. Over time, Lupe saw me every day walking my dog or on my visits to Trail's End and Twin Oaks from my home in Ramos y Ramos just blocks away. Eventually I became regular companions with Lupe and her sister Mara, both of whom seldom left the park while their family members were at work. After a month in the Alvin parks Lupe took a side job as my translator for longer interviews with other residents. My friendship with Lupe allowed me to develop familiar relationships with a broader network of residents, so that by the time of my departure I was not only visiting residents every day but also frequently attending dinners and parties as I had been in Florida. Additionally, because word of vacancies in the Alvin parks often spreads through networks of family and close friends, many park residents were either related to each other or regarded each other as *primos,* cousins. Lupe's initial vouching for me secured me access to many in Trail's End who were related or well acquainted with her family (her mother, father, two sisters, their spouses, and several *primos* all lived in Trail's End) and in Twin Oaks where some residents knew members of her family. Indeed, by the time I moved away, her own mother frequently referred to me as *mi cuarta hija,* my fourth daughter.

Over the course of fieldwork, I spent time every day with residents: cooking together, taking walks and riding bikes, attending and hosting dinners, visiting homebound neighbors, doing laundry in the communal laundry room, sitting beside them at the hospital or the VA, and simply relaxing on their patios or screened-in porches. I also spent many days going over relocation forms, helping people pack and unpack, driving them to look at apartments or other parks, attempting to navigate state websites, looking at other For Sale mobile homes, talking with managers of other parks, driving with them as they followed their moving mobile home, hosting them in my trailer as their home was being installed, and accompanying them on meetings with their landlord, with the developer of their park (in Florida), or with public officials.

Residents came to know me both as a researcher and as a neighbor. They saw me as I went about my daily activities and they knew where I lived and slept. They could knock on my door, enter my screened-in porch, or call to me from outside my trailer at any time, and they did. This meant that I did not always control the terms of my interactions with residents. The ethnography took place both when I was on the clock—outside in the park, doing laundry in the laundry room, looking for someone to talk to—and when I was off—late in the evening, when residents had a personal emergency, or before I had gotten out of bed.

During this time I also spent days with movers and installers of mobile homes. In Texas, residents used mobile home movers that were inexpensive one- or two-person crews. The jobs were done quickly and I spoke with several movers, but did not have time to work with moving crews. In Florida, however, I became acquainted with entire work crews. Eventually I was allowed to come on workdays with the crews, meeting in the morning before the workday, "working" (i.e., watching work) during the day, riding along in the cab of trucks as we hauled homes, and on one occasion even being snuck by a crew into Sawgrass Estates, which at the time (due to negative publicity about the closure) was highly restricted, guarded by Seminole Police, and required a daily-issued permit for entrance.

In total I had close involvement with 59 residents in Silver Sands in Florida and 29 residents in Twin Oaks (14) and Trail's End (15) in Texas. I also interacted with and formally interviewed (oftentimes more than once) 11 correctional officers being evicted from mobile home staff housing at four different Florida correctional facilities; 14 residents in Ocean Breeze, Florida; 19 residents in Sawgrass Estates, Florida; 10 residents in Sunny Acres, Florida; 6 residents in Ramos y Ramos, Texas; dozens of residents in the 24 potentially closing mobile home parks in Alvin, Texas; and 12 mobile home movers, installers, and owners of moving companies in both states. In total, this universe of people living and working inside closing or potentially closing parks included about 180 residents and 200 people total who actively engaged in my ethnographic fieldwork and many more who came in and went out of my orbit in the parks.

All participants knew the central focus and research questions of the study and gave verbal consent. The names of the primary parks and all residents are pseudonyms to protect their confidentiality; however, the names of places and towns are not, since they are important for context. Also, in keeping with my original IRB proposal, I use pseudonyms for all key informants, professionals, and companies I met during my initial two years of fieldwork. Lakeshore Communities, the national corporate park company, is an exception because the company is easy to identify, as it is the largest owner of mobile home parks in Florida. Frank Rolfe and the Mobile Home Park Boot Camp are similar exceptions. Their real names are used, although all attendees at the boot camp are given pseudonyms.

In every park, in addition to written notes, I audio-recorded all conversations and interactions relating to the relocation, which resulted in about a thousand individual audio recordings, over three hundred hours of MP3 files, and hundreds of pages of field notes including direct transcription of recorded conversations every day. I transcribed every hour of recordings and interviews myself without assistance. These transcriptions were done during my years living in the parks, and revisiting recorded conversations and events each evening guided my interactions and shaped my questions to residents when we next met.

In addition to one-on-one interactions with residents, I recorded all group interactions of which I was a part. These recordings were exhaustive, as I learned each night when I transcribed for hours on end. Sometimes I would pause the recording if we ventured into long conversations that were completely unrelated to the topic of housing and eviction, but most often I continued to record and then made decisions about what was relevant that evening as I transcribed. I recorded using an app on my phone and kept the phone out and visible during all my recorded interactions. While recording, the app displays a large visible icon of a microphone. This, plus residents' frequent checks ("Did you get that on your device?" "Are you sure that's recording?"), assured me that even once we became comfortable with each other after months and even years, residents always knew I was actively collecting data.

The ethnography I set out to conduct seemed to me very different from the ethnographic works I had read as a graduate student, which often took the form of small-group ethnography set within a bounded place. I quickly came to see that residents living in closing mobile home parks existed within a broader field of interested actors. The parks, the stigma, and the insecurity were all shaped in part by the interrelations between city officials, state laws, private actors, and residents. My neighbors were only one set of players in this web of relations. At the outset of the project, I quickly saw that the ethnographic phase of the research would be an extension of the geospatial work I had started two years earlier. I was mapping a field.

This field was not bound by the interactional processes that took place between residents and landlords in individual parks. It was not bound by the geography of park properties, or even the geography of the cities where they were located. This field was configured by the demands of urban growth, the private companies that have a stake in redevelopment, the state laws that structure residents' rights to their communities, and the federal policies that support the private poverty housing market. Conducting comparative ethnography within a large group that is in turn embedded in processes determined by multiple actors at multiple scales required an orientation toward these larger theoretical concerns from the outset of the project. Thus, in both the collection and analysis of this data, I combined Lofland's (1995) approach to "analytic ethnography" with Emirbayer's (1997) approach to "relational sociology," which is taken up in Desmond's (2014) call for "relational ethnography."

I focused from the outset on housing insecurity not as a static condition, but rather as "a dynamic, unfolding process" (Emirbayer 1997: 287). As an object of analysis, I understood this process to be a relational one. Thus during data collection, I gave analytic primacy to the configurations of relations (Desmond 2014) that make up a mass eviction and structure the outcome for residents. But I did so strategically, positioning mobile home park housing insecurity not only within the interactions and transactions that occur in and around mobile home parks (those between residents, landlords, developers, and city officials), but also within the historic legacy of mobile home finance, construction, and regulation (covered in this book's first chapter) as well as the political economy of the mobile home empire, which is driven by the dictates of financialized capital, the shift from wage labor to passive income, and the federal withdrawal of public support for affordable housing (covered in the book's final chapter). This orientation avoids reducing structural processes to transactions within a bounded field and moves toward a theoretically grounded, structural form of relational ethnography in which "the ethnographer seeks out the macro conditions of micro processes, but those micro processes always remain in focus" (Burawoy 2017: 275).

During fieldwork, I investigated how the process of forced removal is determined by "chains of interdependence" (Weber, Nice, and Wacquant 2001) that form a web of mutual reliance between evicted residents, the surrounding community, the private actors that administer relocation services, the state regimes that regulate park closures, and the national corporations that own parks or redevelop them. This required that in addition to gathering the housing histories and daily experiences of residents, I focused my data collection on moments of interaction between residents, landlords, developers, private contractors, agency officials, and state and local representatives. I conducted participant observation alongside actors at different positions in the matrix of mobile home housing insecurity, both inside and outside closing parks all the way to the seminar rooms of the Mobile Home Park Investors Boot Camp.

Ethnography sited at multiple points in a web of relations has many analytic rewards. It is what allowed me to understand mobile home park housing insecurity in relation to the historic laws and contemporary policies described in chapters 1 and 2, and the broader markets in mobility described in chapters 5 and 6. It also has challenges. One challenge was that in including so many respondents and comparing so many experiences, I often feared that this book lacked adequate attention to the nuances and contradictions that are intrinsic to any individual experience, which small-group ethnographies are often so good at capturing. Another challenge was that residents sometimes looked to me as an expert, knowing I spoke with agency representatives, movers, and owners of large companies. This challenge was ethical as much as it was practical. I had to be real with myself, acknowledging that I did not want to withhold essential information from residents, even if that could be seen as shaping interactions in the field and undermining supposed objectivity. In this regard, I was fortunate that I often found myself as confused as residents over various policies regarding their relocation (especially in Florida where there were simply more policies to understand). Because of my own confusion, I felt comfortable telling residents that I could not be of help gleaning information they requested (for example, how moving dates were being chosen in Florida, or whether the city would grant variances to the ordinance and allow residents to remain in their parks longer in Texas). Instead I genuinely focused on helping where I could. This meant doing things like reading and interpreting policies; looking things up online; assisting with packing and moving; and, in a couple of cases in Alvin, posting and selling a resident's abandoned mobile home for cash on Craigslist.

Only in one case did I answer a resident's request to be a liaison with a landlord, when Silver Sands resident Stella asked me if I could relay her desperate situation and ask her landlord for more time before the final eviction date. Stella was in her late 80s, blind, homebound, and on the verge of losing her home, which could not be moved, without any other arrangements. I did as she asked, speaking with her landlord to the best of my ability but to no avail. She was not granted any more time, though eventually her son forced his own roommate to find new housing and she was able to move in to his apartment. Perhaps, for the sake of sociological purity, I should have never intervened. In Stella's case, the outcome did not change. But perhaps, say, if I did not offer to post a resident's home on Craigslist, the outcome would have been different. Perhaps the resident would have remained fruitlessly posting paper ads in the nearby grocery and I would have recorded this extra data point, one more loss on top of the mountain of losses my research had documented. But in cases like this I chose to offer help, and I do not believe any effect on the outcomes outweighs the obligation to do the little I could.

LOOKING BACK

Mobile home parks are unique places where socio-spatial closeness produces both gossip and the maxim that everybody knows everybody's business in the park. It also produces a sense of intimacy that expressed itself in park residents' habit of just dropping by, in the conversations neighbors held with each other from across lots, and in the networks of community ties that led park residents in both states to consistently check in on each other. These practices worked to my advantage as an ethnographer, especially as residents came to know me as a neighbor. Moving in and living in parks without a break helped me establish myself as a fixture in the parks, which surely aided in the process of building trust and becoming a neighbor.

Throughout this process my position as a 30-something, white woman shaped my interactions differently with different residents at different times. With the exception of two households, Silver Sands was entirely white. Trail's End and Twin Oaks were both entirely Latino/a. My whiteness made me less of an anomaly than I already was (because of my age) in Silver Sands and it likely contributed to my acceptance there. Being a youngish woman living on my own made me stand out, but I also believe it made me seem unthreatening; Silver Sands residents sometimes referred to me as a college student. In Trail's End (and perhaps Twin Oaks), my whiteness produced the initial skepticism noted above from Lupe, who first thought I worked for social services. But my age and gender likely also helped me overcome this skepticism as I got to know the young mothers and elderly grandmothers who were the primary population in Twin Oaks and Trail's End during the quiet daytimes while all other men and women were at work. These women, like Lupe and Señora Reyes, were central in my getting to know other households in these parks over time, establishing rapport, and requesting individual interviews.

In both states, I believe my working class-background helped me bridge some of the divides of age and ethnicity. I was raised as one of nine children in Pennsylvania's Appalachia. We lived in a three-bedroom house where the girls slept five to a room. During my childhood, only my father brought in income for our large family and we relied on federal assistance for food. I knew that some called me white trash. But I also sensed, even then, that this was much different than being called trailer trash. My interactions with residents were informed by my own background, by an appreciation of the very singular stigma that is projected on them, and by the understanding I hope this gives me.

I do not believe that perfect synergy between the background of the researcher and the people they study produces a better ethnography. I think there is value in studying people different from ourselves. In many ways though, my working-class background meshed with the residents in parks and helped me establish deep rapport. I was comfortable in their homes, even if the electric wasn't working or if cockroaches ran across the floors. In fact, during one phase I became useful to Texas residents as an amateur exterminator using the tricks and tools my dad, a maintenance man, had taught me and that I used to exterminate in my own mobile home. In some ways, I recognized some of resident's struggles in the life of my own family. In other ways, of course, their experience was worlds apart from my own. This was especially true in Texas where many residents were undocumented immigrants. I tried to never lose sight of these differences, to never kid myself that I was a true member of these communities, even though residents treated me like a neighbor. I didn't try to "fit in" in the shallow ways some ethnographers have proposed, by adopting dialect or dress. Instead I undertook the dogged task of just being there, day after day, month after month, all my waking hours except for those before bed when I would transcribe the day's recordings. I gratefully received the friendship and acceptance of my neighbors and focused wholeheartedly on being the instrument of record for this traumatic period in their lives.

In the middle of these traumatic moments, these residents showed me the true meaning of community and neighborliness. Even as they were being evicted, as they budgeted precious dollars to restock their fridges after the move, the people in this book checked in on me and made me part of their dinner plans. Residents in both states did this with such consistency that it became a hallmark of my fieldwork: people making sure I had a good meal. At first I skeptically thought they were needlessly worried that I could cook for myself, but I came to see that they were just kind, just very good neighbors.

Residents demonstrated this kindness even during the most trying moments of the evictions. In the final months that they lived in their boxed-up home, three months before Mattie's death, she and Walter remembered my birthday from some conversation we'd once had and hosted a party for me on their screened-in porch. On the day he abandoned his home and began sleeping on the street, Randall met me for a beer. As a moving gift he presented me with a small box, inside of which was a gorgeous artisanal cupcake topped with a sugar Tyrannosaurus Rex, which likely cost Randall what he made in an hour. He said he knew I would love it and he was right. Lupe and her sisters taught me recipes that I still use today. They hosted a goodbye party for me, and neighbors who I had met only during the most hectic days of the relocation came and celebrated long into the night.

I am grateful to every one of these residents who allowed me into their lives during one of their most difficult periods. This book would not have been possible without their help, and my own life inside mobile home parks would not have been as enjoyable without their generosity, humor, and warmth.

Notes

INTRODUCTION

1. The names of all mobile home parks, residents, local companies, and industry representatives are pseudonyms; the names of places and towns are not.

2. A note on terminology: The term "manufactured home" technically refers to an industrially produced home fabricated after 1976 when HUD introduced manufactured home performance standards, and the term "mobile home" refers to a home manufactured before 1976. In practice, however, the two terms are synonyms used to describe a prefabricated home of at least 320 square feet that is attached to a permanent chassis (Manufactured Home Construction and Safety Standards, 24 CFR § 3280). This definition distinguishes mobile / manufactured homes from other forms of modular housing that are assembled on site. The term manufactured home is preferred by industry representatives and some housing advocates in attempts to increase the marketability of the homes or to downplay the notion that they are transient structures. Residents in this study were far more likely to use the term "trailer," although they also frequently used "mobile home." In this book, I follow historians of the mobile home in using the common term "mobile home," not only because "manufactured home" was never used by a single resident participating in this study, but also because the term "conveys better than any other the basic hybrid character of the innovation and the essential basis for the conflicts it has engendered" (Wallis 1991: viii).

3. Manufactured housing is also an especially important source of rural housing (see Salamon and MacTavish 2017 on rural mobile home parks). About 14 percent of all occupied units located outside of metropolitan areas are mobile homes, which are concentrated in more rural county jurisdictions (CFPB 2014). Indeed in 112 U.S. counties (primarily in Southern and Western states) over one-third of all homes are mobile homes (ibid.). Nonetheless, mobile home park evictions are primarily an urban problem. In more populous states, a large share of manufactured housing is located in urban areas (60 percent and 78

percent in Texas and Florida respectively). More importantly, most *rural* manufactured housing (over two-thirds) is sited on privately owned land where residents own the home and the property and are thus protected from the evictions described in this book (Apgar et al. 2002). Meanwhile, the location of mobile home within *parks* and the development pressures that contribute to park closures are both primarily urban phenomena. All parks in this study were located within metropolitan areas.

4. The study of mobile home park closures not only expands the study of eviction but also broadens current understandings of U.S. poverty, which have remained focused on the economics of how poverty is produced and is dominated by research on neighborhood structure, labor markets, and welfare reform (see O'Conner 2000; Newman and Massengill 2006). This body of research emphasizes transformations in the urban environment including deindustrialization, urban to suburban migration, and the geography of job opportunities (Wilson 1987, 1996; Massey and Denton 1993; Jargowsky 1997), as well as macro shifts in the political economy of poverty governance, especially the reform and redefinition of the American welfare state (Piven and Cloward 1993; Hays 2003; Katz [2001] 2008). Qualitative research on poverty remains rooted in these macro-level processes, exploring the destabilization of low-wage, low-benefit work (Tilly 1996; Fine and Weis 1998; Newman 1999), as well as strategies of "making ends meet," either on meager welfare benefits (Oliker 1995; Edin and Lein 1997; Edin and Shaefer 2015) or in absence of any aid (Bourgois 1995; Dohan 2003; Venkatesh 2006). Ethnography within closing mobile home parks expands research on the production of poverty by situating housing within this literature. Doing so speaks specifically to the *reproduction* of poverty and offers opportunities to uncover the socio-legal mechanisms that entrench and perpetuate economic inequality.

5. Jonathon McClellan, senior director of the national manufactured home communities group at Marcus & Millichap, cited in "Low-Cost Housing Demand Boosts Mobile-Home Park Operators," *Wall Street Journal*, April 21, 2015.

6. Frank Rolfe, founder of Mobile Home University, cited in "Goldman Alum Gives Up Funds to Become Trailer-Park Mogul," *Bloomberg*, April 10, 2014, www.bloomberg.com/news/articles/2014-04-10/trailer-parks-lure-investors-pursuing-double-wide-returns.

7. I refer to these parks as "closing" mobile home parks because, as I describe in the following chapters and in the methodological appendix, each of these parks was slated to close for various reasons during the time of this study. In the end, all of the Florida parks did close but some of the Texas parks remained open.

8. Clifford Geertz (1988: 2–3) called on ethnographers to dispel the illusion that ethnography is simply a matter of sorting "strange and irregular" field data into orderly categories and replace this illusion with a picture of "being there" and what that entails. *Being there* is not simply a question of time spent in the field; it is an epistemological question that carries through to how ethnographers write and how their writing pulls from the narratives they collect from those who take part in their research. "It is not that everything ethnographers

say is accepted once and for all simply because they say it. A very great deal, thank God, is not . . . Unable to recover the immediacies of field work for empirical reinsertion, we listen to some voices and ignore others . . . we do so because some ethnographers are more effective than others in conveying in their prose the impression that they have had close-in contact with far-out lives" (ibid., 6): in other words, the impression that they have been there.

This is a task of writing as much as of fieldwork. This task structures the way field notes are reproduced in this book. Geertz calls on ethnographers to scrutinized textual matters that are often overlooked in favor of setting down scientific discourse, "such matters as imagery, metaphor, phraseology, or voice" (ibid., 2). In the chapters that follow, I incorporate the rhetoric of respondents directly into the text in long verbatim field notes. During fieldwork, I transcribed all daily audio recordings myself, without assistance and with a detailed ear toward accuracy of both language and tone. Included in these transcripts are notes on the sounds, sighs, pauses, and shifts respondents made in their speech.

Following Geertz, I believe the craft of ethnography should be attuned to both the substance of respondents' narratives and how they deploy these narratives. Thus, in the following chapters I reproduce both extended quotes and long passages from field notes verbatim, including myself on the page, with very little editing (primarily for length). I do so both to highlight the direct recording of interactions with and between individuals in this study and to encourage alternate interpretations of what they said and how they said it—to allow the reader to be there, or in Geertz's words, "to rescue the 'said' of such discourse from its perishing occasions and fix it in perusable terms" (ibid., 20).

9. Social space—a geographic metaphor for the classification of people according to the material and symbolic capitals they wield—is Bourdieu's response to existing theories of social stratification through a revised relational and perceptual understanding of social structure (Bourdieu 1989). Bourdieu argues that the organization of physical space directly mediates social distancing and proves foundational to social inequality since the structures of the social order are perceived, experienced, and thus incorporated "through a prolonged and indefinitely repeated experience of the spatial distance that affirms social distance" (Bourdieu 1999: 126).

10. Goffman's theory is also useful in offering a relational understanding of how stigma is produced. Place-based stigma is an analogous relational object. In the study of marginalized communities, the very concept of marginalization presupposes a relation to some imagined center. In the words of the housing industry, "conventional" housing has long been defined by such a site-built standard, with all the property-owning, single-family, "domestic privatism" (Hayden 1995) that it entails.

1. THE MOBILE HOME IN AMERICA AND AMERICANA

1. I did not personally interview the former inhabitants of the home I rented in Silver Sands. I pieced their story together from several of their neighbors and

from the landlord of Silver Sands, as well as from items they left behind in the home.

2. This is not to say that mobile homes only exist in the United States. The United Kingdom, Ireland, Canada, and Australia have significant numbers of mobile homes and parks as well. However, many of these are used for seasonal housing, and none of these countries has the manufactured housing history or industry size that exists in the United States.

3. The same technologies that created the earliest prefabricated houses were adopted by other sectors of the housing industry. These technologies streamlined and cheapened the mass production of single-family homes through assembly-line grading, cutting, and prepackaging. Sold through companies such as Pacific Systems Homes and Sears, Roebuck, and Co., these homes were factory produced and then built on site. The standardized methods forged in prefabricated housing allowed for economies of scale that made these "kit houses" affordable. An estimated hundred thousand kit houses were built throughout the United States between 1908 and 1940 (NTHP 2016), including the first home my own parents were able to purchase, the Sears, Roebuck home where I was raised.

4. Hallet v. Sumpter, 106 F.Supp. 996 (D. Alaska 1952).

5. Pagel v. Gisi, 132 Colo. 181, 286 P.2d 636 (1955).

6. 251 Iowa 969, 103 N.W.2d 364 (1960).

7. 28 Ohio Misc. 47, 272 N.E.2d 181 (C.P. 1971).

2. SOCIO-SPATIAL STIGMA AND TRAILER TRASH

1. Methods of coupling ethnographic data with geographic information systems (GIS) technologies have been formulated in research on low-income families and their use of welfare programs. Those methods, termed *geo-ethnography*, are argued to better situate households' experiences in real space (Matthews, Detwiler, and Burton 2005). A similar approach to pairing spatial conceptualization of park closures with ethnographic understanding of their effects is presented in this chapter to gain a deeper understanding of the external pressures facing urban mobile home park residents (for a more in-depth discussion of this geospatial analysis see Sullivan 2017b).

2. Texas has an estimated 1,895,932 people living in mobile homes according to 2010–14 estimates from the American Community Survey. It is followed by Florida (1,422,104), North Carolina (1,321,877), and California (1,134,241). Source: U.S. Census Bureau, "2010–2014 American Community Survey 5-Year Estimates," http://factfinder.census.gov/faces/tableservices/jsf/pages /productview.xhtml?pid = ACS_14_5YR_B25033&prodType = table.

3. The use of Harris County as a study site does require one important caveat. Houston is the only unzoned major U.S. city. This has meant that Houston's urban development (like neighboring Alvin's) occurs without the centralized land use planning that shapes other U.S. cities. However, the lack of zoning in Houston has not meant that development occurs in a wholly

distinctive way from other U.S. cities. In fact, researchers investigating the "uniqueness" of this unzoned metropolis consistently find that (a) Houston's laissez-faire land regulation provides economic incentives for segregation of uses and produces patterns of development similar to what is found under zoning (Siegan 1972) and (b) despite a lack of zoning, local land use regulatory policies continue to shape urban development in ways similar to other U.S. metros (Qian 2010).

Indeed, scholars argue that Houston's lack of zoning makes the city the most "appropriate symbol of urban growth in the late twentieth century in the United States" (Fisher 1989: 144). This is precisely *because* without the mask of zoning the outcomes of a constellation of public and private interests that are at work in many city planning offices are more readily on display. While the lack of zoning in Harris County limits direct comparison in important ways, it also provides a unique opportunity to trace the full contours of mobile home park closure and redevelopment without compulsory external constraints.

4. To map the current and former locations of mobile home parks from 2002–11, I used yearly historic records of land use codes taken from the tax rolls of Houston's local appraisal district (Harris County Appraisal District or HCAD). In most jurisdictions, appraisal districts assess property taxes using land use codes attached to each lot (or parcel) in the appraisal district. These codes are carefully reassessed each year for taxation purposes. This provides an especially accurate and nuanced historical record of changing land use patterns. Using GIS, these tax records can be geo-referenced, or spatially joined, to property maps maintained by states and localities. This process creates a geographically accurate record of shifting land use patterns.

5. With respect to similar uses of GIS methods to create proxy measures for data otherwise unavailable, see McKenzie 2013. In addition to these steps, I performed a two-part validation process using digital ortho-imagery and Google Earth™ to verify that parks had indeed closed on these properties. For a detailed, step-by-step record of this analysis and the geospatial methodology I used to perform it, see Sullivan 2017b.

6. I used the spatial analyst tools ANND and Getis-Ord Gi* analysis to identify where specific spatial features (lost park parcels) were clustered and found significant clustering of lost mobile home park parcels in areas along the city limit in the northeastern portion of the county. Average Nearest Neighbor Distance (ANND) analysis identifies the presence of statistically significant clusters of spatial features (closed mobile home parks) by measuring the distance between each feature and the nearest feature of the same type, then comparing that average distance to a hypothetical random distribution. The ANND calculation results (inset Map 3) show that lost park parcels have a nearest neighbor ratio of .59 with a highly significant z-score (a nearest neighbor ratio of less than 1 classifies a pattern as geographically clustered), i.e., closed mobile home park parcels in Harris County are geospatially clustered and there is a less than one percent chance that the observed clustering is random.

In addition to ANND analysis, I performed Getis-Ord Gi* analysis, which detects "hot spots" where areas with high counts of lost mobile home park parcels are clustered. The resultant z-scores and p-values identify where features with either high or low values cluster spatially. For statistically significant positive z-scores, the larger the z-score, the more intense the clustering of high values. To identify areas most affected by mobile home park closure, I selected census tracts with high counts of lost mobile home park parcels within close distance of one another—in other words, areas with high positive z-scores (greater than 2.58) and low p-values (less than 0.05) (see Map 3). Then, because areas where more mobile home parks are located may experience more mobile home park closures over time, I performed modified Getis-Ord Gi* analysis on the ratio of lost mobile home parks to total mobile home parks to control for the total number of mobile home park parcels in an area. This analysis identified areas that lost significantly high numbers of mobile home park parcels accounting for the total number of mobile home parks in the area. Maps 3 and 4 show significant clusters of lost mobile home park parcels both with and without controlling for the total number of mobile homes in the area.

7. The 2011 land use codes are an incomplete record because development must be complete for a property to be reappraised and recoded in the tax roll records. Property redevelopment takes time to be completed and recorded with the appraisal district, so the most common 2011 land use code on closed park parcels is "residential vacant table value," which denotes vacant residential land awaiting development (i.e., a new house or structure). In the inset in Map 4, the combined categories of residential land with improvements (N = 28) and residential land awaiting development (N = 8) comprise 41 percent of the former mobile home park parcels for which 2011 land use codes were entered. This indicates, simply, that redevelopment was still taking place and the nature of this redevelopment was not yet finalized in the tax records.

8. For a more in-depth assessment of public perception and media portrayal of trailer park residents as a "transient and deficient" racialized class of other, see Kusenbach 2009.

9. Florida Statutes 723.083.

3. DAILY LIFE UNDER THE SPECTER OF DISLOCATION

1. Interestingly, Walmart's application was held up because a nearby neighborhood association had vocally opposed the development of a Walmart near their community. The neighborhood associations stated opposition to the Walmart did not include any vocal support for the residents of the mobile home park or concern over their eviction.

2. This attitude is similar to the one Herbert Gans found in his classic study of the West End, the Italian-American Boston neighborhood that would eventually be cleared by urban renewal. There most residents knew about the city's plan for redevelopment, although no one could remember when they had first

heard about these plans. Even though residents were "unanimously opposed" to the redevelopment plans and "had no desire to leave" they also did not feel "sufficiently threatened to be alarmed" (Gans 1962: 288–98).

3. The Wind Zone Rating for manufactured housing, introduced in 1994 and designated by HUD, consists of three categories. Wind Zone III is recommended for zones where winds reach up to 110 mph. This zone includes the Gulf coasts of Texas, Louisiana, Mississippi, Alabama, and Florida as well as the Atlantic coast of Florida.

4. Kai Erikson (1976) describes a similar psychic reaction in his study of displacement after the flooding of an Appalachian mining community. Erikson argued that the trauma of the flood and the resulting dislocation reshaped residents' sense of self, power, and agency so that they were left feeling "numbed and depleted" (159). Similar to Josefina's emergent sense that "we are all just passing by," one middle-aged Appalachian woman in his study said, "it will make you feel like that—washed away, just about washed away" (ibid.).

4. "WE ARE NOT FOR SURE WHEREVER WE ARE"

1. City of Alvin, Texas Ordinance No. 11-C Amending Chapter 241/2.

2. Phenomenological theories of space hold that place is essential to human understandings of the self. The more contemporary, multidisciplinary literature on *place attachment*—the affective bond between people and landscapes—argues that place informs a sense of identity, facilitates shared cultural meaning, enables community bonds, and influences individual action (Mah 2009; Manzo and Devine-Wright 2014). Home, as "an experience of being in the world," is emotionally and cognitively important to identity (Mallett 2004). The formative role of place in structuring identity sheds light on the process by which mobile home residents internalize the socio-spatial stigma that characterizes mobile home communities.

3. Heidegger (1958), for instance, conceptualizes place-making as "dwelling" and establishing "roots," which he argues is the fundamental human essence of "Being." In his history of the tramp as a social type, geographer Tim Cresswell (2001: 14–16) describes how "moral geographies of mobility" construct the figure of the vagrant: "Place, in its ideal form, is seen as a moral world, as an ensurer of authentic existence and as a centre of meaning for people . . . Place, home and roots are profoundly moral concepts in the humanist lexicon. By implication, mobility appears to involve a number of absences—the absence of commitment, attachment and involvement—a lack of significance."

4. Indeed, Atuahene (2016) argues for the need to retain analytic specificity when determining whether a dignity taking has occurred. Dignity takings must entail the various elements of: (1) a state action that directly or indirectly (2) destroys or confiscates property (3) of individuals it deems to be subpersons (4) through processes of dehumanization or infantilization (5) without paying just compensation or without a legitimate public purpose.

5. RELOCATION AND THE PARADOX OF
STATE INTERVENTIONS

1. I did not personally witness this meeting; however, Tabitha recorded it on a digital recorder and gave the recording to me.

2. In an overzealous effort to comply with the state requirements, Flagler sent out as many as eight copies of the eviction notice to individual households.

6. COMMUNITIES AS CURRENCY WITHIN
THE MOBILE HOME EMPIRE

1. Mobile Home University, "We Teach Mobile Home Park Investing," www.mobilehomeuniversity.com/.

2. Karl Vick, "The Home of the Future," *Time*, March 23, 2017.

3. This is a common practice in mobile home parks, where landlords oftentimes create uncomfortable or hazardous living conditions for residents in an attempt to get them to move (most often by instituting fines and charging additional fees for pets, cars, and extra occupants or by failing to maintain basic park infrastructure, such as water, sewer, and gas). In Desmond's (2016) study, informal evictions also made up almost half of all forced moves.

4. Joel Cone, "Mobile Home Parks Are a Viable Investment," *U.S. News and World Report*, July 20, 2016, http://money.usnews.com/money/blogs/the-smarter-mutual-fund-investor/articles/2016–07–20/mobile-home-parks-are-a-viable-investment (accessed March 12, 2017).

5. Warren Buffett, "Chairman's Letter," *Berkshire Hathaway 2012 Annual Report*, p. 3, www.berkshirehathaway.com/letters/2013ltr.pdf (accessed March 13, 2017).

6. Ibid., 17.

7. Ibid.

8. Ibid.

9. www.ffiec.gov/ratespread/aportables.htm.

10. Matt Egan, "Who Owns Wells Fargo Anyway? You, Me, and Warren Buffett," *CNN Money*, September 8, 2016, http://money.cnn.com/2016/09/08/investing/wells-fargo-fake-accounts-warren-buffett/.

11. "Clayton Homes Statement on Mobile-Home Buyer Investigation," *Omaha World-Herald*, April 3, 2015, www.omaha.com/clayton-homes-statement-on-mobile-home-buyer-investigation/article_7052e0c4-da3b-11e4-8abd-5f0b53380837.html.

12. There are also REITs that do not trade on the stock exchange. These nontraded REITs can yield higher dividends compared to those of publicly traded REITs, but involve unique risks related to illiquidity of the asset, nontransparency of the investment, and potential conflicts of interest (U.S. Securities and Exchange Commission, *Investor.gov*, https://investor.gov/additional-resources/news-alerts/alerts-bulletins/real-estate-investment-trusts-reits).

CONCLUSION

1. A renter earning the federal minimum wage of $7.25 per hour would need to work 94.5 hours per week (for all 52 weeks of the year) to afford a one-bedroom rental home at the Fair Market Rent and 117 hours per week to afford a two-bedroom (National Low Income Housing Coalition 2017).

2. "Extremely low-income households" have an income at or below the Poverty Guideline or 30% of Area Median Income (the median family income in the metropolitan or nonmetropolitan area), whichever is higher. "Very low-income households" have an income between 31% and 50% of AMI. "Low-income households" have an income between 51% and 80% of AMI, and "middle-income households" have an income between 81% and 100% of AMI.

3. Washington State, Office of the Attorney General, Manufactured Housing Dispute Resolution Program, www.atg.wa.gov/manufactured-housing-dispute-resolution-program.

4. Both homeowners and community owners can file a complaint with the attorney general if they believe the other party has violated the state's Manufactured/Mobile Home Landlord Tenant Act (RCW 59.20). The AG will accept complaints either online or via the telephone. They will review the complaint, determine whether or not the other party has violated the act, and take appropriate action—either contacting the complaining party to state that the act has not been violated, or if the act has been violated, they will attempt over-the-phone mediation with both parties; if one party ignores the opportunity to mediate, the AG will carry out further investigation and can issue fines until the violating party comes into compliance. Either party can appeal the AG's decision to the Administrative Law Judge and ultimately to Superior Court. The AG provides an annual report to the legislature and makes statistics on its rulings publicly available on their website: www.atg.wa.gov/manufactured-housing-dispute-resolution-program#Start.

5. For a complete comparative list of state protections for mobile home park residents and state laws that promote resident-owned communities, see Prosperity Now's Resource Guide, "Promoting Resident Ownership of Communities," at https://prosperitynow.org/files/resources/Promoting_Resident_Ownership_Resource_Guide.pdf.

6. Quotes taken from the *National Public Radio* story "When Residents Take Ownership, A Mobile Home Community Thrives" by Daniel Zwerdling, December 27, 2016.

7. As President Trump's 2017 Tax Cuts and Jobs Act is implemented, the cap for the MID will be lowered from interest on up to $1 million in mortgage debt to interest on up to $750,000 in mortgage debt for homes bought between December 15, 2017 and December 15, 2026. Barring new legislation the cap will revert to $1 million in mortgage debt in 2026. The MID will continue to apply to both first and second homes. This change will not likely impact the fundamental inequalities of the MID discussed here.

8. These programs include Public Housing, Housing Choice Vouchers, Section 8 Project Based Rental Assistance, Section 202 Supportive Housing for the Elderly, and Section 811 Supportive Housing for People with Disabilities.

METHODOLOGICAL APPENDIX

1. www.tcpalm.com/news/2009/jul/28/no-headline——mc_gates/.
2. While the names of all residents in this study (and all other mobile homes parks) are pseudonyms, the name of Ocean Breeze is not a pseudonym because the very public nature of its closure made the park impossible to anonymize.

References

Adams, Vincanne. 2012. *Markets of Sorrow, Labors of Faith: New Orleans in the Wake of Katrina*. Durham, NC: Duke University Press.

———, Taslim Van Hattum, and Diana English. 2009. "Chronic Disaster Syndrome: Displacement, Disaster Capitalism, and the Eviction of the Poor from New Orleans." *American Ethnologist* 63(4): 615–36.

Allen, Barbara L. 2007. "Environmental Justice and Expert Knowledge in the Wake of a Disaster." *Social Studies of Science* 37(1): 103–10.

Allen, Chris. 2008. *Housing Market Renewal and Social Class Formation*. London: Routledge.

Aman, D.D., and B. Yarnal. 2010. "Home Sweet Mobile Home? Benefits and Challenges of Mobile Home Ownership in Rural Pennsylvania." *Applied Geography* 30: 84–95.

APA (American Planning Association). 2001. "Policy Guide on Factory Built Housing." Ratified by the APA Board of Directors, March 12, 2001, New Orleans, LA.

Apgar, William, Allegra Calder, Michael Collins, and Mark Duda. 2002. *An Examination of Manufactured Housing as a Community and Asset Building Strategy*. Washington, DC: Neighborhood Reinvestment Corporation in collaboration with the Joint Center for Housing Studies of Harvard University.

Appraisal Institute. 2014. *The Appraisal of Real Estate, 14th Edition*. Chicago: Appraisal Institute.

Atuahene, Bernadette. 2014. *We Want What's Ours: Learning from South Africa's Land Restitution Program*. Oxford: Oxford University Pres.

———. 2016. "Takings as a Sociolegal Concept: An Interdisciplinary Examination of Involuntary Property Loss." *Annual Review of Law and Social Science* 12: 15.1–15.27

Aurand, Andrew, Dan Emmanuel, Diane Yentel, and Ellen Errico. 2017. *The Gap: A Shortage of Affordable Homes*. National Low Income Housing Coalition, March 17. http://nlihc.org/sites/default/files/Gap-Report_2017.pdf.

Auyero, Javier. 2012. *Patients of the State: The Politics of Waiting in Argentina.* Durham, NC: Duke University Press.

Avery, Robert B., Glenn B. Canner, and Robert E. Cook. 2005. "New Information Reported under HMDA and Its Application in Fair Lending Enforcement." *Federal Reserve Bulletin* 91 (Summer): 344–94.

Baldwin, Carliss Y., and Kim B. Clark. 2000. *Design Rules, Volume 1: The Power of Modularity.* Cambridge, MA: MIT Press.

Barajas, Michael. 2017. "Here's What Happens When 'Urban Redevelopment' Displaces a Trailer Park Full of People." *San Antonio Current,* May 5. www .sacurrent.com/the-daily/archives/2017/05/05/heres-what-happens-when-urban-redevelopment-displaces-a-trailer-park-full-of-people.

Beamish, Julia, Rosemary Goss, Jorge H. Atiles, and Youngjoo Kim. 2001. "Not a Trailer Anymore: Perceptions of Manufactured Housing." *Housing Policy Debate* 12(2): 373–91.

Bernhardt, Arthur D. 1981. *Building Tomorrow: The Mobile / Manufactured Housing Industry.* Cambridge, MA: MIT Press.

Bettie, Julie. 1995. "Class Dismissed? Roseanne and the Changing Face of Working-Class Iconography." *Social Text* 45: 125–49.

Birk, Chris. 2014. "Using a VA Loan for Manufactured or Modular Housing." *Veterans United Network.* www.veteransunited.com/valoans/how-to-buy-a-modular-home-with-a-va-loan/.

Blomley, Nicholas. 2004. *Unsettling the City: Urban Land and the Politics of Property.* New York: Routledge.

———. 2017. "Taking Up Property: Comments on Ananya Roy." *Geoforum* 80: A20–A21.

Boorstin, Daniel. 1966. *The Americans: The National Experience.* New York: Vintage Books.

Borchersen-Keto, Sarah. 2017. "Favorable Supply Picture Boosts Manufactured Housing REITs." *REIT.com,* April 20. www.reit.com/news/articles/favorable-supply-picture-boosts-manufactured-housing-reits.

Bourdieu, Pierre. 1989. "Social Space and Symbolic Power." *Sociological Theory* 7(1): 14–25.

———. 2000. *Pascalian Meditations.* Stanford, CA: Stanford University Press.

———, et al. 1999. *The Weight of the World: Social Suffering in Contemporary Society.* Stanford, CA: Stanford University Press.

Bourgois, Philip. 1995. *In Search of Respect: Selling Crack in El Barrio.* New York: Cambridge University Press.

Braithwaite, John, Cary Coglianese, and David Levi-Faur. 2007. "Can Regulation and Governance Make a Difference?" *Regulation and Governance* 1: 1–7.

Bratt, Rachel G., Michael E. Stone, and Chester Hartman. 2006. *A Right to Housing: Foundation for a New Social Agenda.* Philadelphia: Temple University Press.

Brown, Wendy. 2006. "American Nightmare: Neoliberalism, Neoconservatism, and De-Democratization." *Political Theory* 34(6): 690–714.

Brunsma, David L., David Overfelt, and J. Steven Picou. 2007. *The Sociology of Katrina: Perspectives on a Modern Catastrophe.* Lanham, MD: Rowman & Littlefield.

Burawoy, Michael. 2017. "On Desmond: The Limits of Spontaneous Sociology." *Theory and Society* 26: 261–84.

Burby, R.J., T. Beatley, P.R. Berke, R.E. Deyle, S.P. French, D.R. Godschalk, E.J. Kaiser, J.D. Kartez, P.J. May, R. Olshansky, R.G. Paterson, and R.H. Platt (1999). "Unleashing the Power of Planning to Create Disaster Resistant Communities." *Journal of the American Planning Association* 65(3): 247–58.

Burby, R.J., R.E. Deyle, D.R. Godschalk, and R.B. Olshansky (2000). "Creating Hazard-Resilient Communities through Land-Use Planning." *Natural Hazards Review* 1(2): 99–106.

Burkhart, Ann M. 2010. "Bringing Manufactured Housing into the Real Estate Finance System." *Pepperdine Law Review* 37: 427–58.

Carter, Carolyn L., Odette Williamson, Elizabeth DeArmond, and Jonathan Sheldon. 2004. "Manufactured Housing Community Tenants: Shifting the Balance of Power." Washington, DC: AARP Public Policy Institute.

Centeno, Miguel A., and Joseph N. Cohen. 2012. "The Arc of Neoliberalism." *Annual Review of Sociology* 38: 317–40.

CFED (Corporation for Enterprise Development). 2011. *Promoting Resident Ownership of Communities.* Washington, DC: CFED. https://prosperitynow.org/files/resources/purchaseopportunity_resourceguide_AppA_10_2011.pdf.

———. 2015. *Titling Homes as Real Property.* Washington, DC: CFED. https://prosperitynow.org/files/resources/Updated_Titling_Brief_2015.pdf.

CFPB (Consumer Financial Protection Bureau). 2014. *Manufactured-Housing Consumer Finance in the United States.* Washington, DC: CFPB.

Coleman, James. 1988. "Social Capital in the Creation of Human Capital." *American Journal of Sociology* 94: 95–120.

Collins, Jane, and Victoria Mayer. 2010. *Both Hands Tied: Welfare Reform and the Race to the Bottom of the Low-Wage Labor Market.* Chicago: University of Chicago Press.

Consumers Union. 2001a. "Manufactured Housing Rental Community Tenants Rights." New York: Consumer Reports.

———. 2001b. "Manufactured Homeowners Who Rent Lots Lack Security of Basic Tenants Rights." New York: Consumer Reports.

Cortez, Marisol, María Antonietta Berriozábal, Carlos Cortez, Dennise Frausto, Anayanse Garza, Jessica O. Guerrero, Tamara Pinzon, Raquel Simon, Arturo Trejo, Rachell Tucker, and Lupe Turner. 2017. *Making Displacement Visible: A Case Study Analysis of the "Mission Trail of Tears."* Vecinos de Mission Trails, May 2. https://vecinosdemissiontrails.files.wordpress.com/2017/05/mission-trails-final-report.pdf.

Cresswell, Tim. 2001. *The Tramp in America.* London: Reaktion Books.

Dawkins, Casey J., and C. Theodore Koebel. 2010. "Overcoming Barriers to Placing Manufactured Housing in Metropolitan Communities." *Journal of the American Planning Association* 76(1): 73–88.

Denvir, Daniel. 2015. "One Thing HUD Can Do to Save Trailer Parks." *Atlantic CityLab*, September 25. www.citylab.com/equity/2015/09/one-thing-hud-can-do-to-save-trailer-parks/407395/.

Desmond, Matthew. 2012. "Eviction and the Reproduction of Urban Poverty." *American Journal of Sociology* 118(1): 88–133.

———. 2014. "Relational Ethnography." *Theory and Society* 43(5): 547–79.

———. 2015. "Unaffordable America: Poverty, Housing, and Eviction." Fast Focus no. 22–2015. Institute for Research on Poverty: University of Wisconsin–Madison.

———. 2016. *Evicted: Poverty and Profit in the American City*. New York: Penguin Random House.

——— and Monica Bell. 2015. "Housing, Poverty, and the Law." *Annual Review of Law and Social Science* 11: 15–35.

———, Weihua An, Richelle Winkler, and Thomas Ferriss. 2013. "Evicting Children." *Social Forces* 92(1): 303–27.

Detzour, Mark, Terry Grissom, Crocker Liu, and Thomas Pearson. 1990. "Highest and Best Use: The Evolving Paradigm." *Journal of Real Estate Research* 5(1): 17–32.

Dohan, Daniel. 2003. *The Price of Poverty: Money, Work, and Culture in the Mexican American Barrio*. Berkeley: University of California Press.

Drury, Margaret. 1967. "Mobile Homes: The Unrecognized Revolution in American Housing." PhD dissertation, Department of Housing and Design, Cornell University.

———. 1972. *Mobile Homes: The Unrecognized Revolution in American Housing*. New York: Praeger.

Edin, Kathryn, and Laura Lein. 1997. *Making Ends Meet: How Single Mothers Survive Welfare and Low-Wage Work*. New York: Russell Sage.

Edin, Kathryn, and Luke Shaefer. 2015. *$2.00 a Day: Living on Almost Nothing in America*. New York: Houghton Mifflin Harcourt.

Edwards, Carlton. 1963. "Mobile Home Journal, Consumer Survey." Study conducted at Michigan State University in conjunction with Ross Federal Research Corporation. New York: Davis.

Effinger, Anthony, and Katherine Burton. 2014. "Why Wall Street Loves Trailer Parks." *Bloomberg Markets Magazine*, May.

Emirbayer, Mustafa. 1997. "Manifesto for a Relational Sociology." *American Journal of Sociology* 103(2): 281–317.

Erikson, Kai. 1976. *Everything in Its Path: Destruction of Community in the Buffalo Creek Flood*. New York: Simon & Schuster.

Fassin, Didier, and Richard Rechtman. 2009. *The Empire of Trauma: An Inquiry into the Condition of Victimhood*. Princeton, NJ: Princeton University Press.

Fine, Michelle, and Lois Weis. 1998. *The Unknown City: Lives of Poor and Working-Class Young Adults*. Boston: Beacon.

Fischer, Claude S. 2002. "Ever-more Rooted Americans." *City and Community* 1(2): 177–98.

Fischer, Will, and Chye-Ching Huang. 2017. *Mortgage Interest Deduction Is Ripe for Reform*. Washington, DC: Center on Budget and Policy Priorities.

Fischer, Will, and Barbara Sard. 2016. *Chart Book: Federal Housing Spending Is Poorly Matched to Need*. Washington, DC: Center on Budget and Policy Priorities.

Fisher, Robert. 1989. "Urban Policy in Houston, Texas." *Urban Studies* 26: 144–54.

Flaherty, Jordan. 2010. *Floodlines: Community and Resistance from Katrina to the Jena Six*. Chicago: Haymarket.

Forbes. 1965. "Trailers No More: Mobile Homes Have Grown into a Billion-Dollar Industry." *Forbes* 95 (March 15): 36.

———. 2017a. "Forbes 400." Accessed March 12, 2017. www.forbes.com /profile/sam-zell/.

———. 2017b. "Forbes 400." Accessed March 12, 2017. www.forbes.com/profile /warren-buffett/.

Fraser, Nancy, and Axel Honneth. 2003. *Redistribution or Recognition: A Politico-Philosophical Exchange*. London: Verso.

Fridman, Daniel. 2017. *Freedom from Work: Embracing Financial Self-Help in the United States and Argentina*. Stanford, CA: Stanford University Press.

Fried, Marc. 1966. "Grieving for a Lost Home: Psychological Costs of Relocation." In *Urban Renewal: The Record and the Controversy*, edited by James Q. Wilson, 359–79. Cambridge, MA: MIT Press.

Fullilove, Mindy Thompson. 2005. *Root Shock: How Tearing Up City Neighborhoods Hurts America, and What We Can Do about It*. New York: One World / Ballantine.

Galster, George, and Stephen Peacock. 1986. "Urban Gentrification: Evaluating Alternative Indicators." *Social Indicators Research* 18: 321–37.

Gans, Herbert. 1962. *The Urban Villagers: Group and Class in the Life of Italian-Americans*. New York: Free Press.

Geertz, Clifford. 1978. *The Interpretation of Cultures*. New York: Basic Books.

———. 1988. *Work and Lives: The Anthropologist as Author*. Stanford, CA: Stanford University Press.

Genz, Richard. 2001. "Why Advocates Need to Rethink Manufactured Housing." *Housing Policy Debate* 12(2): 393–414.

Gieryn, Thomas F. 2000. "A Place for Space in Sociology." *Annual Review of Sociology* 26: 463–96.

Glynn, Sarah. 2009. *Where the Other Half Lives: Lower Income Housing in a Neoliberal World*. New York: Pluto Press.

Godschalk, D.R., E.J. Kaiser, and P.R. Berke. 1998. "Integrating Hazard Mitigation and Local Land Use Planning." In *Cooperating with Nature: Confronting Natural Hazards with Land Use Planning for Sustainable Communities*, edited by R.J. Burby. Washington, DC: John Henry Press.

Godschalk, D.R., and W.A. Anderson (2012). *Sustaining Places: The Role of the Comprehensive Plan*. Planning Advisory Service Report no. 567. Chicago: American Planning Association.

Goetz, Edward G. 2010. "Desegregation in 3D: Displacement, Dispersal and Development in American Public Housing." *Housing Studies* 25(2): 137–58.

Goffman, Erving. 1963. *Stigma: Notes on the Management of a Spoiled Identity*. New York: Simon & Schuster.

Gordon, Avery F. 2008. *Ghostly Matters: Haunting and the Sociological Imagination*. Minneapolis: University of Minnesota Press.

Greenhouse, Carol, ed. 2009. *Ethnographies of Neoliberalism*. Philadelphia: University of Pennsylvania Press.

Grissim, John. 2003. *The Complete Buyer's Guide to Manufactured Homes and Land*. Sequim, WA: Rainshadow.

Gutman, Leslie M., and Carol Midgley. 2000. "The Role of Protective Factors in Supporting the Academic Achievement of Poor African American Students during the Middle School Transition." *Journal of Youth and Adolescence* 29: 223–48.

HAC (Housing Assistance Council). 2011. *Rural Housing Research Note Preserving Affordable Manufactured Home Communities in Rural America: A Case Study*. Washington, DC: HAC.

Hackworth, Jason. 2002. "Postrecession Gentrification in New York City." *Urban Affairs Review* 37(6): 815–43.

———. 2007. *The Neoliberal City: Governance, Ideology, and Development in American Urbanism*. Ithaca, NY: Cornell University Press.

———. 2009. "Destroyed by Hope: Public Housing, Neoliberalism, and Progressive Housing Activism in the US." In *Where the Other Half Lives: Lower Income Housing in a Neoliberal World*, edited by Sarah Glynn. New York: Pluto Press.

Hagan, John, Ross MacMillan, and Blair Wheaton. 1996. "New Kid in Town: Social Capital and the Life Course Effects of Family Migration on Children." *American Sociological Review* 61: 368–85.

Hager, Don J. 1954. "The Construction Worker and Trailer Living in Bucks County, Pennsylvania." *Housing Research* 7: 60.

Hartman, Chester, and David Robinson. 2003. "Evictions: The Hidden Housing Problem." *Housing Policy Debate* 14(4): 461–501.

Hartman, Rebecca. 2011. "Immobile Dreams." *Encore* (Fall/Winter). http://oregonhumanities.org/magazine/encore-fall-winter-2011/immobile-dreams /344/.

Harvey, David. 2005. *A Brief History of Neoliberalism*. New York: Oxford University Press.

Hayden, Delores. 1995. *The Power of Place: Urban Landscapes as Public History*. Boston: MIT Press.

Haynie, Dana L., and Scott J. South. 2005. "Geographic Mobility and Adolescent Violence: Evaluating the Mechanisms." *Social Forces* 84(1): 363–76.

Hays, Sharon. 2003. *Flat Broke with Children: Women in the Age of Welfare Reform*. New York: Oxford University Press.

Heidegger, Martin. 1958. *The Question of Being*. New York: Rowman & Littlefield.

Herbert, Gilbert. 1978. *Pioneers of Prefabrication: The British Contribution in the Nineteenth Century*. Baltimore and London: Johns Hopkins University Press.

Hirsch, W.Z., and A.M. Rufolo. 1999. "The Regulation of Immobile Housing Assets under Divided Asset Ownership." *International Review of Land and Economics* 19(3): 383–97.

Hoang, Kimberly. 2015. *Dealing in Desire: Asian Ascendancy, Western Decline, and the Hidden Currencies of Global Sex Work*. Oakland: University of California Press.

Hoffmann, John P., and Robert A. Johnson. 1998. "A National Portrait of Family Structure and Adolescent Drug Use." *Journal of Marriage and the Family* 60: 633–45.

Holland, John H. 1992. "Complex Adaptive Systems." *Daedalus* 121(1): 17–30.

———. 2012. *Housing Our Heroes: Veterans in Rural America*. HAC Rural Research Brief. www.ruralhome.org/storage/documents/rrbriefs/rrb_veterans.pdf.

Houston Business Journal. 2011. "Harris County Median Home Price Just above 130K." September 23. www.bizjournals.com/houston/news/2011/09/23/harris-county-average-home-price-just.html.

Hoya Capital Real Estate. 2016. "REIT Rankings: Manufactured Housing." *Seeking Alpha*, September 14. https://seekingalpha.com/article/4006168-reit-rankings-manufactured-housing?page = 2.

Huss-Ashmore, R., and C. Behrman. 1999. "Traditional Environments: Health and the Perception of Permanence in Urban Micro-Environments." In *Urbanism, Health and Human Biology in Industrialized Countries*, edited by Lawrence Schell and Stanley Ulijaszek. Cambridge: Cambridge University Press.

Jacobs, Jane. 1961. *The Life and Death of Great American Cities*. New York: Random House.

Jargowsky, Paul A. 1997. *Poverty and Place: Ghettos, Barrios, and the American City*. Lincoln: University of Nebraska Press.

Jewell, Kevin. 2001. "Manufactured Homeowners Who Rent Lots Lack Security of Basic Tenants Rights." Austin, TX: Consumers Union.

Joint Committee on Taxation. 2017. *Estimates of Federal Tax Expenditures for Fiscal Years 2016–2020*. January 30. Congress of the United States. www.jct.gov/publications.html?func=select&id=5.

Kallin, Hamish, and Tom Slater. 2014. "Activating Territorial Stigma: Gentrifying Marginality in Edinburgh's 'Other' Fringe." *Environment and Planning A* 46(6): 1351–68.

Katz, Michael B. [2001] 2008. *The Price of Citizenship: Redefining the American Welfare State*. Philadelphia: University of Pennsylvania Press.

Kaufmann, Daniel, Aart Kraay, and Pablo Zoido-Lobaton. 1999. *Governance Matters*. World Bank Policy Research, Working Paper no. 2196. Accessed October 13, 2015. http://info.worldbank.org/governance/wgi/pdf/govmatters1.pdf.

Kelly, Burnham. 1952. *The Prefabrication of Houses*. Cambridge, MA: MIT Press.

Klein, Naomi. 2007. *Shock Doctrine: The Rise of Disaster Capitalism*. New York: Metropolitan.

Klinenberg, Eric. 2002. *Heat Wave: A Social Autopsy of Disaster in Chicago*. Chicago: University of Chicago Press.

Kochera, Andrew. 2001. *Issues in Manufactured Housing*. Washington, DC: Public Policy Institute, American Association of Retired Persons (AARP).

Kusenbach, Margarethe. 2009. "Salvaging Decency: Mobile Home Residents' Strategies of Managing the Stigma of 'Trailer' Living." *Qualitative Sociology* 32: 399–428.

———. 2017. "'Look at My House!'—Home-Making and Identity among Latino/a Owners of Mobile Homes." *Journal of Housing and the Built Environment* 32(1): 29–47.

Lake, Robert. 2003. "The Power of Culture and the Culture of Power in Urban Geography in the 1990s." *Urban Geography* 24: 461–64.

Langer, Susanne. 1953. *Feeling and Form*. New York: Charles Scriber's Sons.

Lees, Loretta, Tom Slater, and Elvin Wyly, eds. 2010. *The Gentrification Reader*. London and New York: Routledge.

Lens, Michael C., and Paavo Monkkonen. 2016. "Do Strict Land Use Regulations Make Metropolitan Areas More Segregated by Income?" *Journal of the American Planning Association* 82(1): 6–21.

Levine, Jonathan. 2006. *Zoned Out: Regulation, Markets, and Choices in Transportation and Metropolitan Land-Use*. Washington, DC: Resources for the Future.

Lewis, Oscar. 1959. *Five Families: Mexican Case Studies in the Culture of Poverty*. New York: Basic Books.

Lofland, John. 1995. "Analytic Ethnography: Features, Failings, and Futures." *Journal of Contemporary Ethnography* 24(1): 30–67.

Logan, John R., and Harvey I. Molotch. [1987] 2007. *Urban Fortunes: The Political Economy of Place*. Chicago: University of Chicago Press.

MacTavish, Katherine, Michelle Eley, and Sonya Salamon. 2006. "Housing Vulnerability among Rural Trailer-Park Households." *Georgetown Journal on Poverty Law and Policy* 13(4): 95–117.

Mah, Alice. 2009. "Devastation but Also Home: Place Attachment in Areas of Industrial Decline." *Home Cultures* 6(3): 287–310.

Mallett, Shelley. 2004. "Understanding Home: A Critical Review of the Literature." *Sociological Review* 52(1): 62–89.

Manzo, Lynne C., and Patrick Devine-Wright, eds. 2014. *Place Attachment: Advances in Theory, Methods and Applications*. New York: Routledge.

Massey, Douglas S., and Nancy A. Denton. 1993. *American Apartheid: Segregation and the Making of the Underclass*. Cambridge, MA: Harvard University Press.

Matthews, Stephen, James Detwiler, and Linda Burton. 2005. "Geo-ethnography: Coupling Geographic Information Analysis Techniques with Ethnographic Methods in Urban Research." *Cartographica* 40(4): 75–90.

McKenzie, Brian S. 2013. "Neighborhood Access to Transit by Race, Ethnicity and Poverty in Portland, OR." *City and Community* 12(2): 134–55.

Merrill, Thomas W. 1998. "Property and the Right to Exclude." *Nebraska Law Review* 77: 730–55.

Merton, Robert K. 1948. "The Social Psychology of Housing." In *Current Trends in Social Psychology*, edited by Wayne Dennis, 163–217. Pittsburg: University of Pittsburgh Press.

MHI (Manufactured Housing Institute). 2012. "Manufactured Housing: An Industry Overview." Presentation to the National Association of Counties Rural Housing Forum Western Interstate Region Conference, May 16, 2012, Santa Fe, NM.

Michel, Lawrence, Jared Bernstein, and John Schmitt. 1999. *The State of Working America, 1998–99*. Ithaca, NY: Cornell University Press.

Mileti, Dennis. 1999. *Disasters by Design: A Reassessment of Natural Hazards in the United States*. Washington, DC: Joseph Henry Press.

Moore, Marvin M. 1973. "The Mobile Home and the Law." *Akron Law Review* 6(1): 1–22.

Morgan, Jennifer M. 1995. "Zoning for All: Using Inclusionary Zoning Techniques to Promote Affordable Housing." *Emory Law Journal* 44: 359.

Mumford, Lewis. 1961. *The City in History: Its Origins, Its Transformations, and Its Prospects*. Orlando, FL: Harcourt.

National Conference of State Legislatures. 2007. "Manufactured Housing: Not What You Think." www.ncsl.org/IssuesResearch/EconomicDevelopment TradeCulturalAffairs/ManufacturedHousingNotWhatYouThink/tabid/12742 /Default.aspx#charts.

National Consumer Law Center. 2011. *Promoting Resident Ownership of Communities*. NCLC Policy Brief. www.nclc.org/images/pdf/manufactured _housing/cfed-purchase_guide.pdf.

National Low Income Housing Coalition. 2017. *Out of Reach 2017*. http:// nlihc.org/sites/default/files/oor/OOR_2017.pdf.

NCMH (National Commission on Manufactured Housing). 1996. *National Commission on Manufactured Housing Final Report*. Washington, DC: NCMH.

Newman, Katherine. 1999. *No Shame in My Game: The Working Poor in the Inner City*. New York: Knopf / Russell Sage.

——— and Rebekah Peeples Massengill. 2006. "The Texture of Hardship: Qualitative Sociology of Poverty, 1995–2005." *Annual Review of Sociology* 32: 423–46.

NTHP (National Trust for Historic Preservation). 2016. "Kit Houses." National Trust for Historic Preservation Library Collection, University of Maryland.

NTPB (National Resources Planning Board). 1941. *Family Expenditures in the United States*. Table 1, p. 1. Washington, DC.

O'Connor, Alice. 2000. "Poverty Research and Policy for the Post-Welfare Era." *Annual Review of Sociology* 26: 547–62.

Oliker, S.J. 1995. "Work Commitment and Constraint among Mothers on Workfare." *Journal of Contemporary Ethnography* 24: 165–94.

Oliver-Smith, Anthony. 1990. "Post-Disaster Housing Reconstruction and Social Inequality: A Challenge to Policy and Practice." *Disasters* 14: 7–19.

Oregon.gov. 2017. "Mobile Home Park Living Resources." www.oregon.gov /ohcs/pages/manufactured-dwelling-park-living-resources.aspx.

Orfield, M. 2002. *American Metropolitics: The New Suburban Reality.* Washington, DC: Brookings Institution Press.

Peck, Jamie. 2002. "Political Economies of Scale: Fast Policy, Interscalar Relations, and Neoliberal Workfare." *Economic Geography* 78(3): 331–60.

———. 2005. "Struggling with the Creative Class." *International Journal of Urban and Regional Research* 29(4): 740–70.

Peck, Jamie, and Adam Tickell. 1994. "Jungle Law Breaks Out: Neoliberalism and the Global-Local Disorder." *Area* 26(4): 317–26.

———. 2012. "Apparitions of Neoliberalism: Revisiting 'Jungle Law Breaks Out.'" *Area* 44(2): 245–49.

Pattillo, Mary. 2013. "Housing: Commodity versus Right." *Annual Review of Sociology* 39: 509–31.

Pendall, Rolf, Robert Puentes, and Jonathan Martin. 2007. *From Traditional to Reformed: A Review of the Land Use Regulations in the Nation's 50 Largest Metropolitan Areas.* Research Brief. Washington, DC: Brookings Institution, Metropolitan Policy Program.

Persin, Susan. 2015. "Manufactured Housing Leads 2015 REIT Sector Performance." *Urban Land: The Magazine of the Urban Land Institute,* July 27. https://urbanland.uli.org/economy-markets-trends/.

Peterson, Charles E. 1948. "Early American Prefabrication." *Gazette des beaux-arts* 33, series VI.

Piketty, Thomas. 2014. *Capital in the Twenty-First Century.* Cambridge, MA: Belknap Press of Harvard University Press.

Piven, Frances Fox, and Richard Cloward. 1993. *Regulating the Poor: The Functions of Public Welfare.* New York: Vintage Books.

Pribesh, Shana, and Douglas B. Downey. 1999. "Why Are Residential and School Moves Associated with Poor School Performance?" *Demography* 36(4): 521–34.

Purser, Gretchen. 2016. "The Circle of Dispossession: Evicting the Urban Poor in Baltimore." *Critical Sociology* 42(3): 393–415.

Qian, Zhu. 2010. "Without Zoning: Urban Development and Land Use Controls in Houston." *Cities* 27(1): 31–41.

Relph, Edward. 1976. *Place and Placelessness.* London: Pion.

Rivlin, Gary. 2014. "The Cold, Hard Lessons of Mobile Home U." *New York Times Magazine,* March 13. www.nytimes.com/2014/03/16/magazine/the-cold-hard-lessons-of-mobile-home-u.html.

Rolfe, Frank. 2011. "Why Investors Like Warren Buffett Are Bullish on Mobile Home Parks." *National Real Estate Investor.* http://nreionline.com/finance-amp-investment/why-investors-warren-buffett-are-bullish-mobile-home-parks.

Rothwell, Jonathan T., and Douglas S. Massey. 2010. "Density Zoning and Class Segregation in U.S. Metropolitan Areas." *Social Science Quarterly* 91(5): 1123–43.

Roy, Ananya. 2003. "Paradigms of Propertied Citizenship: Transnational Techniques of Analysis." *Urban Affairs Review* 38(4): 463–91.

Ruggles, Steven J., Trent Alexander, Katie Genadek, Ronald Goeken, Matthew B. Schroeder, and Matthew Sobek. 2010. *Integrated Public Use Microdata Series: Version 5.0.* Minneapolis: University of Minnesota.

Salamon, Sonya, and Katherine T. MacTavish. 2017. *Singlewide: Chasing the American Dream in a Rural Trailer Park.* Ithaca, NY: Cornell University Press.

Sanders, Welford. 1986. *Regulating Manufactured Housing.* American Planning Association, PAS Reports Archive, no. 398.

Sassen, Saskia. 2014. *Expulsions: Brutality and Complexity in the Global Economy.* Cambridge, MA: Harvard University Press.

Schneider, Kenneth R. 2005. *Autokind vs. Mankind: An Analysis of Tyranny, a Proposal for Rebellion, a Plan for Reconstruction.* London: Authors Choice Press.

Schorr, Alvin L. 1956, "Mobile Family Living." *Social Casework* 37(4): 175–80.

Schwab, James C. 2010. *Hazard Mitigation: Integrating Best Practices into Planning.* Chicago: APA Press.

Schwartz, Barry. 1974. "Waiting, Exchange, and Power: The Distributions of Time in Social System." *American Journal of Sociology* 79: 841–70.

Scommegna, Paola. 2004. "Study Finds U.S. Manufactured-Home Owners Face 'Quasi-Homelessness.'" Population Reference Bureau. www.prb.org/Publications/Articles/2004/StudyFindsUSManufacturedHomeOwnersFaceQuasiHomelessness.aspx.

Sheehan, Michael, and Roger Colton. 1994. "The Problem of Mass Evictions in Mobile Home Parks Subject to Conversion." Fisher, Sheehan and Colton: Public Finance and General Economics.

Shen, G. 2005. "Location of Manufactured Housing and Its Accessibility to Community Services: A GIS-Assisted Spatial Analysis." *Socio-Economic Planning Sciences* 39: 25–41.

Siegan, Bernard. 1972. *Land Use without Zoning.* Lexington, MA: Lexington Books.

Slater, Tom. 2010. "Ghetto Blasting: On Loïc Wacquant's Urban Outcasts." *Urban Geography* 31(2): 162–68.

———. 2015. "Planetary Rent Gaps." *Antipode* 49(Suppl. 1): 114–37.

———. Forthcoming. "Territorial Stigmatization: Symbolic Defamation and the Contemporary Metropolis." In *The Handbook of New Urban Studies,* edited by John Hannigan and Greg Richards. Thousand Oaks, CA: Sage.

Sluzki, Carlos E. 1992. "Disruption and Reconstruction of Networks Following Migration / Relocation." *Family Systems Medicine* 10(4): 359–63.

Somers, Margaret. 2008. *Genealogies of Citizenship: Markets, Statelessness, and the Right to Have Rights.* New York: Cambridge University Press.

Soss, Joe, Richard C. Fording, and Sanford F. Schram. 2011. *Disciplining the Poor: Neoliberal Paternalism and the Persistent Power of Race.* Chicago: University of Chicago Press.

Stein, Walter J. 1973. *California and the Dust Bowl Migration.* London: Greenwood Press.

Stone, Michael E. 2006. "Social Ownership." In *A Right to Housing,* edited by Rachel G. Bratt, Michael E. Stone, and Chester Hartman. Philadelphia: Temple University Press.

Sullivan, Esther. 2017a. "Displaced in Place: Manufactured Housing, Mass Eviction, and the Paradox of State Intervention." *American Sociological Review* 82(2): 243–69.

———. 2017b. "Moving Out: Mapping Mobile Home Park Closures to Analyze Spatial Patterns of Low-Income Residential Displacement." *City and Community* 16(3): 304–29.

———. 2017c. "Dignity Takings and Trailer Trash: The Case of Mobile Home Park Mass Evictions." *Chicago-Kent Law Review* 92(3).

Thébault, Elisa, and Colin Fontaine. 2010. "Stability of Ecological Communities and the Architecture of Mutualistic and Trophic Networks." *Science* 329(5993): 853–56.

Tilly, Chris. 1996. *Half a Job: Bad and Good Part-Time Jobs in a Changing Labor Market.* Philadelphia: Temple University Press.

Tuan, Yi-Fu. [1977] 2001. *Space and Place: The Perspective of Experience.* Minneapolis: University of Minnesota Press.

Tucker, C. Jack, Jonathan Marx, and Larry Long. 1998. "'Moving On': Residential Mobility and Children's School Lives." *Sociology of Education* 71: 111–29.

U.S. Census Bureau. 2010. "2010–2014 American Community Survey 5-Year Estimates." http://factfinder.census.gov/faces/tableservices/jsf/pages/productview.xhtml?pid = ACS_14_5YR_B25033&prodType = table\.

———. 2014. "Energy Boom Fuels Rapid Population Growth in Parts of Great Plains; Gulf Coast Also Has High Growth Areas." www.census.gov/newsroom/releases/archives/population/cb14-51.html.

———. 2016a. "Median and Average Sales Prices of New Homes Sold in United States." www.census.gov/construction/nrs/historical_data/index.html.

———. 2016b. "Total Populations in Occupied Housing Units by Tenure by Units in Structure, 2016." American Community Survey 1-Year Estimates. https://factfinder.census.gov/faces/tableservices/jsf/pages/productview.xhtml?pid=ACS_16_1YR_C25033&prodType=table.

U.S. Department of Commerce. 2015. "Cost and Size Comparison for Manufactured and Site Built Homes: 2007–2015." www2.census.gov/programs-surveys/mhs/tables/time-series/sitebuiltvsmh.xls.

U.S. Department of Housing and Urban Development. 1998. *Factory and Site-built Housing: A Comparison for the 21st Century.* www.huduser.gov/Publications/pdf/factory.pdf.

U. S. Securities and Exchange Commission. 2017. "Real Estate Investment Trusts (REITs)." Investor.gov. www.google.com/search?q = real+estate +investment+trusts&ie = utf-8&oe = utf-8.

Valverde, Marianna. 2012. *Everyday Law on the Street: City Governance in an Age of Diversity.* Chicago: University of Chicago Press.

Venkatesh, Sudhir. 2006. *Off the Books: The Underground Economy of the Urban Poor.* Boston: Harvard University Press.

Vick, Karl. 2017. "The Home of the Future." *Time,* April 3, pp. 46–51.

Wacquant, Loïc. 2007. "Territorial Stigmatization in the Age of Advanced Marginality." *Thesis Eleven* 91: 66–77.

———. 2008a. *Urban Outcasts: A Comparative Sociology of Advanced Marginality.* Cambridge: Polity.

———. 2008b. "Relocating Gentrification: The Working Class, Science, and the State in Recent Urban Research." *International Journal of Urban and Regional Research* 32: 198–205.

———. 2009. *Punishing the Poor: The Neoliberal Government of Social Insecurity.* Durham, NC: Duke University Press.

———. 2015. "Class, Ethnicity, and State in the Making of Marginality: Revisiting Territories of Urban Relegation." In *Territories of Poverty: Rethinking North and South,* edited by Ananya Roy and Emma Shaw Crane. Athens: University of Georgia Press.

———. 2016. "Revisiting Territories of Relegation: Class, Ethnicity and State in the Making of Advanced Marginality." *Urban Studies* 53(6): 1077–88.

———, Tom Slater, and Virgílio Borges Pereira. 2014. "Territorial Stigmatization in Action." *Environment and Planning A* 46: 1270–80.

Wagner, Daniel, and Mike Baker. 2015a. "Warren Buffett's Mobile Home Empire Preys on the Poor." Center for Public Integrity. Accessed March 12, 2017. www.publicintegrity.org/2015/04/03/17024/warren-buffetts-mobile-home-empire-preys-poor.

———. 2015b. "A Look at Berkshire Hathaway's Response to 'Mobile Home Trap' Investigation." Center for Public Integrity. Accessed March 12, 2017. www.publicintegrity.org/2015/04/06/17081/look-berkshire-hathaways-response-mobile-home-trap-investigation.

Wallis, Allan. 1991. *Wheel Estate: The Rise and Decline of Mobile Homes.* Oxford: Oxford University Press.

Weber, Florence, Richard Nice, and Loïc Wacquant. 2001. "Settings, Interactions and Things: A Plea for Multi-integrative Ethnography." *Ethnography* 2(4): 475–99.

Wellington, Alexander C. 1951. "Trailer Camp Slums, A New Kind of Slum: The Permanent Trailer Camp Offers All the Bad Features of the Urban Blighted Area, None of the Vacation Advantages for Which Trailers Were Made." *Survey* 87: 418–21.

Willat, N. 1955. "Trailer Parks: They Mushroom into a Thriving Business across the Nation." *Barron's National Business and Financial Weekly,* September 26, p. 15.

Wilson, William J. 1987. *The Truly Disadvantaged: The Inner City, The Underclass, and Public Policy.* Chicago: University of Chicago Press.

———. 1996. *When Work Disappears: The World of the New Urban Poor.* New York: Alfred A. Knopf.

Wray, Matt, and Annalee Newitz, eds. 1997. *White Trash: Race and Class in America.* New York: Routledge.

Wyly, E. 2004. "The Accidental Relevance of American Urban Geography." *Urban Geography* 25: 738–41.

Zukin, Sharon. 1987. "Gentrification: Culture and Capital in the Urban Core." *Annual Review of Sociology* 13: 129–47.

Index

Geographic information systems (GIS)
(geospatial), 55, 59–61, 65, 74, 207
Goffman, Erving, 24, 27–28, 73
Gordon, Avery, 78, 85, 97

halfway homeowners, 1, 5, 16, 25,
27–28, 50, 200
health, 188, 189, 191–192, 197; anxiety,
39, 72, 80–82, 90, 97, 122–124, 136,
139, 146, 157, 189; hospitalizations,
2, 4, 8, 10, 122, 147, 150, 189; mental,
102, 116, 122, 124, 204; physical, 2,
26, 32, 102, 116, 122, 124, 148, 165,
189, 204
homelessness, 12–14, 94, 154, 188
homeownership, 16–17, 50–51, 128,
190, 202–203, 205; as an emotional
investment, 1, 80
housing insecurity, 11, 17–18, 189–190,
193–194; and resident understanding
of rights, 97, 163; and undocumented
status, 11, 21, 72, 115–116, 119, 195,
214, 221; as a *specter of dislocation*,
75–99, 105, 108; expectation of
permanence, 79–80, 85; residents'
sense of, 104–106

immobility of mobile homes, 3–6, 16,
20, 86, 94, 128, 144, 152, 164–165,
189–190
investing in mobile home parks, 23,
159–160, 162, 173–178; as passive
income, 173, 176–177, 179;
commercial mortgage-backed
securities (CMBSs), 182–184; real
estate investment trusts (REITs),
182–184

Lakeshore Communities, 133–135,
137, 139–140, 142, 152, 154, 157,
216
Legal Aid organizations, 9–10, 77, 153,
163, 211
Lofland, John, 217
Los Alamos Mobile Home Park, 89
Low Income Housing Tax Credit
(LIHTC), 46, 61, 63, 65

MacTavish, Katherine, 55, 79–80, 97
media images of mobile home parks,
106, 174; coverage after natural
disasters, 75–76, 80–82; coverage of
park closures, 129, 141; historical
coverage of mobile homes, 37, 44
Merton, Robert K., 40
Mission Trails Mobile Home Park,
186–193. *See also* Vecinos de
Mission Trails
mobile home history: 1970s–2000s,
46–47, 48–50; birth of mobile home
parks, 43; Dust Bowl, 38, 42, 50;
early factory-built mobile homes,
36–40; early mobile home history,
35–36; early research on mobile
homes, 41, 42, 44; Gold Rush of
1848, 36, 42; Great Depression, 38,
40, 51; introduction of the single and
doublewide, 43; of importing mobile
homes, 36–37; post-WWII, 46, 50,
57; World War II, 41–42
mobile home movers, 3, 5–6, 23, 29,
112, 133, 165, 168, 199, 216
mobile home park policy reforms, 30,
198, 201, 204
mobile home reinstallation, 143, 148,
150, 162, 167, 190, 199
Mobile Home University (Boot
Camp), 23, 30, 159–162, 173–177,
179–182, 216, 218. *See also*
Reynolds, Dave; Rolfe, Frank
modularity, 35–46, 51, 167, 203
mortgage interest deduction (MID),
202, 231
municipal ordinance, 28, 30, 40, 48,
55–56, 69, 191; and mobile home
invisibility, 194–195; court cases
challenging, 48; in Florida, 65–66,
68, 219; in Texas, 50, 53–54, 67–68,
72, 87–91, 100, 104–108, 114, 127,
187, 212–213, 219

natural disasters, 76, 80, 155–156,
195
neoliberalism, 25–27, 29, 46–47, 130–
131, 156–158, 176, 199, 200